(more)

"Nobody writes about the Corps like a Marine—General "Brute" Krulak is obviously one of the gifted few who does it so well. . . . A keen sense of humor. . . . *First to Fight* is intensely personal, yet historically factual. . . . Anyone who reads it will be very satisfied."

—*Battle Cry*

"Krulak is a clear and vivid writer."

—*West Coast Review of Books*

"*First to Fight* makes for wonderful reading. It is faced-paced; often stirring; always informed, interesting, and enlightening. Marines will zip through it, delight in it, and wish it was far longer."

—*Marine Corps Gazette*

"A complex, intriguing tale. . . . Blunt, controversial and to the point. And 110 percent Marine."

—*The Hook*

"The variety and wealth of General Krulak's own experience in the Marine Corps makes him an important interpreter of what being a Marine means and what the Corps stands for."

> —Allan R. Millet, Colonel, USMC Reserves
> author of *Semper Fidelis*

"Krulak is an excellent writer. *First to Fight* is informative, interesting and fast-moving."

> —*Military Review*

"Enjoyably provocative."

> —*The Burbank Times*

"Fortunately for the nation, these amphibious, airborne, ground-pounding warriors consistently live up to their public reputation. . . . In *First to Fight,* mystique is moved aside, the alchemy opened up, and elitism rationalized until the core of this 200-year-old American institution is ready for inspection. . . . Although Krulak barks and bites throughout the book, it is from experience and wisdom and—in the absolute spirit of fraternity—never at the expense of the Marines he so obviously loves and respects."

> —*Los Angeles Times Book Review*

FIRST
TO
FIGHT

AN INSIDE VIEW
OF THE
U.S. MARINE CORPS

LT. GEN.
VICTOR H. KRULAK
**USMC
(RET.)**

POCKET BOOKS

New York   London   Toronto   Sydney   Tokyo   Singapore

POCKET BOOKS, a division of Simon & Schuster
1230 Avenue of the Americas, New York, NY 10020

ISBN: 0-671-73012-6

First Pocket Books printing April 1991

10 9 8 7 6 5 4 3 2 1

POCKET and colophon are registered trademarks of
Simon & Schuster.

Printed in the U.S.A.

To the steady legions of Marines who over the years, by their fidelity, resourcefulness, courage, and willingness to sacrifice on land, at sea, and in the air, created not just a distinguished Corps but a national institution.

CONTENTS

FOREWORD

Since the birth of our nation, the steady performance of the Marine Corps in fighting America's battles has made it the very symbol of military excellence. The Corps has come to be recognized worldwide as an elite force of fighting men, renowned for their physical endurance, for their high level of obedience, and for the fierce pride they take, as individuals, in the capacity for self-discipline. The reasons for their high repute, however, go much deeper.

General V. H. Krulak, in *First to Fight*, seeks to bring those reasons to the surface. He describes the book as "a series of simple vignettes, part history, part legend, and part opinion" illuminating those qualities that have caused the Corps to survive and flourish. In fact the book is much more than that, providing an intimate cross-sectional view of how the Corps thinks and acts under stress, how its attention to the welfare of the individual and its high standards of performance have sustained it through good times and bad. And in telling his story the author shows an unusual ability to merge interesting detail with personal experience and opinion.

There is a stern reality in Krulak's portrayal of what military experience has always shown: "easy training—hard combat, hard training—easy combat." He takes his reader into the inner workings of the rigorous recruit training system that has turned many a generation of soft young Americans into the legendary "leathernecks," and he explains the passionate determination of the Corps's leaders to bring those in its ranks up to the best spiritual qualities of loyalty to Corps and Country and fraternal love for each other.

I learned something of this almost mystical spirit many years ago. My only brother enlisted in the Marine Corps at the age of eighteen when the United States entered World War I. His letters from "boot camp" at Parris Island filled me with pity and alarm, so much did they sound like epistles from a slave labor camp or a military gulag. But gradually I became aware that the note of self-pity and the plaintive "I-me" seemed to disappear from his letters, to be replaced by a more confident "we-us." Ultimately the proud day came when he wrote that his group had completed their training and, "We are shipping out for France." Strangely enough his letters from the war zone complained more about the cruel Simon Legree-like character of his battalion's colonel than about the food, the privations, the fierceness of the Boche enemy he and his comrades were facing, or the wound he received at Belleau Wood. When the war was over, and my brother returned on leave to regale us with his war experiences, I asked him about that terrible colonel. Whereupon something very strange happened. "Oh," he said in the flattest of flat voices, "he was killed." And then, after a silent moment, his young eyes grew moist. "Sorry, Sis," he said, furtively wiping away a pair of tears, "but we loved that SOB; he took such damn good care of us."

First to Fight underscores this fact—that the qualities that make for military excellence consist not only of hard training, exceptional physical fitness, and stern discipline, but of human solidarity. General Krulak makes clear that the U.S. Marine Corps is more than a crack military machine. It is a fraternity bonded in blood. The roots of that brotherhood are nourished by the Marines' solitude among the armed forces. Readers who were not previously aware of Marine Corps history will learn of the efforts by the Army and the Navy to limit or alter the functions of the Corps by subsuming, assimilating, or absorbing it into one or the other, or both of their services. General Krulak gives a lucid and unresentful account of when and why these attempts were made in times past to diminish the identity of the Corps. We learn that General Marshall and General Eisenhower, two of the great organizers of our World War II victory, were among those who tried to rationalize the Marine Corps out of meaningful existence on military, economic, or institutional grounds. It is significant that again and again the Congress has come to the rescue of the threatened Corps, not as an act of pity or of emotion, but to preserve a precious American resource.

These and other episodes recounted in the book are reminders that the pursuit of excellence follows a hard and rocky road. The story of the Marines' development of the tools and techniques involved in amphibious warfare in the face of apathy and parsimony is told in a quiet and richly detailed way. The reader is convinced of the enduring magnitude of this contribution to the art of war and of the vision and stubborn resolution of the men who did it.

It is in the matter of the Marines' attitude on fighting, however, that the book is at its best. The story of the battle of Khe Sanh in Vietnam is an unforgettable portrait of dedicated professionals at war, an inspiring story of spirit and valor under brutal circumstances. It is told with flair and fire. Other stories of Marine Corps combat during the two centuries it has existed are tragic testimony to the fact that the United States is part of a society that is centuries away from the Utopian goal of "One World" of peaceable nations. In those two centuries our country has averaged involvement in major land or naval warfare during one year out of every six. Nor have we known any dearth of limited hostilities and undeclared wars. War Department records show that over the decades American servicemen have responded to about 100 calls to combatant duty somewhere in the world, and the Marines have been involved in most of them. Several of these "minor" combats were costlier, in loss of lives and money, than our larger wars, and the cost has often been a monument to our unpreparedness.

Americans seem to be amnesiac about the price of being unready for the brief-notice challenge of war. We persist in thinking of ourselves as a peaceable and peace-loving people and, during the years when our sons and brothers are not fighting and dying in war, our politicians enthusiastically foster this self-delusion with patriotic rhetoric. And all too often they keep their promises to pare down our military services. Despite the debilitating actions of peace-at-any-price civil leadership, the Marines have somehow been able to make and keep themselves ready to answer their country's call. General Krulak's story of the 1950 Inchon landing in Korea is a moving example, telling how the Corps, with their brothers in the Navy, managed to produce from nowhere the men and means to make one of the most complex and decisive amphibious operations in history.

The Marines' constant readiness to perform runs counter to the great illusion which has been cherished by our countrymen—the dream of nonmilitary "collective security." Since the end of World War I millions of Americans have held to the belief that an organization of all the nations into a single body, acting and voting under a democratic charter, would ensure "peace on earth and good will to men." Despite the dismal failure of the League of Nations to prevent World War II, and its ignominious collapse at Geneva, the true believers tried again. They created the United Nations even before the battlesmoke of World War II had cleared. In the task of preventing wars among its 156 members, the U.N. has been a colossal failure. Since it came into being, there have been more than fifty wars involving the smaller powers, a number of which are raging today. To be sure, there has been no shooting war between any of the European powers, or between the super nuclear powers, the United States and the Soviet Union. And the credit for this goes to one thing—readiness, in this case in the form of the well-armed military alliance of the West.

Preparedness is one thing the Marines do understand, and General Krulak's book drives home its importance. *First to Fight* is the distilled reasoning of a good fighting man who has spent his lifetime in the profession of arms, with a hands-on involvement in combat and a clear perception of the value of being ready to go when the call to arms is sounded. In his retirement General Krulak has felt compelled by his experience in war to think hard—and to write lucidly—about it. His is the work of a first-class soldier repelled by bureaucracy and deeply desirous of seeing our nation safe and strong.

He brings his work to a close on a poignant note, worrying about the future of the Corps and the country itself. Today, he writes with unerring perception, our nation's problems, the Marine Corps' problems, "reside in the times themselves, in a national erosion of the work and service ethics, in a failure across the land to provide incentives for excellence, in a dimmed sense of industry and frugality, and, most seriously, in a degraded sense of national commitment." He sees this condition as a "sobering challenge" not just to the Corps but to all Americans—a challenge that, I am sure, will be met only by a true renewal of our sense of national purpose and the strengthening of our national will.

CLARE BOOTHE LUCE

PREFACE

This book had its beginning in an exchange of correspondence in 1957. The then-commandant of the Marine Corps, General Randolph McC. Pate, addressed the following brief note to me:

Headquarters U.S. Marine Corps
Office of the Commandant
Washington, D.C.

30 Oct. 1957.

Dear Brute:

Why does the U.S. need a Marine Corps?
When convenient, would you jot down some answers to the above question? . . .

Thanks,

Ran

To this I responded five days later, in part as follows:

Dear General:

Why does the United States need a Marine Corps?

In 1946, when serving as one of a group of officers engaged in studying ways and means to prevent our summary destruction, this question came in for much discussion. As one means of exploring the matter, we hit on the idea of taking the enemy's viewpoint.

So, we spent a little time seeking answers to the converse question—"Why does the United States *not* need a Marine Corps?"—and from those reflections came a few conclusions which apply to your question.

The United States does not need a Marine Corps mainly because she has a fine modern Army and a vigorous Air Force. Her Army fights on the ground— on any kind of ground—and does it well. Her Air Force fights in the air and does it well too. Marines are designed to fight on the ground and in the air just like the Army and Air Force, and have no corner on skill in either place.

The Marines claim to have a mystical competence in landing operations, but they really don't. There are thousands and thousands of soldiers who have been carefully trained and thoroughly drilled in amphibious matters too, and they can do anything Marines can do. And Marine aviators have no corner on tactical air operations in support of the infantry either. Our Air Force has done a lot of it, and can do it again.

Now, I know that all of these things are unpleasant to read, and we don't like to even think that they are said. But they *are* said. More serious still, they *are not entirely false!* There is a little tiny element of truth in each and every one—just enough to be frustrating—just enough to make our case a hard one to argue on technical facts alone. It makes little difference that the functions discharged by the Marines are more important in this day of missile diplomacy than ever before; that they would have to be done by *someone* under any circumstances, or that if there weren't a Marine Corps we would find our country having to improvise one in time of need. These truths are still very hard things to argue in technical terms, and the fact is, if I had to stick to pure and unqualified military technicalities, I would find it most difficult to prove, beyond question, that the United States does truly *need* a Marine Corps.

But we are not talking about technicalities or any cold comparison of weapons, organizations, functions, or pure mechanical capabilities. When you talk of the Marine Corps and the United States, you are not operating in the realm of technicality. You are operating in the realm of reality.

Technically it probably can be demonstrated that we don't *need* a U.S. Senate—there being some 400-odd Representatives ready and willing to do all the legislating needed.

Technically it probably can be demonstrated that we don't *need* woman suffrage—that our elective processes would produce the same results whether women voted or not, and that it is thus just a needless expense. But women do vote—not because of any technical reasoning—but because of something deeper, stronger, and far more compelling—because the American people want it that way!

And that is the case with the Marine Corps. We exist today—we flourish today—not because of what *we* know we are, or what *we* know we can do, but because of what the grassroots of our country *believes* we are and *believes* we can do.

These thousands—millions—of people don't understand much about "the comprehensive exercise of sea power" or "the security needs of a maritime nation," and they don't even absorb the full implication of "the balanced fleet." But that isn't too important, because what they do understand and believe about the Marine Corps is more powerful by far than these technical things.

Essentially, as a result of the unfailing conduct of our Corps over the years, they believe three things about the Marines. First, they believe that when trouble comes to our country there will be Marines—somewhere—who, through hard work, have made and kept themselves ready to do something useful about it, and do it *at once*. They picture these Marines as men—individual components of a lean, serious, professional outfit. I am sure that the grassroots reaction to our recent evidences of readiness vis-à-vis Suez and the Middle East were instinctively accepted by the American people as a matter of course. "How else would Marines act?"

Second, they believe that when the Marines go to war they invariably turn in a performance that is dramatically and decisively successful—not most of the time, but always. Their faith and their convictions in this regard are almost mystical. The mere association of the word *Marines* with a crisis is an automatic source of encouragement and confidence everywhere.

The third thing they believe about the Marines is that our Corps is downright good for the manhood of our country; that the Marines are masters of a form of unfailing alchemy which converts unoriented youths into proud, self-reliant stable citizens—citizens into whose hands the nation's affairs may safely be entrusted.

The people believe these three things. They believe them deeply and honestly—to the extent that they want the Marines around—in either peace or war. They want them so much that they are ready to pay for them—and to fight for them too, if need be.

Now we have heard it said that it isn't really the people who do all this—that they really don't much care—but that it is actually the Congress; or more properly a group of avid Marine-bitten, Marine-influenced, Marine-guided Congressmen who maneuver to keep the Marines on the top of the heap in the face of counter-maneuvering on all sides.

Nothing could be further from the fact. Oh, there is no doubt that the Congressmen are a powerful sounding board, but they are by no means just puppets dancing to Marine-controlled strings. They are doing exactly what they believe the people want them to do; no more, and certainly no less.

I believe the burden of all this can be summarized by saying that, while the functions which we discharge must always be done by someone, and while an organization such as ours is the correct one to do it, still, in terms of cold mechanical logic, the United States does not *need* a Marine Corps. However, for good reasons which completely transcend cold logic, the United States *wants* a Marine Corps.

Those reasons are strong; they are honest, they are deep-rooted and they are above question or criticism. So long as they exist—so long as the people are convinced that we can really do the three things I have mentioned—we are going to *have* a Marine Corps. I feel that is a certainty. And, likewise, should the people ever lose that conviction—as a result of our failure to meet their high—almost spiritual—standards, the Marine Corps will then quickly disappear.

Is there a chance that such a thing might happen? I think there is. I think that we ourselves can shake those convictions and the accompanying faith which really sustain us. By a lack of attention we can lose the inspirational personal relationship among our officers and our rank and file—a relationship quite different than that found in other services and one which heretofore has distinguished our Corps. In certain respects I fear we have, and I am sure that it is not going unnoticed. Also, by carelessness or by inordinate attention to less important things, we can lose those characteristics of lean professional simplicity and unfailing preparedness which, in the years past, have deservedly made the Marines one of America's treasures. In this respect, too, I feel we have lost some of our wealth of good will.

How serious it is, I don't profess to estimate to you, but it certainly worries me. It does, General, because, as I said before, if the United States *wanted* to try, she could get along without a Marine Corps.

(signed)
BRUTE KRULAK

In the years that followed I thought many times that my letter to Commandant Pate had not adequately analyzed the rich and complex soil in which the durability of the Marines is rooted. This book, therefore, is an effort to set down what I perceive to be the qaulities that have caused the Marine Corps to survive and to flourish. I have not written an accolade—which the Marines do not need—nor a full dress historical portrait of the Corps, complete with sword, braid, and medals. Rather, I aim through the amalgamation of fact, legend, anecdote, and interpretation to create a faithful image of what the Marine Corps is and a rationalization of the mystique of this altogether American institution. The book is a series of simple vignettes, part history, part legend, and part opinion.

While the mystique of the Corps transcends individuals, there were—in the early days, in my day, and still—people whose behavior exemplifies one or more of the qualities that characterize the Corps. Also, the Corps is in a sense like a primitive tribe where each generation has its medicine men—keepers of the tribal mythology, protectors of the tribal customs, and guardians of the tribal standards. Without them the tribe would wither, suffering from poverty of the soul. These medicine men come often to the fore in the following pages. In describing them, I hope that I have not, either by omission or inclusion, done violence to the memory of those departed or the sensibilities of those still breathing. Certainly, none is intended.

ACKNOWLEDGMENTS

The pleasure of writing this book was heightened by the quality and depth of the help I received.

I am grateful to three commandants, Generals Shepherd, Wilson, and Barrow, for their encouragement and professional reflections, and particularly to General Shepherd for making available to me his diary to help in reconstructing what really happened in the preparations for Inchon; also to Lieutenant General Charles G. Cooper and Major General Wesley H. Rice for their administrative support at the Marine Corps Recruit Depot, San Diego.

The History and Museums Division of Marine Corps Headquarters provided a wealth of resource material and was constant and unfailing in their desire to be helpful. It is an immense and well-organized repository of historical treasure and its director, Brigadier General E. H. Simmons, along with his able staff, were tireless in their determination to make it all available to me.

Those parts of the book that are the distillate of the minds and memories of others could not have materialized without their willing assistance. I wrote several score letters to probe the recollection of people who were actually there.

The responses were heartwarming—a significant contribution to the text.

I received valuable help from Lieutenant General Alpha L. Bowser, Admiral Arleigh A. Burke, Colonel Marion C. Dalby, Major General Ross T. Dwyer, Colonel Robert Elder, Brigadier General Leonard E. Fribourg, Brigadier General Samuel B. Griffith, Mrs. W. P. T. Hill, General Robert E. Hogaboom, Colonel Wilson E. Hunt, Brigadier General Homer G. Hutchinson, Lieutenant General William K. Jones, Major General Avery Kier, the Honorable Clare Boothe Luce, Major General James J. McMonagle, Captain Grayson Merrill, U.S.N., Dr. Arthur G. B. Metcalf, Lieutenant General Louis Metzger, Dr. Allan R. Millett, Admiral Thomas Moorer, Major General Raymond L. Murray, General Alfred H. Noble, Brigadier General Chandler Olson, Master Gunnery Sergeant Grant V. Pace, Admiral U. S. G. Sharp, Brigadier General Samuel R. Shaw, General Gerald C. Thomas, General Merrill B. Twining, Major General Donald M. Weller, Lieutenant General Richard G. Weede, and Lieutenant General William J. Van Ryzin.

Particular thanks are due also to Brigadier General E. H. Simmons and Evelyn A. Englander of the History and Museums Division and to Deborah Guberti of the U.S. Naval Institute for their thoughtful comments on the manuscript as it evolved through its several incarnations, to Cynthia Barry for her painstaking editing, and to Judith Moore for her help in research and in typing the multiple drafts of the manuscript.

FIRST
TO
FIGHT

Introduction

In 1935 I asked venerable Gunnery Sergeant Walter Holzworth just how the Marine Corps came by its reputation as one of the world's greatest fighting formations. "Well, lieutenant," the sergeant said, "they started right out telling everybody how great they were. Pretty soon they got to believing it themselves. And they have been busy ever since proving they were right."

A classic marine, Holzworth had seen every side of the Corps, from the 1st Aviation Company in World War I to the Fleet Marine Force. With service "in far off foreign lands" —China, Haiti, Guam, Cuba—and in the continental posts of the Corps—Norfolk, Quantico, San Diego, Lakehurst, Philadelphia—he epitomized the hard professional marine, the beau ideal of every new wearer of the Globe and Anchor, myself included.

His explanation, however, had little in common with actual early Marine Corps history. The pride and self-confidence that today is the Marines' hallmark did not emerge fully matured at Philadelphia's Tun Tavern* in 1775, as he suggests. To the contrary, the Marines got off to a shaky start, and they soon had more enemies than friends. The Corps's beginning could hardly have been less auspicious.

The "first and second battalions of American Marines" authorized by the Continental Congress on 10 November 1775, primarily to seize the British base at Halifax, were still a dream at the war's end, and the "Colonel and two Lieutenant Colonels" authorized in the same resolution did not appear until well into the nineteenth century. The Corps acquired, in the first months of its existence, only ten officers and about two hundred rank and file. None—officers or men—had much knowledge of war, and none, despite the injunction of the Continental Congress, were "so acquainted with maritime affairs as to be able to serve to advantage by sea when required." Their first leader, Samuel Nicholas, managed a barroom, the other officers were artisans and merchants, and the enlisted men were uneducated and largely unskilled immigrants.

Material conditions suggested that the Corps would not survive even the duration of the Revolution. The first enlistees were without weapons for several months, and there was no such thing as a Marine uniform for a year. In a pungent foretaste of problems so often encountered in the ensuing two hundred years, the Army and Navy had more money than the Corps and higher priority on the country's limited munitions stock.

The initial mission of the Marine Corps was to provide security for the ships in which Marines were embarked. This mainly meant helping ships' officers impose discipline on the crews. It also meant doing whatever the ship or squadron commanders might take into their heads to prescribe, including firing on enemy ships at close range with their muskets or taking part in a landing party along with sailors, such as occurred at New Providence in the Bahamas in

---

* Tun Tavern, owned by Robert Mullan, later to become an officer in the Continental marines, is linked traditionally with the earliest recruiting efforts for the Corps. Actually, there is much to support the conclusion that the first marines were recruited at the Conestogoe Waggon on Chestnut Street, although later recruiting—in mid-1776—was conducted from Tun Tavern.

March 1776 and at Penobscot Bay in July 1779. Neither seaman nor soldier, with few skills to recommend him, the marine was regarded with suspicion and sometimes animosity by his sailor peers. They resented him on general principles, but mostly they resented his portion of prize money.* The Corps itself was seen as an economic threat by the Continental Army and Navy, who objected to the diversion of precious funds for purchase of Marine equipment and supplies.

Did the Marines begin their life on a boastful note, as Gunnery Sergeant Holzworth told it? The War of Independence, where they did little fighting and suffered a total of 119 casualties, seems to have given them little to boast about. In fact, the Continental Marines actually disappeared following the Treaty of Paris in 1783. They were revived in an anemic sort of way, along with the Navy, by the Frigate Act of 1794 when Congress authorized construction of eight frigates, and their position was further solidified by law in 1798.

The Marines were still needed as seagoing police to help the revitalized post-Revolutionary Navy maintain discipline in its ships. This mission little endeared the Marines to their Navy associates, who realized they were there primarily to keep desertion-minded sailors from jumping ship, to guard the rum supply, and to protect the officers against a mutinous crew. They were obliged to do the last more than once, as exemplified by celebrated mutinies in the sloop *Ranger* in 1778, the frigate *Alliance* in 1783, and the *Constitution* in 1807.

Along with understandable antagonisms in the Navy, there was some doubt in the Congress, as well as in budget-conscious President Jefferson's White House, as to the long-term need for Marines. As yet, no one envisioned the elite amphibious landing force it would later become. Thus, forty years after the Continental Marines first appeared, the Corps's existence was still shaky with no more than one thousand Marines of all ranks in uniform, drawing a pittance for pay ($6.60 a month for a private, $25.00 for a

---

* The principal function of the Continental navy, at least as seen by its rank and file if not by the Continental Congress, was to prey upon British commerce for profit rather than for a popular cause.

captain), with very little combat experience or institutional pride behind them. The Corps was still a long, long way from the proud and boastful portrait painted by Sergeant Holzworth. Its mere survival was uncertain.

Yet the Marines did survive. In the American military establishment, they were perennially the smallest kid on the block in a hostile neighborhood. They seemed to have an extraordinary propensity for shooting themselves in the foot, but they still managed to stay alive—and to flourish. In a century and a half, they evolved an elite, almost mystical institutional personality. Partaking variously of pride, aggressiveness, dedication, loyalty, discipline, and courage, this complex personality was—and is—dominated by a conviction that battle is the Marines' only reason for existence and that they must be ready to respond promptly and effectively whenever given an opportunity to fight. Finally, they came to accept, as an article of faith, that marines must not only be better than everyone else but different as well. Some of their critics claim they are even eccentric, but, as John Stuart Mill explains in his essay *On Liberty,* the border between eccentricity and genius is drawn precious fine.

Over the years the Marines have slowly acquired many faces, many qualities of substance that they seem to possess in greater measure than do their military counterparts. No single quality is a true personification of the Marine Corps. It is only in the sensitive mixture of all of them that the Marines' real character and, consequently, their durability resides. The mixture has been flavored over the years by a procession of exceptional personalities—the right man for the right task at the right moment.

There was Commandant William Burrows (1798–1804), who made a religion out of the honor of the Corps, who gave the nation the Marine Band, and who delighted a frugal president and secretary of the navy by willingly building the Washington Marine Barracks for a total of $20,000, using his Marines to do the job.

There was Commandant Franklin Wharton (1804–18), who, despite some contemporary question about his courage, was the first to underscore the virtue of administering uniform discipline, of providing education, of ensuring the health and welfare of the troops, and of protecting the institutional honor of the Corps.

Then there was Commandant Archibald Henderson (1820–59). Vain, headstrong, intensely loyal to the Corps, he fought Congress and the Navy at every turn for the welfare of his men. He seized every opportunity to involve the Marines in combat—against the Indians in Florida and Georgia (where Henderson himself led the Marine force), at Chapultepec in Mexico, in China, or in disturbances at home. He campaigned continually for a larger Corps, demanded frugality, and worked tirelessly to improve the quality of both officers and enlisted men. And he outlawed swearing in the Marine Corps.

There was Commandant Charles Heywood (1891–1903), who created the first genuine Marine Officers' School. But his most popular success was making the marine's ration allowance equal to a sailor's—for the first time in 115 years!

Another was Commandant George Barnett (1914–20). Though deeply committed to the mission of capturing and defending advanced bases for the Navy, he had an unerring instinct for the battle, and over the objections of the War Department and of AEF Commander General Pershing, he managed to get a brigade of Marines into the western front battles of World War I. The brigade's skill, heroism, and triumphs at Belleau Wood, Blanc Mont, and the Meuse-Argonne contributed to a growing institutional pride, to a feeling of elitism, and to the fighting traditions of the Corps. He also, with great foresight, proposed creation of a Marine aviation unit primarily to "support the 4th Brigade in combat in France." As it turned out, the 1st Marine Aviation Force did not fly in support of the 4th Brigade. Instead, as recommended by Captain A. A. Cunningham, the first Marine aviator, the force served as the Day Wing of the U.S. Navy Northern Bombing Group, near Calais, France.

Commandant John A. Lejeune (1920–29) was determined to make the Corps a paternal organization, where an officer's first concern was the care of his men. He saw the need for a significant mission for his Corps, a mission attuned to the maritime nature of America's destiny, one intertwined with the purposes and the fortunes of the U.S. Navy. Long before he became commandant, Lejeune saw the task of not just defending but of seizing advanced bases for the fleet as a logical Marine Corps mission, central to our national security. With vision, he proposed the reorganization of the Corps as "one organic whole" to do the advanced base force job.

There were other commandants whose energy and wisdom epitomized one or another of the qualities that constitute the Marines' particular cachet. Major General John H. Russell (1934–36) nourished the Fleet Marine Force to health, emphasizing its function of seizing advanced naval and air bases and thus establishing the foundation for the Marines' air and ground triumphs in World War II and thereafter. General Thomas Holcomb (1936–43), as much as any other, saw the virtue of comprehensive, quality education. Generals Alexander A. Vandegrift (1944–48), Clifton B. Cates (1948–51), and Lemuel C. Shepherd (1952–55) all fought tirelessly to carve out a permanent statutory place in the Defense Department for the three combat divisions and three aircraft wings of the Fleet Marine Force.

Still another "personality" has influenced the Marines' evolution—Lady Luck. Certainly, it was luck that placed Lieutenant Presly N. O'Bannon and a half-dozen marines at Derna to make "To the Shores of Tripoli" an American legend. It was luck that caused the AEF censors in 1918 to believe, wrongly, that famed war reporter Floyd Gibbons had been killed and to pass, as his "last story," Gibbons's stirring account of the Marines' valor at Belleau Wood. And it had to be luck that placed photographer Joe Rosenthal on the top of Mt. Suribachi at the precise moment when five Marines and a Navy hospital corpsman made American history with a flag.

Each of these personalities, Lady Luck included, has illuminated one or more of the prime qualities— brotherhood, valor, institutional pride, loyalty, intellect, obedience, originality, and parsimony—that contribute to the American people's perception of their Marine Corps. For the Marines' own part, those qualities have translated into a hunger for excellence, a conviction that there is no room in their lexicon for the word *complacency,* and that there is no bank account of indulgence or good will owed the Corps for past performance, most particularly from their sister services and sometimes from the executive branch of government. Two centuries of experience have caused Marines to be continually wary of the aspirations of others where the survival of their Corps is concerned.

Marine Corps legend addresses that matter directly in a tale of the first two Marine recruits. Sitting at a table at Tun Tavern, so the story goes, they were enjoying several tankards of ale, when one is supposed to have exclaimed to the other, "They're after us! They're after us!"

"Who's after us?"

"The Army and the Navy, that's who."

It probably didn't happen—at least not at Tun Tavern. But it is true that the Continental Marines did run afoul quickly of the larger services, setting a pattern that has persisted, in one way or another, throughout the two centuries of the Marines' existence.

Only a fortnight after that historic Friday, 10 November 1775, when the Continental Congress resolved that there should be "two battalions of American Marines" among the Continental armed forces, General Washington let the Congress know that he saw the proposition of raising two battalions of Marines from his tiny army as a bad idea. He would have to pick over the entire army to find them and this "would not only cost the army time, anxiety, and pain, but would also weaken it."[1]

Washington had his way. By 30 November he was relieved of the responsibility for finding the troops for the Marine units and, as it turned out, the two battalions provided for in the resolution were never formed. The Marines had experienced their first interservice conflict. It would not be the last, nor the worst.

A year later, New York City had fallen to the British and Washington was retreating through New Jersey with British forces hot on his heels. Philadelphia was in peril. On 30 November Washington called for reinforcements— militiamen from Philadelphia, seamen from two frigates, *and* three companies of Marines. It is interesting that Washington enjoined Colonel Cadwalader, his commander on the spot, to "let me know in the meanwhile if they [the

Marines] came out resolved to act upon Land or meant to confine their Services to the Water Only."² Only five months after the Liberty Bell rang out, and the Marines already have a reputation as prima donnas!

As it turned out, the Marines responded promptly, some 131 of them, and were on their way, on 2 December, to join General Washington's forces before Trenton. It would be romantic to report that on this first occasion when the Army called on them for help the Marines were in the van of the attack at Trenton or that they saved the day at Princeton. Alas, the truth is less dramatic. The Marine detachment from the privateer Hancock occupied Burlington, New Jersey, without bloodshed, and the battalion under Major Nicholas was among those engaged at Princeton, where they lost an officer and four marines. And that is about it.

The historically significant fact, however, is that the Marines were called upon for the first time by the Army, and they responded willingly, as they have ever since.

The Marines' interaction with the Navy both during and following the Revolution was more complex, perhaps because it was a closer relationship. There were questions about what the Marines should do, and what authority should be assigned to the Navy and what reserved for the Marine commandant. There was continual Navy resentment of the Marines' shipboard tasks of preventing arson, theft, and desertion and of protecting officers from unruly crew members. On occasion, service pride and personal jealousies even gave rise to duels between Navy and Marine officers.

One articulate spokesman for those in the Navy antagonistic toward the Marines was Captain Thomas Truxtun, variously of the frigates *Constellation* and *President*. Holding strong views on the propriety of a limited and subordinate posture of Marines at sea, he did not hesitate to cross swords with the Marine commandant and the secretary of the navy. In 1801 he said, "It is high time that a good understanding should take place between the sea officers and Marines and that an end be put to their bickerings. If this cannot be done it may be thought best to do without Marines in ships of the U.S. by adding an equal number of ordinary seaman to the crew of each ship." He made his views plain on rank and precedence, too. "The fact is, the youngest sea lieutenant in the Navy takes seniority over the oldest marine officer in service."[3]

Truxtun's words sounded what was to be a century-long running battle with the Marines—a battle that contributed greatly to the paranoia so often identified with the Corps. At issue was what ships' detachments should do and who should have authority over Marines on duty at naval stations ashore. Unfavorable variations in pay and in berthing and messing arrangements offended the Marines. (Until enactment of laws in 1833 and 1834, Marines, both officer and enlisted, were at the bottom of the pay ladder.) The fact that Marines did less work at sea than bluejackets was an understandable affront to the Navy.

In 1821 the Board of Navy Commissioners (senior officers in the Navy) asserted that the marine detachments at shore were "worse than useless" and in 1830 a well-known Navy commander reflected the views of many of his peers, "The abolition of the Marine Corps is absolutely necessary to the efficiency and harmony of our ships."* Also, in 1830, the same year, Secretary of the Navy John Branch reported to the Senate on Marines at sea. While acknowledging that there were strong arguments for abolishing the seagoing detachments, he concluded that the likelihood of mutiny, arising from the roughness of the Navy enlisted men and their daily living and working circumstances warranted retention of the seagoing detachments.

President Andrew Jackson did not care for Marines, either. In 1830, he proposed to the Congress that legislation be enacted merging the Corps with the Army "as the best mode of curing the many defects in its organization." The measure, opposed by Commandant Archibald Henderson (1820–59), the Senate Naval Affairs Committee, and the House Military Affairs Committee, went down to defeat.

Then, in 1833, the Board of Navy Commissioners re-

---

* Commander Alexander Slidell MacKenzie, in *North American Review,* April 1830. MacKenzie earned renown later, in 1842, when he hanged three members of the crew of the brig *Somers* for mutiny, one the son of the secretary of the navy. Incidentally, Commandant Archibald Henderson was quick to point out that *Somers* had no Marine detachment.

drafted the Navy Regulations. Bearing the signature of the president, the Regulations codified what the Marines could and could not do. Marine officers were to be junior to Navy officers of the same rank, regardless of the dates of their commissions. Likewise, no Marine officer could exercise command over a Navy officer, of whatever rank, unless involved in a landing party. Marine officers were foreclosed from commanding either a ship or a naval station, and Marine barracks ashore were to be commanded directly by Navy Yard commandants. This blow to the Marines' pride was even more deeply felt when these restrictions were made law in the Marine Corps Act of 1834.

The wars of the mid-nineteenth century diminished somewhat the intensity of the Navy-Marine Corps conflict, but even when it did, the Corps faced other hazards. At the height of the Civil War two committees of the House of Representatives, inspired by the War Department, considered and rejected the proposition of transferring the Corps to the Army. Stormy debates took place in 1866, 1867, and 1868 on proposals by the White House or the Army to transfer the Corps to the Army or to abolish it altogether.

It is easy to see how such actions created a steadily growing paranoia in the souls of marines during the Corps's first century. The trauma was further intensified by the advent of the steel and steam Navy in the later years of the nineteenth century. Naval officers began to argue that shipboard Marine detachments were an anachronism—not needed to enforce discipline, not needed to man the ship's guns, not needed to comprise landing parties, not needed at all. Sailors, properly trained, they contended, could do anything on board ship the Marines could do.

Their principal spokesman was William F. Fullam, an articulate and respected officer. In terms of his antipathy for Marines, he was a latter day Thomas Truxtun. Fullam proposed, first in 1894 and then in an 1896 article in the U.S. Naval Institute *Proceedings,* that the Marines would make more of a contribution were they removed from the combatant ships and organized as six ready expeditionary battalions to support the fleet of U.S. foreign policy as needed.

Here was an exciting idea, one that should have been

seized by the Marines at once. In fact, it was viewed with suspicion, probably in part because it originated with the hated Fullam group. Commandant Charles Heywood (1891 –1903) saw nothing in the scheme that could approach the importance of service by Marines in ships of the fleet, and he sought and received support from two successive secretaries of the navy, Hilary A. Herbert and John D. Long.

The hard truth was, however, that the case for the Marine ships' detachments was becoming unsupportable. The Corps was rescued, as it had been before and has since, by war—in this case the 1898 war with Spain and the 1900 Boxer Uprising in China. Those conflicts diverted the Navy's attention to more pressing matters. More important, they gave the Corps an opportunity to distinguish itself in the fighting and to earn public renown.

The Marines came out of the war with Spain with a greatly enhanced image. From the start, events developed to their advantage. Private William Anthony, the captain's orderly in the battleship *Maine,* was credited with saving his commander's life. And the exploits of an expeditionary battalion of six hundred and fifty Marines in the seizure of Spanish positions at Guantanamo Bay attracted great attention. The battalion was commanded by Lieutenant Colonel Robert W. Huntington, a sixty-six-year-old Civil War veteran with a fierce disposition. Huntington's second in command was Major Henry Clay Cochrane, renowned throughout the Corps for his colorful, emotional personality. The two of them made good press, and by the time peace was declared the world was well aware of the "Fighting Marines" in Cuba.

Further luster was added to the Corps's repute by their participation in the defense of the Foreign Legation in Peking in 1900. During the seventy-five-day seige of the Legation Quarter, where the foreign troops were outnumbered a hundred to one by the fanatical Boxers, the Marines behaved with skill and steadiness. Along with detachments of Russians and British Royal Marines, they held the key position on the Tartar Wall that separated the Legation Quarter from the rest of the city. The leader of the composite international group was dashing, mustachioed Marine Captain John Twiggs "Handsome Jack" Meyers, who led his force with such reckless valor that it won praise from President McKinley and members of Congress and a permanent memorial from the British government. These triumphs, along with effective performance in the Philippine Insurrection and the Cuban pacification, further endeared the Marines to the American public and to Congress. This attachment would serve as a protective shield for the Corps in the years ahead.

A mere fourteen years later, Navy planners, led still by Fullam, now a commander, proposed once again that the Marines be removed from ships. This time the opposition was to be the most serious the Corps had yet faced in its century and a quarter of existence. Neither the secretary of the navy, Victor Metcalf, nor the president, Theodore Roosevelt, was favorably disposed to the Corps. (Roosevelt had, in 1896, when he was assistant secretary of the navy, caused a Navy personnel board to consider not only the removal of the Marine ships' detachments but absorption of the Corps into the line of the Navy.) Commander Fullam and his associates reiterated their argument of 1894—that Marine detachments aboard ship were as anachronistic as sail, and the Corps would be far more effective were it reorganized into expeditionary battalions, with their own assigned transport ships, trained and ready to serve with the fleet in the seizure or defense of advanced bases.

While most Marines saw Fullam's expeditionary force idea as nothing more than a straw man, a few more perceptive Marine officers—among them Eli K. Cole, John A. Lejeune, and Dion Williams—were impressed with the horizons that would open up for the Corps were it to become the nation's principal overseas expeditionary force. Their voices were muted, however, by widespread apprehensions that the Fullamites wanted to see the Corps destroyed.

While many naval officers did not share Fullam's antagonistic views, the Navy leadership, including the secretary himself, were insistent on seeing the Marines off the ships. It was able to persuade an already willing president to withdraw the shipboard guards by Executive Order. To mollify the marine commandant, George F. Elliott (1903–10), Roosevelt offered him the opportunity to draft a new charter, detailing what the Marine Corps should do in the defense of the United States in place of service aboard ships of the fleet.

A staff group led by Lieutenant Colonel Eli K. Cole put together a simple document that laid the foundation for the Marines' subsequent employment and their primacy in the amphibious field. According to the draft, the Marines would thereafter, among other things, garrison naval installations, provide the first line of defense of naval bases beyond the continental limits, as well as man the fixed defenses for those bases, garrison the Panama Canal Zone and, most important in the long run, provide expeditionary forces as needed. Roosevelt accepted Elliott's proposal and published it as Executive Order 969 on 12 November 1908.

It was a historic reorientation, greatly broadening the Corps's horizons, and it should have been welcomed. Instead, knowing the hostility of the president to the Corps, many Marines and a few friends in the Navy concluded that removal from ships of the fleet was the first step in abolishment of the Marine Corps. They flew to the defense of the Corps and sought at once to generate a backfire sentiment in the press and in Congress.

Only 16 days after Executive Order 969 was published the president made clear his real aspirations where the Marines were concerned. Army Major General Leonard Wood, one of the president's favorites, had applauded removal of the Marines from ships of the fleet and had proposed a further step, their absorption into the Army. Roosevelt agreed, saying, "I do not hesitate to say that they should be absorbed into the Army and no vestige of their organization should be allowed to remain."[4] This, of course, sent the friends of the Corps to battle stations.

In January 1909, a subcommittee of the House Naval Affairs Committee presided over by Thomas E. Butler, father of Marine Captain Smedley D. Butler, held hearings on the shipboard Marine detachment issue. The proceedings, as might be expected, were heavily weighted in the Marines' favor. The subcommittee gave minimal consideration to the testimony of the navy secretary, Fullam, and other antiships' guard witnesses. Throughout the hearings, members of the subcommittee brought up the issue of transfer of the Corps to the Army. This put the Navy witnesses in a quandary. They did not want to relent in their determination to have Marines off the ships, but they objected strongly to losing the Corps entirely and were obligated by Butler to say so openly. The subcommittee, predictably, found in favor of returning the Marine shipboard detachments.

The result was a rider to the appropriation bill, that there would be no money for Marine Corps support unless the Marine guards were restored to major ships of the fleet. The bill ultimately went through both houses and was signed by Roosevelt, who wanted no more trouble with the Marines.

The Marines, of course, took satisfaction in seeing the hated Fullam group rebuffed, but in retrospect, it is plain to see that the Corps is actually in Fullam's debt. He offered it a new and important mission, one which has since become its life's blood. The ship's guards the Corps had preserved at such pains could certainly not hold a candle to the usefulness of expeditionary forces, as sketched out in Executive Order 969. This fact was to become clear to even the most reactionary Marines over the course of the next three decades.

Also of long-term benefit was the institutional watchfulness that the shipboard-guard conflict engendered. The Marine leadership came to appreciate the great importance of maintaining the respect and good will of the Congress and the public toward the Corps. By this time, the Marines could not have been unmindful that moves to diminish or to eliminate their Corps had always begun in the executive branch—in the Navy Department, the War Department, or the White House itself. Each time, the Marines found strength and support in a steadfast Congress that saw the Corps as a reliable, austere, essential, and effective combat organization.

There have been some fifteen occasions since the Corps's birth when its preservation has been due wholly to a vigilant Congress. While these encounters have made the Corps stronger, they do explain the often expressed belief on the part of Marines that, as the recruit at Tun Tavern said, "They're after us." They also explain the Marines' confidence in Congress and in the good will of the public to bail them out in time of trouble. That good will has been their shield and buckler for a century and a half. As General Gerald C. Thomas put it, "We have to have the people on our side." What the Marines failed to comprehend, however, was the importance of establishing institutional means of harnessing that popular and congressional strength, to be called upon when needed. This lack of preparation in public and government relations came near to spelling oblivion for a proud Corps in the years immediately following World War II.

PART
I

THE THINKERS

Defend me from my friends.
I can defend myself from my enemies.

The Maréchal de Villars
to Louis XIV

Standing beside Marine Lieutenant General Holland M. Smith on the bridge of the command ship *Mt. Olympus*, off Iwo Jima on the morning of 23 February 1945, Secretary of the Navy James Forrestal said that the raising of our flag atop Mt. Suribachi "means there will be a Marine Corps for the next five hundred years."[1] Moments later, out of Forrestal's hearing, Smith commented, "When the war is over and money is short they will be after the Marines again, and a dozen Iwo Jimas would make no difference."[2]

The resolute general was voicing the frustrations of the many generations of Marines before him who had learned through hard experience that fighting for the right to fight often presented greater challenges than fighting their country's enemies. Viewed more philosophically, it may be said that the unending struggle for survival has done much to strengthen the Marines' character. As in the greyhound races, every time the Corps started to coast, it seemed that the rabbit, in the form of a threat to their survival, sped up and challenged them to higher levels of performance.

Beneficial or not, the continuous struggle for a viable existence fixed clearly one of the distinguishing characteristics of the Corps—a sensitive paranoia, sometimes justified, sometimes not. It is in this atmosphere of institutional vigilance that the Marines have been nourished over the years. This instinctive personal concern of Marines as individuals for the survival of their Corps has certainly been one of the principal factors in its preservation.

CHAPTER 1

Voyage toward Oblivion and Back or How the Marines Were Almost Merged Out of Business

The Marines' survival struggles during their first century and a half were mere skirmishes compared with what was to ensue following the Second World War. The earlier trauma was often simply a product of the nation's growing up, interspersed with an occasional Marine self-inflicted wound. In the early days of the Second World War, however, even as America was still trying to see through the smoke of Pearl Harbor, there were sown the seeds of something far more serious—a carefully designed plan which, if implemented, would destroy the Marine Corps as a fighting force.

The scene is set, at least for me, by three events. In early October 1942, as a member of a team of four Marine officers, I reported to the commanding general of the Army's 25th Infantry Division at Schofield Barracks, Hawaii. We were there at the Army's request to conduct instruction for the division in the various aspects of amphibious warfare and to help them plan, execute, and critique a major amphibious training exercise on the island of Oahu. The other Marines were Colonel LeRoy P. Hunt, who headed the team; Lieutenant Colonel Robert O. Bare, who taught operational subjects; and Captain Rex R. Stillwell, who taught communications. My subjects were logistics and intelligence.

The 25th Division was headed for the South Pacific, Guadalcanal, and while the battle for the island was over, there was still a long overseas road to Tokyo. Time was short, the division had no prior amphibious training, and our little group was very busy.

We completed our teaching task in late November. Preparing to return to the mainland, we paid our parting respects to the division commander, Major General J. L. Collins and his chief of staff, Colonel William P. Bledsoe. Both had been cordial to us from the start and grateful for our help. To our surprise, the courtesy call took an unexpected and significant turn. General Collins chose to speak —probably for the benefit of those of his staff who were present—on how the Army was resolved to eliminate forever its deficiencies in amphibious matters and its dependency on Marines for amphibious expertise. He said that the Army intended to master quickly the intricacies of the specialty which, in any event, were not all that difficult. Collins was polite but so serious as to cause Colonel Hunt later to report the conversation to our commander, Lieutenant General Holland M. (Howlin' Mad) Smith during our oral report to him. The general dismissed it curtly saying, "There's room for everybody."*

The second incident, closely related to the first, took place in Noumea, New Caledonia, about a month later. General Collins, passing through on his way to Guadalcanal with his division, was billeted with a group of senior Army officers, at the quarters of the chief of staff of the Noumea Army Command, Brigadier General Nathan Twining, U.S. Army Air Force. Also present were Major General Rush B. Lincoln, U.S. Army, and Colonel Henry Everest, U.S. Army Air Force. On this evening, 11 December, General Twining was visited by two of his four brothers, an Army reserve intelligence officer, Major Edward B. Twining, and Marine

---

* The incident is from the author's diary. Collins led a high-quality division, not yet greatly diluted by the Army's wartime expansion. At the time we were there, his chief of staff and all four of his principal general staff officers were West Pointers.

Lieutenant Colonel Merrill B. Twining, operations officer of the 1st Marine Division, which had been relieved on Guadalcanal by the Army the day before.

After dinner, as Merrill recounted it to me, Nathan launched into a condemnation of the operations of the Navy and Marines at Guadalcanal.[1] He denied the appropriateness of the Marines being there at all and declared that organizational steps were under way to preclude the Marines from further preempting the functions of the other services. According to Merrill, Collins joined vigorously in the discussion, concurring in Nathan's views to the point where it was plain that there was something more sinister afoot than an ordinary professional discussion. Merrill said, "This was no simple family interservice argument, of which my family had had many. This was serious." He subsequently reported the incident to General Vandegrift, and he to Admiral William F. Halsey, neither of whom had much time for interservice quarreling and said so.

The third occasion took place in Washington in December 1943. Army Chief of Staff George C. Marshall had just presented to the Joint Chiefs of Staff his concept of a unified Defense Department, including a separate Air Force, where a single chief of staff and an armed forces general staff would manage all the nation's military affairs.* Captain William D. Chandler, USN, my father-in-law, was secretary of the Navy General Board, and he told me that Admiral Claude C. Bloch, the General Board president, was furious about Marshall's reorganization proposal. "It is a disgrace," Bloch said, "that when we still have a war to win the Army is already trying to pick up the pieces when it's over."

Notwithstanding the admiral's lamentation, the Marshall

---

* This was not the first time this idea saw daylight. It was first proposed in 1925 by Congressman Albert R. Hall of Indiana and again in 1935 by Senator Bennet Champ Clark of Missouri. In neither case was there much support, and the Marine Corps gave it little concern. A similar bill, offered in 1932, was challenged by General MacArthur, then chief of staff, because of his opposition to a separate Air Force. He said, "Pass this bill and every potential enemy of the United States will rejoice." These words were quoted scores—perhaps hundreds—of times by the Navy and Marine Corps in the 1946–47 merger crisis.

proposal was the foundation for several War Department-generated hearings in both the House and Senate during the remainder of the war. All were conducted in the context of seeking greater efficiency, greater economy, and greater readiness to meet short notice crises ("Remember Pearl Harbor"). The schemes before the House and Senate divided warfare into three elements—land, sea, and air. The Army would be responsible for combat on the land, the Navy for combat at sea, and the Air Force for combat in the air. A Defense Department would be created—headed by its secretary—and there would be a single military chief of staff with direct access to the president. The three elemental services would have their chiefs of staff, and there would be a chief of a Service of Supply. The chief of staff to the president and the four service chiefs would constitute the "United States General Staff," and there would be a Joint Staff to serve them. And as for the Marine Corps? No mention at all. Army witnesses dismissed the Marine issue in testimony as not important. The Marshall idea elicited some favorable congressional reaction, mainly because nobody in uniform who might have objected had the time or the inclination to do so.

In March 1944, as a result of quiet War Department encouragement, Representative James Wadsworth introduced a resolution to create a "Select Committee on Postwar Military Policy." The resolution passed, and the Speaker of the House appointed a committee to examine the wisdom of consolidating the armed forces in some way—"streamlining" was the popular word. The Army, claiming to be the exponents of economy and efficiency, made the most of the opportunity, presenting the committee with only a slightly different version of the Marshall proposal.

Known as the McNarney plan, after Army Lieutenant General Joseph McNarney who presented it, the plan favored an independent Air Force and an authoritarian arrangement that gave an overall military service chief a direct link to the president on strategic and budgetary matters, bypassing the new secretary of defense and the civilian hierarchy. Also like the Marshall proposal, it gave no evidence that a Marine Corps existed. When queried on the omission of the Marine Corps, McNarney dismissed it as "a detail of organization I don't believe I care to comment on."[2]

Other Army witnesses and Representative Wadsworth contended that now was the time for unification and the attendant efficiencies. Navy witnesses, on the other hand, expressed the view—best articulated by Assistant Secretary Artemus L. Gates—that centralization was not necessarily synonymous with efficiency, that the preservation of civilian control was essential, and that, in any case, the problem deserved careful study only after the war had ended.[3]

The war in Europe was nearing its Normandy crisis, the Pacific war was at the bitter stage—still to come were New Guinea, the Marianas, the Philippines, Iwo Jima, and Okinawa. Congress had little stomach for an interservice conflict, which the hearings clearly promised to generate. In this atmosphere, General Vandegrift, commandant of the Marine Corps, neatly summarized the sentiments of a majority of the House committee in his testimony on 11 May, "With the entire record of this war available to us after its termination, we should study and plan, we should clarify obscure incidents, and we should keep our minds open in the interim, to ensure the best organization when we adopt it. Otherwise, we may adopt one prematurely that would appear less desirable, when all the facts are at hand as a basis of judgment."[4]

The committee concluded hearings on 19 May, and a month later issued its report. Although wartime was not the proper moment, it said, reorganization was necessary and the services should begin developing answers.[5] Plainly, the Navy and Marines had done little more than delay an Army program that had popular appeal and a growing head of steam.

In an effort to develop some answers on its own, the Joint Chiefs of Staff (JCS) appointed a committee of Army and Navy officers, headed by Admiral J. O. Richardson, USN (Ret.), to study the issue. The committee traveled widely and interviewed some eighty officers, but its report read as if it had been authored by the same penman who crafted the Marshall scheme. It proposed to diminish greatly civilian influence over military affairs, eliminating the secretaries of the military departments and establishing a "commander of the armed forces" who had direct access to the White House as "chief of staff to the president." The Joint Chiefs of Staff (the service chiefs and a chief of a Service of Supply) would advise the president on strategy and budgetary matters, but only through the chief of staff. The secretary of defense and his civilian associates would hold positions of little substance.[6]

Although the majority of the committee agreed with these extreme proposals, Chairman Richardson did not, expressing his dissent in strong terms. At the JCS level, the chiefs themselves split down the middle, Generals George C. Marshall and Henry H. Arnold concurring and Admirals William D. Leahy and Ernest J. King dissenting.[7] Because of this basic disagreement among the chiefs themselves the report collapsed and disappeared within the JCS structure.

The Richardson Committee report disturbed Navy Secretary Forrestal, who became further distressed after discussing armed forces unification with President Truman on two occasions. The former captain of Battery D had long been known to entertain ideas of his own on armed forces organization—ideas decidedly inimical to the Marines. Now he confirmed in private to Forrestal what he had already declared publicly—that he favored unification in the exact terms proposed by General Marshall. Forrestal realized that the military could benefit from some organizational changes, but he was critical of the overcentralization basic to the Marshall concept and its inherent limits in meshing military decision making with foreign policy. Deeply troubled, he commissioned Ferdinand Eberstadt, a well-known investment banker, to study the structure of the American government as it related to national security and to recommend an optimum organization.

A most conscientious man, Eberstadt spent twelve weeks painstakingly researching the subject. His penetrating report surprised even Forrestal in its comprehensiveness, and his conclusions were strikingly unusual. He declared that the narrow issue of amalgamation of the military into a single unified department did not address the real problem and that it would not be beneficial in any case. The real challenge, he said, lay in creating a system that brought together harmoniously all elements of the government involved in national security. Specifically, he argued for the integration of intelligence, resources, administration, diplomacy, and fighting, and he proposed the creation of agencies that, working together, would achieve this purpose. As to the military itself, he recommended three cabinet-level departments—War, Navy, and Air, each with direct access to the president. He said that the Joint Chiefs of Staff organization should be retained but that no post of overall commander of the armed forces should be created. Where the uniformed military was concerned, therefore, Eberstadt emphasized the need for civilian checks and balances, essentially the reverse of the Marshall concept. So, even before the war ended, the stage was set for a major controversy.

Then came VJ Day and with it a wave of victory-borne euphoria. Those who had won the conflict were true heroes, enjoying the gratitude of the nation. Their views on military affairs deserved respectful attention, and the warm afterglow of global victory left no room for suspicion that one arm had any desire to profit at the expense of another.

It was in this atmosphere that the Marshall idea resurfaced in two bills (S. 84 and S. 1482) before the Senate Military Affairs Committee. The bills were coupled with a well-organized press campaign, launched in late October 1945, that emphasized the president's favorable reaction to the Marshall scheme and his dissatisfaction with any military man who opposed it. The Army's array of spokesmen included, among others, the secretary of war, General Marshall, and, most visibly, the same 25th Infantry Division General J. L. Collins whom I had met in Hawaii in 1942. Now a lieutenant general, and known as "Lightning Joe," Collins presented a polished, articulate, and persuasive argument.* The simple symmetry of the plan arrested attention and, at least superficially, promised both efficiency and economy.

The Collins plan exhibited to all that the War Department saw the Marines not as a separate component of the Department of the Navy, their true statutory position, but as a subordinate included element of the U.S. Navy. The

---

* Collins says he was given the spokesman job to keep the heat off General Marshall.

effect of such an arrangement would insulate the Marines from the secretary of the navy in all departmental matters. Beyond that, there was a broader and more serious issue in the Collins proposal. It would isolate the president, as commander in chief, from broad military advice. A single secretary would counsel the president, supplanting both the civilian secretaries of the military departments and the chiefs of the services. The new defense secretary would have the responsibility of formulating a single military budget, which the service chiefs would be called upon to defend but which they would not have had a hand in creating. In its intense concentration of advice, the idea was inconsistent with the way our country runs or, as Navy Secretary Forrestal put it, "fundamentally against the spirit and genius of American institutions."[8]

Some of us in the Marine Corps were worried about the Corps' well-being as an American institution under the Collins arrangement. From both philosophical and practical points of view, we could see that there would be no place for a dynamic Marine Corps in such a system. By the time Marine operational views filtered through successive meshes at the levels of chief of naval operations, chief of staff of the armed forces, and defense secretary, such as survived would likely be undistinguishable.

Opposition witnesses, including Secretary Forrestal and Admiral King, struggled to resist the Army proposal while trying not to appear negative about improvements in the overall defense organization. Their testimony, measured against that of War Secretary Patterson, General Marshall, and General Collins, was not persuasive. Their weakness underscored the hazard to the Marines, who were not even included in the Navy Department's list of witnesses.

From the Marines' standpoint, this threat to their survival could not have come at a worse time. While demobilizing from a wartime peak strength of 485,000 to a peacetime level of 100,000 (later reduced to 65,000), they were still trying to preserve a vestige of their combatant capability. They were rolling up their large Pacific logistic system, they were struggling to meet a heavy occupation commitment in China with too few people, and they were beginning to face the intellectual reality that the atom would have a massive influence on their future professional affairs. For many Marines, still feeling the euphoria of the great Pacific victory and caught up in their new tasks, it was hard to accept the idea that anybody would try to organize the Corps into a position of military ineffectiveness. They had no time for such concerns and they didn't want to believe them anyhow.

That is why the successful 1945–47 battle for Marine Corps survival was actively fought by so few people—a fact later to become obscure because "success has a thousand fathers while failure is an orphan."

The top-ranking Marine during the fight in 1945 was Commandant Alexander Archer Vandegrift (1944–47) of Guadalcanal fame. A Virginian, he was born in 1887 into a gentle tidewater family—an architect father and an artist mother. Sturdy, devout southerners, they prayed to "the God of Abraham, Isaac, Jacob, Robert E. Lee, and Stonewall Jackson." Vandegrift became interested in a military life thanks to his grandfather, a Confederate veteran who fascinated the young man with accounts of his Civil War campaigns. He ended up in the Marine Corps in 1909 only because he failed the physical examination for entrance to West Point in 1907. His satisfaction at passing the demanding qualifying examinations for a Marine Corps appointment was tempered by his grandfather's parochial disapproval. "I never thought I would see the day when a grandson of mine would be wearing a *blue* uniform," he said.[9] Vandegrift's patrician background and his gentle, dignified heritage ill-fitted him for the gut fight that he faced in the unification controversy. This was to hurt the Marines before it was all over.

Advising Vandegrift directly and enjoying his full confidence was Brigadier General Gerald Carthrae Thomas. Also a veteran of Guadalcanal, where he was Vandegrift's operations officer and later chief of staff, Thomas had a wholly different personality. Enlisting in the Corps from Illinois Wesleyan University immediately after war was declared in 1917, he fought as an enlisted man in France for a year as intelligence chief of a battalion of the 6th Marine Regiment. After performing with distinction in the crucibles of Belleau Wood, Soissons, and the Meuse-Argonne—a Silver Star for heroism and a Purple Heart—he was commissioned in September 1918. He began what would be a brilliant and well-rounded career that would fit him well for his role in the unification battle. Fighting in Haiti, China, and Guadalcanal gave him a practical soldier's background. (Later he fought in Korea, where he commanded the 1st Marine Division.) Studying at the Army Infantry School at Fort Benning, Georgia, and a two-year course at the Army Command and General Staff School at Fort Leavenworth, Kansas, polished his intellect and gave him an opportunity to meet many Army (and later Air Force) officers with whom he would renew acquaintances in Washington and in various combat assignments. Teaching intelligence and history at the Marine Corps Schools in Quantico, Virginia, where he became the resident expert on Gallipoli, gave him a solid grounding in the origins of his Corps's specialty. Thomas matured into a poised, thoughtful, open-minded man who could see through a problem with lightning speed, whose solutions were practical and strong, and whose ability to express himself in clear and persuasive terms was legend. Vandegrift could not have had a better viceroy for the merger issue.

Thomas returned to Marine Headquarters from the southwest Pacific in late 1943 and, in a brief moment, was aware of the implications of General Marshall's unification plan. He described it to me as "pure militarism in the German image and a direct threat to the Corps." He knew it would have to be dealt with, and to help him he turned to another distinguished Guadalcanal veteran, one of the truly great minds of the modern Marine Corps.

Merrill B. Twining, USNA '23, was the pivotal man in the critical 1945–47 phase of the Marine Corps's struggle for survival. What the Corps got out of the battle was, in no small measure, Twining's doing. Quiet, reflective, and practical, he possessed a reservoir of natural wisdom and vision, an impressive intellect, and a broad professional background that made him ideal for the task at hand. He had been alert to the Army's designs on the Marines since his conversation with his brother in Noumea in 1942. Trained as a lawyer, he was a master of logical and articulate expression and a tireless worker. He possessed that rare quality of leadership that inspired everyone, from the sober-sided fighter to the eccentric dilettante, to trust and follow him, a quality that would serve the Corps well in the trying months ahead.

At the time, early October 1945, I was serving as the operations officer of the 6th Marine Division in Tsingtao, China. One morning a brief message was received directing that I proceed without delay to Marine Headquarters in Washington. Upon arrival I reported to General Thomas, who told me that he was the cause of my summary transfer. Then he described the grave situation facing the Corps, said that Twining would design our defensive program, and that I would be Twining's assistant.

Under the coordination of Thomas and the direction of Twining, and with only limited knowledge by Vandegrift, there grew up a small group of activists who, each in his own way and often at some personal sacrifice, poured his efforts into the battle. Others in the group included Brigadier General Merritt A. Edson, a fighter in the purest Marine tradition, famed for his leadership in Nicaragua and winner of the Medal of Honor for his intrepid conduct at Bloody Ridge on Guadalcanal. Fearless and truly patriotic, he ultimately sacrificed his career to see the truth made public. Additionally, there were Colonels Robert E. Hogaboom and James E. Kerr; Lieutenant Colonel James C. Murray, who had an innovative brain, an agile pen, and a great capacity for work; Lieutenant Colonel James D. Hittle, an articulate writer and a tireless lobbyist whose Capitol Hill contacts were critical in the battle; Lieutenant Colonel DeWolf Schatzel, Lieutenant Colonel Samuel R. Shaw, Lieutenant Colonel Robert D. Heinl, Lieutenant Colonel E. H. Hurst, Major Jonas M. Platt; and Reserve officers Russell Blandford, Arthur Hansen, Lyford Hutchins, and William McCahill.

One day, in a conversation with Twining and me, Colonel Kerr referred to the loose-knit group as "The Little Men's Chowder and Marching Society" after a mythical institution appearing in a popular comic strip "Barnaby." The name stuck and it was not long before the products of our minds and pencils came to be known as "chowder."

The Society was anything but a team. There were times

when we were more like a log floating downstream with a thousand ants on it—each of them convinced that he was steering. At best, we were a group of individuals who had a reasonable understanding of the problem and shared similar goals. With a minimum of direction, we each worked in our own way to help build the backfire that stemmed what at first looked like an unstoppable conflagration. The trouble was, however, that at the outset none of us had any experience in congressional lobbying, which was to become the critical factor. The Corps itself, moreover, had no plan or system for mustering congressional help or for generating favorable press support.

To make matters worse, we were often misunderstood by our peers and sometimes by our superiors. Twining and I, for example, were working at the Marine Corps Educational Center in Quantico, Virginia, as members of a Marine Corps Board assigned to study amphibious concepts. To a much greater degree, we were engrossed in analyzing Army, Navy, and Joint Chiefs of Staff documents, writing memorandums for others to use to educate the public and members of Congress as to the hazards of the proposed legislation, composing speeches for senior Marine officers, and, later, organizing some of the congressional lobbying effort. Our immediate commander was Brigadier General Oliver P. Smith, a quiet, straightforward, God-fearing gentleman who found it hard to ascribe antagonistic motives to others and who deplored our behind-the-scenes activity. "Wheels within wheels," he called it. It was necessary, from time to time, for Twining to solicit the intercession of General Thomas to reassure General Smith that we were not engaged in a witch hunt, that what we were doing had real meaning. But Smith was never altogether sure.

In discussing the issues, Twining and I agreed that the time had come for a U.S. Air Force as a separate armed service. World War II had proved that, and for us to oppose it would be both imprudent and parochial. We did feel strongly that there should never be any doubt that the Marine Corps saw, as the most important thing of all in the controversy, the preservation of unquestioned civil authority over military affairs and unfiltered access by the military to the topmost civilian echelon. Second to that, but of critical importance to the Marine Corps, was the procurement of statutory protection for the Corps. This was no more than any service would logically seek for itself.

The Marine antiunification organization, if it could be called an organization at all, made itself felt for the first time through a statement to the Senate Military Affairs Committee by Commandant Vandegrift in late October 1945. It dealt the Collins plan its first small setback. In a tightly written speech, composed by Colonel Twining, General Vandegrift attacked the proposed invasion of the civilian sphere by the military, the erosion of congressional influence over military affairs, and the unmetered control of the budget by the supreme military commander, whose presence, the general declared, would project "the military hierarchy upward into fields which profoundly affect the political, economic and social aspects of national security and national life." The statement was an open declation that the survival of the Marine Corps as an institution was in the center of the Army's sights, the initial shot in a counterattack that was ultimately to humble the War Department and bring into being a national military establishment that protects the existence, the capability, and the function of the Marine Corps.

Vandegrift's statement was followed by a welter of conflicting testimony by Army and Navy witnesses over the meaning of "unification," "civilian control," "merger," and other euphemisms. I heard much of the testimony and could not fail to note that every uniformed Army witness, from General Eisenhower down, made unfavorable references to or implications about the Marines. Nor did the Corps find great comfort in the testimony of Navy leaders—Admirals King, Nimitz, and Sherman—none of whom took occasion in their statements to underscore the Marines' important naval functions and useful wartime performances. An exception was Admiral Halsey, whose applause of the Corps's combat contribution matched his own aggressive temperament. "The fightingest of fighting men," he called them.

Another opportunity to strike a blow soon came to the Marines' behind-the-scenes antiunification team. Lieutenant General Roy S. Geiger, commanding general of all the Marines in the Pacific, came from his headquarters in

Honolulu at the Senate committee's invitation to give his views on the pending bills. Geiger, a gruff, plain-talking man of impressive physical proportions, snow-white hair, and ice-blue eyes, gave the committee its money's worth, and more.

Geiger's credentials for speaking were excellent. He was a renowned pioneer Marine aviator, seasoned in air and ground combat, and had commanded an amphibious corps of two Marine divisions with distinction for the entire eighty-two-day Okinawa campaign. He had not forgotten about his experience in June 1945 at Okinawa when the overall commander of the U.S. invasion force, 10th Army Commanding General Simon Bolivar Buckner, was killed in an enemy artillery barrage. By virtue of his seniority, Geiger automatically succeeded to command of the 10th Army, consisting of four Army and two Marine divisions. We then witnessed the War Department break all records in flying General Joseph Stillwell from the United States to take over the command to avoid having the world see a Marine in command of a field army of six divisions.

General Thomas arranged for Twining and me to speak to General Geiger about preparing him a statement. He was blunt. He wanted to oppose the legislation strongly, particularly its proposed removal of air components from the Army but also its envisioned basic reorganization. We prepared him a hard-nosed speech that he studied, accepted without any comment, and delivered with relish. The statement made three points. First, that the Collins plan was retrospective—"nothing more than a pantographic enlargement of the present War Department organization; a simple elevation of that backward-looking framework to the national level." Second, that the scheme was fatally narrow, failing to provide "a framework within which the president, the Armed Services, the State Department and representatives of labor, industry, science and production could all make their special contributions toward the protection of our country." And, finally, that the unwillingness of the Army Air Force to serve in a supporting role for the Army stood in contrast to the attitude of the Marines, "In . . . 170 years we have never acquired the view that to support another arm in performance of a service to the country was to suffer either indignity or loss of prestige. I wish everybody could share this same healthy outlook."

The Senate committee and the press viewed Geiger's testimony as in the classic Marine style—plain talk with the bark on. By his candor, Geiger did several important things. He alerted the committee to some hard reality that had been glossed over in the orchestrated testimony in favor of the merger legislation. He put the Army on notice that the Marines were not going to take lying down the humiliation planned for them. He notified the Navy that the Marines, strong and loyal allies in opposing the general merger proposition, would stand on their own feet in defense of the Corps. And he told those Marines who took the time to listen that their Corps was in trouble.

That trouble deepened in December 1945 when President Truman sent a message to Congress stressing his desire to see a reorganization of the military along the lines recommended by the War Department. He saw the single chief of staff as a central figure and, while his message declared that the Marines "should be continued as an integral part of the Navy," he privately described the Corps as a duplication, the Navy's "own little Army that talks Navy and is known as the Marine Corps."[10] Thus, the 1945 Senate committee hearings and the president's statements caused the lines to be drawn clearly.

The Army, with presidential support, was determined to see a single department comprising three elemental services —land, sea, and air—with a single administrative secretary at the top. The Joint Chiefs of Staff would manage budget and strategy, with the sole link to the president on these matters being the single chief of staff of the armed forces, who would also adjudicate all budgetary disagreements among the armed forces. The Army, with the exception of some internal grousing about the loss of Army aviation, loyally and aggressively supported these proposals. Why the Army did so had more to do with money than with common rank-and-file jealousies or even with suspicions by General Marshall and Eisenhower that the Marines were bent on creating "a second land Army." Although vigorously held, these views were less significant than the oppressive economics of sustaining an Army in peacetime. Every Marine who was enlisted, every Marine unit provided for in the budget, every Marine tank, artillery piece, fighter, or attack aircraft was a threat to a hungry Army—and budding Air Force—struggling on a peacetime budget.

As for the Navy's position, the testimony of its leaders showed that the Navy was opposed to a single Department of Defense and, most definitely, to a single chief of staff who would have control of the Navy's budget. The Navy believed in the preservation of civilian authority over the services in the form of secretaries of the military departments and disagreed completely with the concept of tri-elemental organization. Navy spokesmen contended that the services should be organized on a functional basis, with each assigned those means needed to discharge its combatant duties. Central to the Navy's concern was the preservation of naval aviation. In the matter of appropriations, where the cost of fighting off obsolescence in a highly technical fleet during peacetime was sobering, the Navy was inclined to see the Marines, good and useful though they were, as siphoning off precious dollars from ship, aircraft, and weapons projects.

The Marines' general attitude was consistent with that expressed by the Navy, except that the Corps held even more strongly to the need for civilian control over the military at large. Particularly, the Marines wanted civilian control of the budget, and they wanted assurance of direct —not circuitous—access to civilian officialdom. Close and continuing congressional influence over military affairs, they believed, was also essential. Most emphatically, the Marines held as an article of faith that no Department of the Navy would be correctly constituted without a dynamic air/ground Marine Corps of size and composition adequate to fulfill the expeditionary/amphibious force-in-readiness role. The members of the Chowder Society, in particular, saw that if the Army and the president had their way an effective Marine Corps would have trouble surviving.

With the passage of time, the differences in emphasis between the Navy and the Marines became more pronounced. The Navy, while determined to preserve its own access to the civilian authority, was not equally committed to similar access by the Marines. Finally, while desirous of seeing a meaningful Marine Corps as part of the ultimate solution, most of the Navy leadership—including Secretary Forrestal, it later developed—were willing to sacrifice the Corps if that is what it took to preserve naval aviation. As had so often been the case before, the Marine Corps thus found itself fighting for its life with no real allies in uniform.

Just how alone we were became painfully clear shortly after Christmas 1945. General Thomas sent for Twining and me to confer with Brigadier General Edson, who was serving as the Marine Corps liaison officer in the Office of the Chief of Naval Operations. He showed us a disquieting report by the Joint Strategic Survey Committee—an instrumentality of the Joint Chiefs of Staff—on the subject "Missions of the Land, Sea and Air Forces." It was one of a group of Joint Chiefs of Staff documents designated "JCS 1478 Series."* Running some fifteen pages, it highlighted the differences in organizational concepts between the Army and the Navy that had surfaced in the 1945 Senate hearings. Discussed at some length was the Navy's battle to preserve the whole of naval aviation and the determination of the Army Air Force to restrict the Navy only to aircraft that operate "from ships or the surface of the sea."

Among the conclusions on which the committee agreed there were two points that seized our attention. First, we were distressed to see that the Navy members of the committee had agreed (without any consultation with the Marines) to the following among the stated "Responsibilities of the Navy Department": "To maintain a Marine Corps for the execution of minor operations in war and in peace, and to supply requisite minor garrisons and naval guard services afloat and ashore." We had no illusion as to what the term "minor" could be made to mean when dollars were short and two or three other services were calling the shots.

---

* Joint Chiefs of Staff studies were assigned numbers, with related topics and successive discussions of the same topic each given an individual subordinate number, such as "JCS 1478/1," "JCS 1478/2," and so forth. The document Edson showed us was JCS 1478/8.

Second, we were disturbed to see that the document was classified "Top Secret."† There was no reason to treat it with that high degree of sensitivity but, so long as it was thus classified, we would be unable to use the 1478 Papers to show what the other services were planning for the Marines' future.

Edson told us that the chief of naval operations intended to comment officially to the Joint Chiefs of Staff on JCS 1478/8, and he asked General Thomas to provide him with Marine Corps material the general would like to see included in the Navy comments. Twining and I, with help from Lieutenant Colonel James C. Murray, prepared a paper that rationalized the place of the Marine Corps in the national security system. After the inevitable review, however, very little of our effort survived in the Navy document that went to the JCS. We read it, and felt just about as naked as we had before it was written; not as naked, however, as we felt when we read the corresponding comments by the commander of the Army Air Forces and by the chief of staff, U.S. Army.

In those documents, designated JCS 1478/10 and 1478/11, the two Army leaders, protected by the Top Secret classification, took the gloves off where the Marines were concerned. The Army Air Forces commander, General Carl Spaatz, described the amphibious operations by the Marines in the war just past as "patently an incursion" into the roles of the Army and Air Forces. (There had never been any allegations when the fighting was going on that the Marine conduct was an incursion.) He recommended "that the size of the Marine Corps be limited to small, readily available and lightly armed units no larger than a regiment."[11]

General Eisenhower, the Army chief of staff, was equally blunt. Declaring that the Marines had merely duplicated the role of the Army in the recent war, he proposed to the JCS a new function for the Corps—"initially bridging the gap

---

† At the time there were four security classifications for military documents, in ascending order—"Restricted, Confidential, Secret, and Top Secret. The last classification was reserved for documents which would, if they fell into the hands of the enemy, "compromise seriously the security of the United States." Clearly this debate, which was already in the public domain, did not fit that definition.

between the sailor on the ship and the soldier on the land." He meant, apparently, that the Marines should operate landing craft. While acknowledging "the need of a force within the fleet to provide small, readily available, and lightly armed units to protect U.S. interests ashore in foreign countries," he proposed Marine units "not exceed the regiment in size" and that the Corps, alone among all the armed forces, "not be appreciably expanded in time of war."[12] As to marine aviation, both generals were explicit. If it were identical to and homogeneous with naval aviation, the existence of marine aviation was tolerable; otherwise they saw no place for it.

The two documents, blunt and brutal though they were, proved to be a blessing in disguise, for they removed all doubt of the fate of the Corps as planned by the Army. They stilled for a while those timorous advisors of the commandant who had cautioned that the apprehensions of the Chowder Society were unfounded. General Vandegrift, in a meeting with Thomas, Twining, and me, agreed to demand of the chief of naval operations that he forward to the JCS a letter from the commandant detailing the Marine reaction to the Army analyses we had just read.

And that is the way it worked out. Twining and I prepared a strong memorandum, which General Vandegrift signed. We addressed directly the allegation that the Marines' performance in World War II was "an incursion" into Army affairs, declaring that no part of the Army, either air or ground, was prepared to meet the amphibious need when it arose.

The Marine memorandum, ultimately transmitted as an enclosure to JCS 1478/12, minced no words: "If the Army was not in fact prepared to execute the functions carried out by the Marine Corps," it said, "then clearly no incursion existed. . . . When the urgency arose for an amphibious expedition to seize Guadalcanal, although there were four Army divisions in the vicinity, it was the Marines who were assigned the task. . . . The Army was unprepared to conduct close air support . . . either before the war, during the war or at the end of the war." We reproved the Army for proposing that the Marines be limited to only small, lightly armed units, for protection of our interests in foreign countries, maintaining that the functions, composition, and weapons of elements of the Naval Service were not the Army's business but "a concern of the Congress."[13]

We felt comfortable that everything we had said in the memorandum was accurate and that, if it were ever to see daylight, the result would benefit the Corps. The Army's position would not be equally defensible in the public forum and, as the debate continued, it became even less so.

General Vandegrift's memorandum stung the Army into a violent and detailed assault on the Corps and all it stood for. Still counting on the protective cloak of the Top Secret classification, the Army attacked, with unrestrained malevolence, most of the conclusions of the commandant's memorandum. JCS 1478/14, the Army memorandum, denigrated the significance of Marine Corps amphibious development, challenged the importance of close air support as nourished by the Marines, denied that the Marines had carried the burden of the amphibious march across the Pacific, and declared that the Army had indeed been ready to take part in the amphibious war in the Pacific from the start.

After Twining and I had studied the bitter and wide-ranging Army document, we agreed that its intemperate tone showed that we were not involved in a sober, substantive discussion of sensitive national security issues. We were involved in a cat fight, where the stakes were the preservation of the existing U.S. military structure as well as the survival of the Marine Corps as a national institution. We knew then, since the Top Secret classification was unwarranted and the stakes so important, that nothing on God's earth could keep the documents out of the public domain for long. We determined to answer the Army's attack on the Corps in a calm, detailed, and thoroughly documented form so that the record, whether ultimately public or not, would be accurate and complete. Using the research library facilities at the Marine Corps Schools in Quantico, Virginia, and resources from Marine Corps Headquarters in Washington, we came up with a thirty-four-page paper (JCS 1478/16) that addressed carefully every criticism made by the Army.

We drew heavily on the Army's own publications and

reports to show that they had completely ignored the amphibious warfare field before World War II.* Without the Marines' generation of study and experimentation, the United States would have been unable to prosecute the Pacific War. The words were restrained but stern. "Had the Marine Corps not so devoted itself, there would have been no amphibious doctrine for the Army to follow when the threat of war appeared and the Army, when it evidenced its first sustained interest in the amphibious problem in 1940, would have found itself twenty years late."

We ended the memorandum with words that were to be repeated many times before the merger battle was over: "Had the Marines never fired a shot in this war, had they never sent a man overseas, their existence would have been more than justified by their original and unparalleled contribution to the field of prospective military theory in the development of the amphibious art."[14] And that ended the 1478 series dialog†, but it did not erase the record of how the emasculation of the Marines had been planned.

In the spring of 1946 the Senate Naval Affairs Committee considered the current version of the merger legislation. It varied little from the highly centralized pattern of its predecessors, with one frightening variation—the Army, Navy, and Air Force were described not as services but as "agencies," a term connoting an organization that could be altered or reconstituted by the executive branch without reference to Congress. Navy witnesses attacked the bill on the now-familiar grounds, with one exception. They began to refer, obliquely, to the damning JCS 1478 Papers.

When Twining and I learned that General Vandegrift was scheduled to testify, we set about preparing a speech for him that would, once and for all, focus attention on the motiva-

---

* We pointed out that the 1939 Army Field Service Regulations omitted any mention of amphibious warfare, that as late as 1942 the only Army publication related to amphibious warfare was a direct copy of a Navy/Marine manual, that in 1940 the Army Command and General Staff School devoted a total of only 17 hours to amphibious operations, at a time when the comparable Marine Corps School devoted 635.

† The series, now wholly declassified and available at the Library of Congress, makes fascinating reading.

tions behind the merger movement. Twining set the tune, "Let's make it tough. Tell the truth." And we did.

General Vandegrift, still steaming from his 1478 Papers colloquy with the Army, was nevertheless taken aback by the vigor of our draft and the broad hints it contained of the existence of the Top Secret 1478 Series. Ultimately, through the quiet efforts of General Thomas, in turn encouraged by Twining, the commandant was persuaded to deliver the speech as we had written it. He was still expressing some misgivings at the last minute, even as we rode with him to the Capitol in his limousine.

Thus it was, on 10 May 1946, that the commandant of the Marine Corps delivered the merger legislation a shattering blow. Addressing the broad character of the legislation, he declared in his first few words that the bill was grossly defective in that it reflected "the War Department General Staff theory that the complexities of modern warfare justify an extension of political-military control into fields of government which are essentially civilian in character." He warned Congress that its own prerogatives were in jeopardy and, moreover, that the threat to their position was intentional. Then, turning from the broad issue to the particular case of the Marine Corps, he told the committee that the survival of the Corps was in danger. "This bill (S. 2044) gives the War Department a free hand in accomplishing its expressed desire to reduce the Marine Corps to a position of military insignificance." Alluding to the 1478 Papers, he said, "I know that the War Department's intentions with respect to the Marine Corps are well advanced and carefully integrated. I have seen them in a form emanating from the highest quarters of the War Department." Just in case someone didn't understand how sweeping the legislation was, he said, "Under the provisions of this legislation the single Secretary of Defense and the all-powerful National Chief of Staff are free either to abolish the Marine Corps outright or divest it of all its vital functions."

Following a recital of the Marines' contributions over the years, particularly in the development of amphibious operations, he administered a small goad to keep the Army's attention, "Preceding the recent war the United States possessed the world's top-ranking Marine Corps at an annual cost of $1,500 per Marine and the world's eighteenth place Army at a cost of $2,000 per soldier." Then General Vandegrift struck the crucial note, "In its capacity as a balance wheel the Congress has on five occasions since 1828 reflected the voice of the people in casting aside a motion which would damage or destroy the Marine Corps. Now I believe the cycle has repeated itself and that the fate of the Marine Corps lies solely with the Congress."

He concluded, "The Marine Corps thus believes it has earned this right—to have its future decided by the legislative body which created it—nothing more. . . . The bended knee is not a tradition of our Corps. If the Marine as a fighting man has not made a case for himself after 170 years, he must go. But I think you will agree with me that he has earned the right to depart with dignity and honor, not by subjugation to the status of uselessness and servility planned for him by the War Department."[15]

Subsequent questioning by committee members was spirited, sympathetic with Vandegrift, and generally unfavorable to the legislation. Inevitably, it brought the 1478 Series out in the open. Senator E. V. Robertson, previously briefed by Lieutenant Colonel E. H. Hurst, asked the first questions on the subject. Then Senator David I. Walsh, the chairman, took up the questioning. He had been briefed by Andrew Higgins, an old Marine Corps friend whom I had asked to see him. The senator served up the home-run pitch to the commandant with these words, "Are there documents or papers drawn up by the Joint Chiefs of Staff which confirm your fears about the Marine Corps being rendered ineffective?"[16] That is all it took. General Vandegrift told them the entire story.

The effect was great—on the Congress, the press, and the public. The bill, which had assumed such momentum, was hard aground on a rock called The Marine Corps. Implicit challenges to the authority of Congress surfaced, and the proposed single chief of staff was widely condemned as a "man on horseback." Only nine days after the Vandegrift testimony, the leaders of the Senate and House Naval Affairs Committees jointly declared that the measure would never pass. At the same time Presidential Assistant Clark Clifford advised Assistant Secretary of War for Air Stuart

Symington that he was "convinced the bill could not pass in the near future or, in fact, at any time."

President Truman, stunned by the vigor of adverse public and congressional reaction to the measure, abandoned the idea of a single chief of staff of the armed forces. To salvage something, he directed the secretaries of the Navy and War to get together and summarize for him their specific areas of agreement and disagreement on the merger issue. He gave them eighteen days in which to do it.

They tried, but it did no good. Indeed, six weeks of conferring and compromising and redrafting, from which the Marines were studiously excluded, produced nothing of substance. In mid-July, the president acknowledged what was clear for anyone to see—the War Department's merger plan was dead for that session of the Congress. They would have to start over.

That was the short-run effect. In the long run, the Marines had gained precious time to marshal resistance to a program that only a few months before faced no opposition at all. As it turned out, a critical skirmish had been won, but the battle itself was still in doubt. Much sweat and heartache remained before the issue would be settled.

CHAPTER 2

Wheels within Wheels

In the days following the "bended knee" speech, the Chowder Society took stock. As we reviewed the congressional testimony and the related documents, we became more convinced than ever that the Army was aiming to recast our war-making organization in the German mold—the system employed by a nation that had just lost a great war. In that system, a single chief of staff directed a political-military organization, as war, politics, and economics were regarded as indissoluble. In Germany, the chief of staff, not a constituted civilian echelon, made all war-related decisions and presented the head of state with a set of options—and the bill.

We saw by its testimony that the War Department was convinced that political thinking in military councils would enhance the country's ability to plan for, finance, and conduct war in the modern age. General Vandegrift had called it the "extension of political-military control into fields of government that are essentially civilian in character." We believed that just the opposite was needed. We believed in undiluted military advice at the topmost civilian level; generals and admirals, if they were doing their jobs properly, would have no time to play politicians, too.

We also discerned in the War Department's proposals a desire to project on the national level the same organization under which the Army itself operated. We had already touched on this in the testimony we prepared for General Geiger, where he described the Collins plan as "nothing more than a pantographic enlargement of the present War Department organization; a simple elevation of that backward looking framework to a national level." Reviewing all the testimony, we could see nothing to indicate any retreat on the Army's part from this concept.

Thus, we foresaw a hard fight resulting from fundamental philosophical differences. The issues transcended the narrow matter of protecting the Marine Corps, important though that was. They included the greater question of whether the national security should be managed by civilians or by the military. In our view, "civilian control" was the better way and meant not just control by the executive branch but by Congress as well.

As we formulated our thoughts, we wondered what the next move would be. We did not have to wait long. General Vandegrift, as a result of his outspoken testimony in the Senate, was taken to the woodshed by President Truman. As a result, Twining and I feared that the commandant's freedom to speak out would be permanently circumscribed, an apprehension that turned out to be all too true. The commandant was never again in the forefront of the battle. We were deeply troubled, because muting the voices of opposition within the military was tantamount to denying Congress anything but pro-merger testimony.

During the autumn of 1946, at the president's behest, General Lauris Norstad, representing the Army, Admiral Forrest Sherman, speaking for the Navy, and presidential emissary Clark Clifford met frequently, trying to work out a compromise to come under consideration by the two secretaries—Forrestal and Robert Patterson. The Marines were neither consulted nor advised of what was going on. We were able to glean a few crumbs of information from contacts in the Navy Department, and what we learned gave us no comfort. The Army was still adamantly claiming that the Corps was "an unnecessary duplication" of the Army's rightful combat role.[1] Nobody, as far as we could tell, was beating the drum in the Marines' behalf, but the differences among the conferees on matters such as the power of the proposed defense secretary, the power of the JCS, and the competition between the proposed Air Force and naval aviation had forestalled any agreements that might hurt us.

That was true up until Christmas, 1946. Then, we began to hear rumblings of rapid progress in the talks that had broadened to include the two secretaries. We were unable to learn the details, but we were told that progress toward an accord was being made and that it was a result of an ultimatum from the president.

On 16 January 1947, the bomb dropped in the form of a joint letter from Secretaries Patterson and Forrestal to the president saying that they had reached full accord on the form which our national security organization should take. Twining and I learned what the accord amounted to the next day when General Thomas sent for us. Saying that neither he nor the commandant had been given any advance information on the agreement, he showed us a copy of the letter that the secretaries had sent the president. What it said was bad. What it did not say was worse.

It recommended all the basic elements embodied in the Collins plan except that of a single military commander. It retained the idea of three military departments—Army, Navy, and Air—a Joint Chiefs of Staff supported by a full-time joint staff and a secretary of defense with authority over both the military departments and the Joint Chiefs. For all these elements, imprecise wording left vast opportunities for arbitrary interpretation. There was nothing, for instance, that told what the individual military services were to do and nothing that ensured the existence of the Marines in anything more than name. In that connection, the joint letter declared that the roles and missions of the several armed services should be prescribed by an Executive Order, leaving to the discretion of the president or the secretary of defense what any service might be called on to do. The Army, the Navy, and the Air Force were generally covered by law, as were the positions of defense secretary and a JCS, but, as General Edson later said, "a President, so disposed, could eliminate the effectiveness of the Marine Corps by the stroke of a pen."[2]

It was plain to us that if our functions were not spelled out in law, our survival would be a very dicey thing. Twining believed that the Army and Navy negotiators had struck a deal. The Army negotiators would tolerate the existence of naval aviation if the Navy would accept the risk of having service roles and missions spelled out in an Executive Order, rather than in law.

After discussions with Thomas, Twining, and me, the commandant agreed that, whatever else we did, we had to see to it that the Corps's existence, role, and functions were embodied in law. This would come about only through educating senators and members of Congress to the Marines' need for statutory protection, in short, through lobbying. The Corps, however, was ill prepared to engage in lobbying. As one member of the Chowder Society said, "The Marine Corps did not have a single influential Congressman or Senator who could be contacted on a personal basis and could be counted on to comply with requests for political action."[3]

Gravely concerned over the turn of events, and at General Thomas's instance, the commandant established a "Board to Conduct Research and Prepare Material in Connection with Pending Legislation." Its purpose was simple—to figure out ways to tell the total unification story and to get the facts to the Congress, the media, veterans organizations, and so forth. Headed by Brigadier General M. A. Edson, the board was composed of a dozen dedicated and competent officers, some of whom had already been working on the problem.* The senior member, Brigadier General Edson, came from the first rank of Marine heroes. Icy cool, serious, intelligent, and energetic, with flat blue eyes and a calm, expressionless voice that never greatly exceeded a whisper, he left no doubt as to his sincerity or his determination.

---

* Brigadier General M. A. Edson; Brigadier General G. C. Thomas; Colonel M. B. Twining; Colonel E. C. Dyer; Lieutenant Colonel V. H. Krulak; Lieutenant Colonel S. R. Shaw; Lieutenant Colonel DeW. Schatzel; Lieutenant Colonel J. C. Murray; Lieutenant Colonel J. D. Hittle; Lieutenant Colonel E. H. Hurst; Lieutenant Colonel R. D. Heinl, Jr.; and Major J. M. Platt.

Enjoying the respect of the entire Corps, he was an ideal leader for the group.

Twining and I had only one apprehension regarding this potent little organization. It had been our hope, from the first, to base our principal case on national security as a whole, and not solely on the issue of Marine Corps survival. We were concerned that the new board would lobby almost exclusively on the narrow—albeit altogether valid—question of Marine Corps survival and that that might cast us in a parochial role. As it turned out, while the board did focus mainly on the Marine Corps problem, the total effect was still good. Twining and I were free to concentrate on the broader issues—the danger of too much military influence in national political and economic matters; the hazard of too much power in the office of the secretary of defense; and the need for legislation to spell out explicitly the roles and missions of the services. We were starting almost from scratch in the matter of educating Congress and the media to the realities of the problem. We learned quickly, however, finding powerful allies in the Marine Corps Reserve Officers' Association, the American Legion, and, particularly, the Veterans of Foreign Wars (VFW) as we sought to explain to the Congress why the claims of economy, streamlining, and harmony were unsubstantial.

Information began to flow in—all we could handle and more. It came from former Marines in government such as Budget Director Jim Webb, from Marine friends such as Senator E. V. Robertson of Wyoming, Senator Styles Bridges of New Hampshire, and Representatives Carl Vinson of Georgia, Mike Mansfield of Montana, and F. Edward Hebert of Louisiana. And it came from friends in the press—David Lawrence of *U.S. News and World Report,* columnist Ralph McGill of the Detroit *News* and the Hearst newspapers. On the inside, Brigadier General Arthur Worton, Marine liaison in the Office of Naval Operations, was a useful contact.

From all our sources we learned that Admiral Forrest Sherman, the chief of naval operations, General Lauris Norstad, Army Air Force, and presidential aide Clark Clifford were driving ahead on a compromise for a national security law that followed the lines of the Patterson-

Forrestal letter of 16 January to the president, which they had drafted. We also learned that Army-oriented merger proponents dominated the Senate Armed Services Committee, where such a bill would be heard.

The bill was sent to Congress by the president on 26 February, without a shred of Marine input. As we had feared, it proposed to endow the new secretary of defense with immense and ill-defined authority over the entire military establishment. There was no statutory prescription at all of what the several armed services were expected to do.

Twining felt that while our efforts with individual committee members might improve the bill slightly, nothing we could do would see it defeated or substantially altered in the Senate. Consequently, we agreed to make an all-out effort in the House, while simply trying to limit the damage in the Senate.

We went to work on a draft statement for General Vandegrift—possibly for use before the Senate Armed Services Committee, possibly in the House. It was Twining's idea that we should take heed of the great success achieved by the "bended knee" statement in 1946, but that we should bear down more heavily on the overall national issue—the hazard to our system of excessive concentration of power.

As we prepared the statement, we monitored the Senate hearings, which, from our viewpoint, went badly. Among other things, we learned that General Eisenhower had no reluctance to voice his support for the German political-military system. He portrayed his own World War II function as, "in effect, the Secretary of National Defense in Europe" and contended that "the problem of national defense should always be presented in rounded form from one brain."[4] The under secretary of war, Kenneth Royall, echoed Eisenhower, extolling the virtue of "exercising power by a single hand."[5]

It was incredible to me that such extreme expressions should not have created an outcry of resentment in the Armed Services Committee. However, the chairman, Senator Chan Gurney, whose dignified courtliness did not conceal the bias created by his former service as a reserve officer in the Army, held firm control over the committee's actions.

As the hearings neared their end, there was no indication that General Vandegrift would be called. Through the efforts of one member of the Edson board, Lieutenant Colonel E. H. Hurst, however, Senator Robertson managed to have the commandant invited. We welcomed the opportunity. The draft statement we had been working on was scholarly and thoroughly documented. It focused primarily on the broad issue of whether the civil authority should direct the military leadership or the reverse. Twining and I took the draft to Washington and tried it on Generals Thomas and Edson. They were enthusiastic, seeing it as a worthy sequel to the "bended knee," and Thomas took it at once to the commandant.

We returned to Quantico, I euphoric and Twining somewhat apprehensive, for reasons I did not then understand. We waited two days for a reaction. When it finally came, the news was bad. The commandant, General Thomas told us, did not like the statement. It was too strong and spoke at too great length on matters "above and beyond the Marine Corps."[6] And to crown the rebuff, he did not ask us for a revision. He had turned for his counsel, as we subsequently learned, to his legal advisor, Colonel John W. Knighton, and to Samuel Meeks of the J. Walter Thompson advertising agency.

The hardworking members of the Edson Board were disappointed, and its little Chowder element in Quantico was devastated. Our discouragement deepened when we heard that the commandant was submitting successive drafts of his statement to the Navy Department—to Admiral Nimitz and Secretary Forrestal—who subsequently obliged him to show the final draft to the president as well.[7]

The commandant's appearance before the Senate Armed Services Committee on 22 April bore little resemblance to that of the preceding May. Hostility from several committee members—Senators Chan Gurney and Millard Tydings in particular—placed him on the defensive. In his statement he had proposed amendments intended to give statutory protection to the Marines' functions. Tydings attacked Vandegrift's proposed protective amendments as inadequate and led the committee to suggest wording from the

Norstad-Sherman-Clifford group, which professed to protect the Marine Corps and its functions by saying,

> The provisions of this Act shall not authorize the
> alteration or diminution of the relative status of the
> Marine Corps . . . or of Naval Aviation.[8]

This was a tepid guarantee, indeed, since it failed to give
any clue as to what "relative status" meant or to what it was
tied. Nevertheless, the commandant acquiesced to the proposal during his testimony. Altogether, it was a bad day for
the Marines. Senator Robertson tried, unsuccessfully, to
regain some of the initiative by raising the threat to the
Corps contained in the 1478 Papers. Our activist group
regarded the whole scene as a substantial setback.

In the testimony that followed, some tried to make up the
lost ground. Admiral Halsey, in his characteristic forthright
way, spoke to the importance of a strong and effective
Marine Corps and of the demonstrated need to provide it
with statutory protection. Former House member Melvin
Mass, a major general in the Marine Corps Reserve, represented the Marine Corps Reserve Officers' Association in
a strong, emotional statement that stressed the Marines'
need, alone among the services, for hard protection in
law.

By far, the most persuasive testimony in the Marines'
behalf came on 7 May from Brigadier General Edson who,
with his distinguished fighting background, his Medal of
Honor, and his consummate sincerity, commanded both the
attention and the respect of the committee. He spoke at the
invitation of Senator Robertson and, to shield the Marine
Corps from any fallout, submitted a request for retirement
before his appearance.* Then, speaking as an individual
representing himself only, he made a persuasive statement.
It contained much of the ill-fated talk prepared by Twining
and me for General Vandegrift plus ideas of his own and
ideas of others on the Edson Board. It compared the War
Department's "tri-elemental" philosophy—where everything that fights on land is in the Army, everything that

---

* The commandant declined at first to act favorably on the request.
He was obliged to accept it a month later, prior to Edson's
testimony in the House of Representatives.

fights at sea is in the Navy, and everything that fights in the air is in the Air Force—with the concept of balanced forces, tailored to do the country's defense job. He contrasted the War Department's concept of concentration of military power in the hands of a single man with the more American emphasis on civilian control of our fighting system. He made a strong plea that the nation needed not a secretary of defense as head of the military establishment but a "presidential deputy" who would serve as a "completely impartial" coordinator of the secretaries of the three military departments. He coldly attacked the idea of the Joint Staff, calling it "an embryo National General Staff."[9]

It was a fine effort, but it did not alter the views of the Army-oriented committee, which reported the bill favorably with essentially no changes. Where the Marine Corps was concerned, the committee, in its report, made a key point—the commandant had agreed to the proposed text, including the Norstad-Sherman-Clifford "relative status" language.

The full Senate approved the bill on 9 July, and we then grimly resolved to intensify our efforts in the House of Representatives, where Twining had forecast from the first that our chances were likely to be better. The Edson-Thomas board and its small Quantico contingent—the original Chowder Society—had already been hard at work acquainting the news media and members of the House with the realities as we saw them. We were making steady progress in the face of equally intensive and better organized lobbying efforts by the Army.

We had gotten a favorable break back in February when the War Department friends in the House sought to steer the unification issue away from the Armed Services Committee and into the Committee on Expenditures in the Executive Department. They had reasoned that there might be too much opposition to the measure among members of the Armed Services Committee, in particular from the respected congressman, Carl Vinson. In contrast, the Committee on Executive Expenditures was chaired by an outspoken isolationist, Congressman Clare E. Hoffman of Michigan, a man who had never evinced any interest in defense affairs and had not a single military installation in his district. The War Department strategists believed that

Hoffman would turn the legislation over to a subcommittee headed by a military-minded member, Congressman James W. Wadsworth of New York, known to favor the Army approach.* This move turned out to be a major error. As much as any other single act, it was decisive in preventing the Army from attaining its objectives.

Hoffman, as it turned out, was not the man they thought he was. A quiet, scholarly gentleman, deeply interested in labor legislation (he served on the House Labor Committee), he could have been expected to turn his back on any national defense controversy. And well he might have, were it not for a long-standing acquaintance with the father of one member of the Chowder Society, Lieutenant Colonel James D. Hittle. Along with Twining, Hittle briefed Hoffman on the problem and, while it certainly was not his usual field, the congressman quickly saw the gravity of the matter. In a simple forthright manner, he surprised his colleagues, declaring that the unification legislation would not be turned over to a subcommittee but would be addressed by the committee as a whole. He then proceeded to make himself an expert on the entire subject. The effect of Hoffman's action was described in the Veterans of Foreign Wars National Legislative Letter of May 1947,

> Army big-wigs in pre-80th Congress strategy meeting decided to unofficially lobby unification bill to House Expenditures Committee . . . feared old Naval Affairs lads on House Armed Services . . . were betting that Hoffman would be too busy on labor legislation . . . laying odds that he wouldn't be interested in service legislation . . . would refer bill to subcommittee of national defense expert and top Army pal Wadsworth (R, New York) . . . whoever spawned that idea will soon pack his steamer trunk.

The VFW had been alerted to the legislative struggle two months earlier by Twining, Hittle, and Edson. By April, the

---

* Wadsworth had earlier served in the Senate, where he was a major architect of defense legislation in 1920. His daughter was married to the assistant secretary of war, Stuart Symington.

two million–member organization had taken an official stand. In the words of its national commander,

> The Veterans of Foreign Wars has taken a positive stand with regard to the continuance of the Marine Corps. Our organization urges Congress to so amend the proposed unification bill to the end that the future duties of the Marine Corps and the part they shall play in our armed services be spelled out and not left "dangling" in space, subject to possible whims of interservice intrigue.[10]

In our activities with the VFW we benefited greatly from the fact that John Williamson, assistant to Omar Ketchum, the national legislative representative of the organization, was a first lieutenant in the Marine Corps Reserve. In the following weeks, he was aggressively active, briefing committee members and providing them with questions that would be useful in eliciting the facts during testimony. Williamson's questions were, of course, usually the product of our group. Eventually the questions became so numerous and so pointed in regard to the inherent overconcentration of power and the need for Marine Corps protection that the whole War Department program stood in danger of derailment.

Witness after witness—Secretary Patterson, General Eisenhower, Admiral Sherman, General Norstad—was thrown on the defensive, trying to deal with questions about the excessive power of the proposed secretary of defense, the potential for the Joint Staff to become a National General Staff, the circumvention of the authority of Congress, and the threats to the Marine Corps. Finally, Ferdinand Eberstadt told Secretary Forrestal that the bill would fail to pass "unless there were specific saving clauses for the Marines and Naval Aviation as well as a definition of the powers of the overall Secretary."[11]

Congressman Hoffman laid the groundwork for the final dramatic scene. First, he introduced a series of amendments designed to limit the authority of the defense secretary and to protect the Marine Corps. (The amendments were drafted by various members of the Chowder Society and presented to Hoffman by Williamson of the VFW, assisted by Colonel Hittle). Second, he brought up the JCS 1478 Papers, wherein the chief of staff of the Army had proposed a permanent emasculation of the Marine Corps. With great tenacity, he sought to obtain the papers, declaring that he could not report out the legislation until he examined them. Finally, he wrote to the president, who ultimately produced the documents. Once the committee looked at the 1478 Papers, there could be little doubt in their minds as to the implications of the bill. As Congressman George Bender put it, "Whoever wrote this bill is giving the Marine Corps the bum's rush."[12]

General Vandegrift's testimony on 6 May essentially repeated what he had told the Senate committee earlier. He again offered the same mild protective amendments that he had presented unsuccessfully to the Senate.

At this point, Lady Luck intervened once again in the Marines' behalf. Congressman Hoffman, referring to the Marine Corps protective amendments which he had introduced earlier—the ones our Chowder group had drafted and passed to him through the VFW—asked the commandant how he felt about those amendments. Those of us who were observers at the hearings noticed that the commandant's legal aide, Colonel Knighton, whispered something to him; following which the commandant responded that he favored the amendments, *inasmuch as he had submitted them himself.*

It was obvious that the commandant, his legal aide, or both, were confused. General Vandegrift was referring not to the strong amendments introduced by Congressman Hoffman but to those which he had offered himself. The effect was, however, to anoint Hoffman's proposals, which the Chowder group had designed, with official Marine Corps approval. Whether Hoffman realized the confusion but chose to let the effect stand is unclear. What is clear is that he later said for the record that the commandant's testimony concurred with his amendments, which, of course, was most beneficial.

General Eisenhower followed the commandant. His testimony, like that of others, covered the whole spectrum of questions on the bill. In response to one question he developed an interesting thesis, one which has since been used frequently in advancing the virtue of the Joint Staff and joint education. He said, "You must in advance develop a groundwork of friendship. . . . Then when we come here to Washington we deal as friends and advise our common chief as friends."[13] What he was suggesting was that personal friendships developed in the Joint Staff could result in a serious and productive synthesis of conflicting professional views. We gravely doubted that such harmony could be legislated.

Responding to a carefully phrased question by Chairman Hoffman on the Marine Corps, the general replied that he had not at any time proposed a diminution in the size, roles, or functions of the Corps, saying, "I am nonplussed to find out why I have been considered an enemy of the Marines." Whereupon Congressman Hoffman embarked upon a vigorous line of questioning concerning the Army's views on the Marine Corps. Belatedly, the general recognized the bad news; Hoffman was reading to him directly from the 1478 Papers and had before him Eisenhower's earlier intemperate assertions concerning the Corps! Eisenhower's immediate shift to the cautious defensive was obvious to all of us who were watching the proceedings.

HOFFMAN: Do you realize that the 1478 Papers created the opinions that the Army wanted to eliminate the Corps as an effective combat force?
EISENHOWER: They may have.
HOFFMAN: They did. Do you not know that to be a fact?
EISENHOWER: I suppose they said that, but . . . I don't see why they should be fearful of me.[14]

We concluded afterwards that the general's testimony had to be a solid plus for the Marines.

At about this time—early May—the president made known to Secretaries Forrestal and Patterson and to the service chiefs his dissatisfaction with lobbying by the military services. He made particular reference to the Navy and Marine Corps, telling Vandegrift to "get those Lieutenant

Colonels off the Hill and keep them off."[15] Following this and a conference with General Edson, the commandant dissolved the Edson Board, and from that moment on we were all on our own except for Lieutenant Colonel Hittle. He had become so valuable to Congressman Hoffman that Hoffman requested officially of the Navy Department that he be detailed to duty as a special advisor to the committee. Hittle's presence in Hoffman's office was of great value in all aspects of the legislation—and it certainly made the merger proponents nervous.

The president's open dissatisfaction with antimerger lobbying produced a reverse of his desired effect. Members of the committee—Congressmen Cole, Bender, and Latham—complained of what they described as a "gag" placed almost exclusively on military opposition to the legislation, saying that they were being permitted to hear only one side. Ultimately, and with the president's approval, Secretary Forrestal suspended the provisions of Navy Regulations that stood in the way of open opposition by Navy and Marine officers. The result was a procession of witnesses, largely naval aviators, who were strongly critical of the measure.

Their opposition, however, paled beside the testimony of General Edson. It had been our belief that one powerful witness would be more effective than several of only moderate quality. Edson's talk to the Senate committee had been excellent, but what he laid before Hoffman's committee was even better—the most comprehensive critique of the issue yet articulated. It distilled all the thoughts and arguments we had been developing since the alarm rang almost two years before. In addition to Edson's own views, his testimony embodied the best of Twining and of the rest of us who had been laboring on the project. Its effect was powerful—"an atom bomb in the works," as Congressman Bender later described it.[16]

This time, mindful of the likely impact of his words on the Corps, Edson had resubmitted his request for retirement, and, this time, the commandant accepted it. Then, speaking as a private individual, Edson hammered away—to Twining's satisfaction and mine—at the violence done by the pending bill to civilian control of the military establishment. He showed how military influence would extend into areas that, in our government, were traditionally civilian. He condemned any system that would place a third of our national budget in the hands of a defense secretary whose staff support was predominantly military and whose charter permitted almost unlimited expansion. He criticized the military influence in the proposed Central Intelligence Agency as "a potential Gestapo." He warned the Congress that under the proposed merger system there would no longer be diverse opinions expressed by military witnesses. Rather, he said, the bill would create a "coalition of the armed services" wherein advance agreement would cause all witnesses to testify the same way.[17]

His recommendations, broad in nature and soberly expressed, were impressive on the committee. He proposed:

- that there be no secretary of defense, serving as an advocate at the head of the military establishment; rather that there be a presidential deputy to speak for the president in resolving problems affecting the military departments.
- that the military influence in the National Security Council and Central Intelligence Agency presently provided for in the bill be removed.
- that the size and the functions of the Joint Staff be rigidly delineated, converting it to a secretariat.
- that the roles and missions of all the armed forces be spelled out in law.

Immediately after his testimony, Edson gave Congressman Hoffman a draft unification bill representing his ideas. The draft was a product of the now-disbanded Edson board, all of us having had some hand in its development. After analyzing the proposal carefully, Hoffman decided this was henceforth to be his own bill, and he introduced it as such. The Chowder Society felt rewarded.

Testimony after Edson was anticlimatic. Hearings ended within ten days and then there ensued three weeks of drafting, conference committees, and floor consideration. The Chowder Society strove to ensure that members of the

House were fully briefed and that as many as possible shared Congressman Hoffman's views. Hittle's efforts, particularly, were of great value to Hoffman as the congressman maneuvered the bill, first with his own committee and finally in conference with the Senate.

One benefit during this period of negotiations resulted from the efforts of Lieutenant Colonel DeWolf Schatzel, one of the former Edson board members. He persuaded Sentor Byrd, who was involved in the House-Senate conference, to send a letter to General Vandegrift asking him flat out whether he preferred the Senate or the House version. (The House version was, of course, the Hoffman Bill prepared by our group.) Schatzel drafted the letter for the senator. He then drafted a reply for General Vandegrift, which declared clearly that he preferred the House version of the bill because "it better defined our position." Vandegrift's signature thus neutralized his own earlier Senate testimony and permitted Hoffman to capitalize on the fact that the Marines now officially preferred his bill.

The House-Senate conference adopted Hoffman's version in almost all its details. Most particularly it specified the roles and missions of all the armed forces. Once the conference was concluded, both House and Senate acted quickly and sent the measure to President Truman. On 25 July, he signed the legislation into law. Much that we had fought so hard to achieve was there—the statutory protection of the Marine Corps, air, ground, and Reserve. Additionally, there was protection for naval aviation. What brought me the most pleasure was the articulation of the Marine Corps's roles and missions in these words, most of which our little group had written:

The Marine Corps shall be organized, trained and equipped to provide fleet marine forces of combined arms, together with supporting air components, for service with the fleet in the seizure or defense of advanced naval bases and for the conduct of such land operations as may be essential to the prosecution of a naval campaign.

* * *

Some of the things we had fought to exclude were excluded—most particularly a single chief of staff and most of the military influence in the National Security Council and in the Central Intelligence Agency. Similarly, the size of the Office of the Secretary of Defense and the Joint Staff were sharply limited (100 and 150 persons respectively).

But, as always, much remained to be done. The function of the defense secretary was not adequately defined nor was his relationship with the Joint Chiefs of Staff nor theirs with the president. As for the Marines, their place in the new JCS arrangement was uncertain. Taken all together, however, it was a great Marine Corps triumph. I believe the triumph was due to, more than anything else, the quality of apprehensive vigilance that has characterized the Corps since its birth.

In a Chowder Society "victory celebration" at my house on the day the president signed the bill into law, one member remarked that Truman himself had best articulated our position. In a conversation with Commandant Vandegrift at the height of the controversy, the president eyed him quizzically and said, "You Marines don't trust anybody, do you?" The president was right.

CHAPTER 3

Reprise, Reprise, and Reprise

Understandably, the Marines congratulated themselves on the National Security Act victory. After all, the Corps's existence and its capability to contribute to our country's defense were, at long last, enshrined in law. The celebration was brief, however, as we turned to analyze how the new statute would be regarded by those it affected.

The Navy would probably find little to complain about. The organization was more centralized than Navy leaders wanted, but naval aviation had been accorded the recognition and stature that it needed and deserved.

The Air Force, although undeniably pleased by its new service status, would still have some reservations about the substantial air elements in the Navy and Marine Corps that would not fall within its fiscal or operational orbit. In fact, General Spaatz continued to insist that there should be no differentiation between strategic and tactical air operations and that both should be the responsibility of the Air Force.

The Army would be very unhappy with the legislation. It had fallen far short of attaining their objectives. The defining of roles and missions, which included Marine Corps protection, was a visible affront and an irritation, but more disappointing, to the Army, was the failure to achieve the broader organizational goals. Instead of a highly centralized arrangement where a singular military leadership could confidently face budgetary problems with no fear of internal military dissension, the Army ended up with no chief of staff, a sharply circumscribed General Staff, and a defense secretary with loosely defined jurisdiction. The open charter of the defense secretary could, in fact, turn out to be the greatest problem of all, in the years to follow, not just for the Army but for all the services.

The Marines saw the new law in reverse colors from the Army. They favored more rather than less civilian control, so that the military might confine itself to the planning for and direction of combat operations. The Marines perceived the proper function of the Joint Chiefs to be the expressing of the purely professional military viewpoint, but they feared the invasive potential of the new Office of the Secretary of Defense. Civilian control, they felt, should be exercised by the president and the Congress, not by a departmental chief, whom they regarded as nothing more than an advocate. In his place they wanted a presidential deputy, speaking *for* the chief executive, not *to* him.

Regarding the Marine Corps itself, however, the Marines were apprehensive that the new system provided no assurance that the Corps would be permitted the organizational strength to do its job, no niche for the commandant in the Joint Chiefs of Staff structure, and no assured place for the Marine viewpoint in the Joint Staff. Thus, they were inadequately covered in the critical area of strategic planning, and, they reasoned, "If you're not in the script, you're not in the act." In short, as Commandant Clifton B. Cates put it, the new law was "not a refuge but a battle position which must be defended in full force."[1]

Finally, there were civilians whose aspirations for the defense legislation were not fully met. President Truman, Senators Gurney and Henry Cabot Lodge, and Representative Wadsworth were all stalwart backers of a Chief of Staff/National General Staff system. James Forrestal, elevated from Navy secretary to defense secretary, did not believe that his new position had been endowed with enough power. He had wanted to exercise unquestioned authority over the Joint Chiefs and the Army, Navy, and Air Force departments. To do so, he believed his office should have been larger than the one-hundred-man limitation set by Congress.

Thus, the law, over which so much sweat had been expended, was at best a fragile mutation. Almost at once, to no surprise of the Marines, the centralization advocates initiated a move to advance a step nearer their goal. General Eisenhower fired the opening shot on the occasion of his retirement as chief of staff of the Army in 1948. In a long and sober memorandum to Secretary Forrestal, he voiced his concern with various aspects of the organization for national security, among them the circumscribed scope of the Joint Chiefs of Staff, as he saw it, and the invasive character of the Marine Corps, where the Army was concerned.

Secretary Forrestal followed with an analysis of the system in his report on the first fifteen months of operation of the department. As would be true with all his successors for the next dozen years, he believed that he needed more power. He urged an increase in the size of his office, the establishment of a deputy secretary, and an increase in his "direction, authority and control" over the "departments and agencies of the National Military Establishment." He also, at the prompting of General Eisenhower, proposed the creation of a chairman of the Joint Chiefs of Staff and an increase in the size of its staff from 100 to 210.[2]

A subcommittee of the Hoover Commission on efficiency in the federal government echoed these proposals, as did President Truman, who described the National Security Act as only a "workable basis for beginning the unification of the military services."[3] His recommendations, in the form of a Reorganization Act, included every idea advanced by Secretary Forrestal, plus a proposal that the departments of the Army, Navy, and Air Force be downgraded from the status of executive departments to "military departments."

At the time, I was serving in the 1st Marine Division in

California but was brought back to Washington to work on a plan to oppose the changes. It became plain, however, that there was little stomach in the Congress for concerted opposition to the moves, and the president's proposals became law in August 1949. The Marines recognized the changes as altogether unfavorable—growth in the defense secretary bureaucracy, the possibility of a National Chief of Staff evolving from the newly created JCS chairman position, and, because of the downgrading of the military departments, further insulation of the Corps from the highest decision-making level.

The last point touches on the next significant development. It had its beginnings in the exclusion of Marines from high military councils during the postunification period. In March of 1948, for example, Secretary Forrestal brought together high-ranking defense officials in Key West, Florida, to hammer out details on the services' roles and missions. The Marine commandant, General Cates, was not included. The results were predictable; the conference spoke primarily about what the Marines would *not* do.

* The Corps would not be permitted to expand beyond four division/wing strength in time of war (despite its obvious capability to do more, as exemplified by World War II).
* The Corps would not be permitted to exercise command above the Corps level (evidently to counter what the Army had regarded as a threat in World War II).
* The Corps would not be permitted to create a second land army (it was not lost on the Marines that these same words had appeared in General Eisenhower's memorandum to the Joint Chiefs of Staff in 1946, in JCS document 1478/11).

Parallel with these actions was a trend, initiated in the executive branch, to diminish steadily the personnel strength and consequently the combatant capability of the Corps. Louis Johnson, Forrestal's successor as defense secretary, in his 1959 budget, decreed that the Corps be cut from 100,000 to 65,000 men, its infantry force be cut from eleven to eight battalions, and its aviation squadrons from twenty-three to twelve.

These acts of exclusion and starvation were exactly what the Congress had intended to preclude, and this knowledge inspired Marine supporters in Congress, led by Senator Paul Douglas and Congressmen Carl Vinson and Mike Mansfield, to promote legislation that would make the commandant a member of the Joint Chiefs. Mansfield, in addition, introduced legislation to link the personnel strength of the Corps to that of other services. A bipartisan group of fifty-four House members joined him in this move. General Cates outspokenly supported the congressional movement. He said that without the Joint Chiefs position the Corps did not have "adequate representation in matters of vital concern both to the Corps itself and to the National defense."[4] He also told Congress that "the power of the budget, the power of coordination, and the power of strategic direction of the armed forces have been used as devices to destroy the operating forces of the Marine Corps."

The adverse effects of this policy of exclusion and administrative starvation was dramatically illuminated by the disadvantaged size and condition of the Marine operating forces at the onset of Korea. The situation reinforced the ongoing pressure to see a law passed that would protect the personnel strength of the Corps and place its commandant on the Joint Chiefs of Staff. The mauling of Army units in Korea in late 1950 by onrushing North Korean forces caused one critic of the Truman administration to shift into overdrive. Congressman Gordon S. McDonough of the Fifteenth District in California was a conservative Republican and a fierce and vocal opponent of President Truman and his foreign policy. He declared Truman's policies in the Far East an inept failure and called for the resignation of Secretary of Defense Johnson and Secretary of State Dean Acheson, calling the latter "our Hiss-loving, Russian romancing, world-wooing Secretary of State."[6]

Then, on 21 August, came the heartening news of the

victory of the 1st Marine Brigade in the First Battle of the Naktong in the Pusan perimeter. Congressman McDonough was inspired to take what many now believe to have been the critical step in placing the commandant at the JCS table. He wrote a letter to President Truman, praising the Marines' battlefield performance over the years and applauding particularly their valiant response to the Korean crisis. Emphasizing their importance to the security of the nation, he declared that the Corps "should have its own representative on the Joint Chiefs."[7]

The letter came at a bad time for the president. He was under heavy fire for the evident unpreparedness of our forces in Korea and Japan. Rubbed raw by the widespread attacks on him and his administration, as exemplified by McDonough's letter, he vented his frustrations on the Marines, for whom he had little love anyhow.

He wrote McDonough a furious response, which, imprudently, he failed to show to any of his advisors. In his letter he put the Corps in its place—as he saw it. "For your information," he wrote, "the Marine Corps is the Navy's police force and as long as I am President that is what it will remain. They have a propaganda machine that is almost equal to Stalin's. . . ."[8]

The Truman letter became public knowledge when McDonough inserted it in the *Congressional Record.* And then the fat was in the fire. Senators and representatives on both sides of the aisle excoriated the president's comments. Senator Joseph R. McCarthy called it "a fantastically unpatriotic thing to say about the boys who are dying in Korea."[9] The press followed suit with feature articles, columns, and editorials. Private citizens directed the heaviest volume of mail and telegrams to the White House of the entire Truman administration, save the correspondence on the Taft-Hartley Act of 1947.[10] Finally, the Marine Corps League, which happened to be holding its annual convention in Washington, resolved to demand that the president apologize to the American people for his insult of the Corps.

At first the president did not take the matter too seriously, but the convergence of public outcry and the sober counsel of his own staff caused Truman to put his signature to a carefully qualified letter of apology to Commandant Cates. "I sincerely regret the unfortunate choice of language which I used in my letter to Congressman McDonough. . . . I am certain that the Marine Corps itself does not indulge in such propaganda. . . ." He sent for the commandant and delivered it in person along with a verbal affirmation of his regret. Meanwhile, Presidential Press Secretary Charles Ross urged Truman to go the whole way and appear in person before the Marine Corps League convention. Most of the White House staff opposed the Ross suggestion. General Cates was called to the White House to discuss the matter and, as one observer describes it, after an inconclusive meeting, Cates was instructed to return the following morning.[11] Neither history nor legend explains exactly how it happened, but, when the commandant presented himself at the White House in the morning, he had to advise Truman that he had already told a number of people that the president would, indeed, address the Marine Corps League. Without further debate, the president decided to go.[12]

The Marine Corps League, drawing its membership largely from retired Marines, has always been an extremely independent body. In its fierce loyalty to the Corps, its actions have sometimes given the Marine Corps cause for worry. In this case, its fury at Truman's behavior was so intense that there was concern about how the group would act if the president appeared. The members were not satisfied with the letter of apology, and they were suspicious of Truman because of the 1947 unification issue. The steadying influence, however, of Congressman Melvin Maas of Minnesota, a Reserve major general, and of the league president, Clay Nixon, resulted in a respectful reception for the chief executive. The president spoke at length about the Korean War, his aspirations for peace, and his respect for the Marine Corps. The conventioneers responded with unusual dignity and, on his departure, voted unanimously to accept the president's apology. Then they proceeded to pass another unanimous resolution—calling for Joint Chiefs of Staff status for the commandant!

In the wake of all the attention drawn to the Marine Corps plight, Senator Paul H. Douglas and Congressman Mike Mansfield sponsored a bill providing that the Fleet Marine Force be composed of four combat divisions and four aircraft wings and that the commandant should be a member of the Joint Chiefs of Staff. In introducing his bill, Senator Douglas, reflecting the views of many of his colleagues, said, "We have in the past attempted to provide for this combatant Marine Corps by expressions of Congressional intent. It is clear that expressions of intent are ineffective. We must have direct action in the form of law."[13] The secretary of defense and the Joint Chiefs of Staff opposed the bill. The chief of naval operations, Admiral Sherman, in particular, minced no words. In response to a question from Senator Long, he said:

> The Marine Corps is not being hurt by reason of a lack of Marine membership on the Joint Chiefs of Staff. The Marine Corps is represented in the same manner as is the submarine arm or the air arm . . . in the person of the Chief of Naval Operations . . .

Subsequently, in an exchange with Senators Leverett Saltonstall and James Flanders on the matter of Joint Chiefs participation by the commandant, the admiral's case took a serious blow:

> SENATOR SALTONSTALL: If it were a matter of whether we should undertake an important amphibious operation . . .
> SENATOR FLANDERS: Take as a specific case the Inchon landing.
> ADMIRAL SHERMAN: Yes.
> SENATOR FLANDERS: Was the Commandant present at the Joint Chiefs of Staff meeting when Inchon was discussed?
> ADMIRAL SHERMAN: No, he was not.[14]

Neither the committee nor Congress at large was able to agree with the bill's opponents. As enacted, the legislation

(Public Law 416) provided that the Corps "shall be so organized as to include not less than three combat divisions and three aircraft wings" and

> The Commandant of the Marine Corps shall indicate to the Chairman any matter scheduled for consideration by the Joint Chiefs that directly concerns the Marine Corps. Unless, upon request of the Chairman for a determination, the Secretary of Defense determines that such a matter does not concern the Marine Corps, the Commandant shall meet with the Joint Chiefs of Staff when the matter is under consideration. While the matter is under consideration and with respect to it, the Commandant has co-equal status with the members of the Joint Chiefs of Staff.

Henceforward it would be most difficult to exclude the Corps when matters critical to their statutory function were under discussion. Considering the hostility of President Truman and Defense Secretary Johnson, it is unlikely that the commandant would have achieved JCS status during their tenure without the president's intemperate letter to McDonough. All together, the McDonough incident was, as Commandant Cates said, "One of the luckiest things that ever happened to the Corps."[15]

Public Law 416, signed by President Truman on 20 June 1952, was an essential complement to the National Security Act—in many ways the coming of age event in the Corps's organizational history. While the 1947 act protected the existence of the Corps and stated its functions, it did not guarantee the means to carry out those functions. Public Law 416 did exactly that, by ensuring balanced air/ground forces for the Corps and a seat at the JCS table for the commandant when employment of those forces was deliberated. Furthermore, in its preamble, the law declared that the U.S. Marine Corps was, and had been, a separate military service like all the others, serving within the Department of the Navy along with the U.S. Navy.

Nobody knew just how the "direct concern" provision was to work, and the Corps's new commandant, Lemuel C.

Shepherd (1952–55) had the challenge of establishing a modus operandi with the same Joint Chiefs of Staff who had opposed the law so vigorously. Shepherd's formula was simple—examine all documents involved in Joint Chiefs agenda items (a large staff job in itself) and then declare to be of direct Marine Corps concern only those that fulfilled the criteria without question.

It worked out satisfactorily. At the end of the first year, only 9 percent of the Joint Chiefs agenda items had been declared of direct concern. On those occasions, the chiefs who had opposed the commandant's presence at the table so bitterly welcomed him "warmly and graciously."[16] In 1954, when Admiral Arthur Radford replaced General Omar Bradley as chairman, he often requested that the commandant "remain and discuss matters of no direct concern to the Marine Corps because he valued the Marine viewpoint."[17]

The growth in the Office of the Secretary of Defense, which had begun with the 1949 amendments, quickened in the winter of 1952. Secretary of Defense Robert Lovett, in a letter to the president, deplored his inadequate authority over the Joint Chiefs of Staff and the military departments and lamented his own lack of a military staff. Lovett's solution was threefold: one, to confine the Joint Chiefs of Staff to planning only; two, to provide the Defense Secretary with "a combined military-civilian-staff" that would make the several unified commands responsive directly to the orders of the defense secretary; and, three, to eliminate the statutory provision that the military departments "shall be separately administered."[18]

Lovett's recommendations were a precursor to the Rockefeller Commission, brought into being by President Eisenhower the following spring. The commission's seven members were, in addition to Rockefeller, General Omar Bradley, the president's brother Milton, Lovett, Vannevar Bush, Arthur Fleming, and David Sarnoff. It proposed broadening of the authority of the defense secretary, according the office the characteristics of advisor, executive, and director. The growth was exemplified in the proposed increase of under and assistant defense secretaries from the existing three to nine, plus a general counsel. President Eisenhower, not unexpectedly, applauded the Rockefeller report and, in June 1953, sent to Congress Reorganization Plan No. 6, which sought to give legal effect to the Rockefeller recommendations plus a few items added on the way. The president proposed, for instance, that selection of the director of the Joint Staff should be subject to the approval of the secretary of defense and that the Joint Staff be managed by the chairman and not by the corporate Joint Chiefs.

At the time, Twining and I were both serving on the staff of Commandant Shepherd. We wrote him a statement that exhibited the undesirable implications of the plan to the House Committee on Government Operations. It got their attention, tracing the pressures to enlarge the defense bureaucracy in the Lovett proposal, the Rockefeller report and, finally, the president's reorganization plan. The committee voted (sixteen to fourteen) to reject the entire plan but was overridden by the full House. The plan became law on 30 June 1953.

The Reorganization Plan No. 6 debate was scarcely ended when the Shepherd administration faced a challenge from a different quarter—the Navy. To synchronize the Department of the Navy with the expanded Office of the Secretary of Defense arising from Reorganization Plan No. 6, the secretary of the Navy established a Committee on Organization of the Department of the Navy. Lieutenant General Thomas, then chief of staff at Marine Corps Headquarters, was the Marine representative. I was his staff support.

The committee's recommendations were unremarkable on their face. One, however, created a major departmental whirlwind. It proposed that Navy Department General Order No. 5, the bedrock document that governs the distribution of authority within the department, be revised "to clarify the responsibilities of the Commandant of the Marine Corps to the Secretary of the Navy, and his responsibilities to and relationship with the Chief of Naval Operations."[19]

The chief of naval operations, Admiral Forrest R. Sherman, offered four propositions to apply in a redraft of General Order No. 5:

- That the Marine Corps does not possess operating forces; all Marine Corps combat units being ipso facto a part of the operating forces of the U.S. Navy.
- That the chief of naval operations should exercise general and direct supervision over the Headquarters of the Marine Corps.
- That the chief of naval operations enjoys a broad authority, termed "naval command of the naval establishment," over the entire Department of the Navy, including the Marine Corps.
- That the chief of naval operations should establish the personnel and material requirements of the Marine Corps.

Essentially, the chief of naval operations was contending that he commands the Marine Corps, its forces, and its headquarters and has the authority to establish the Corps requirements for both men and material.

Commandant Shepherd took strong issue with this position, both with the chief of naval operations and Secretary of the Navy Robert A. Anderson. After an inconclusive exchange of views, Secretary Thomas directed that the chief of naval operations and the commandant attempt a redraft of the elements in contention. To do the work, the chief of naval operations appointed Rear Admiral (later Vice Admiral) Ruthven E. Libby. General Shepherd appointed me (at that time a colonel). Both Libby and I had been involved with the Committee on Organization, both knew the high stakes involved, and neither had much stomach for the job.

We began our discussion poles apart, arguing the four issues over five months. Based on review of all applicable laws, we gradually came to agreement on three: that the Marine Corps *does* possess operating forces other than those assigned to the operating forces of the Navy; that the chief of naval operations does *not* exercise supervision over the headquarters of the Marine Corps; and that the commandant of the Marine Corps *does* exercise, on his own, a fraction of the "naval command of the naval establishment." But on the matter of who establishes the personnel and material requirements of the Marine Corps we could not agree. Here was the fundamental issue of appropriations and the apportionment of resources. Libby could make no concession. Nor would I, believing "the power to feed is the power to starve." Accordingly, we laid before our superiors a redraft that favored the Marine Corps on the first three issues, and each offered his own alternative wording on the question of personnel and material requirements.

The commandant and chief of naval operations, now Admiral Robert B. Carney, having debated the issue inconclusively, finally laid their cases before Secretary Anderson. After some deliberation, he found in favor of the Marines, approving the key wording in General Order No. 5 of 20 November 1954 as follows:

The Commandant of the Marine Corps is the senior officer of the United States Marine Corps. He commands the Marine Corps and is directly responsible to the Secretary of the Navy for its administration, discipline, internal organization, unit training, requirements, efficiency, and readiness, and for the total performance of the Marine Corps.

It was a victory for the Corps, and it has stood up for almost three decades.

Meanwhile, President Eisenhower, disgruntled that his goal of giving full legal effect to General Marshall's idea of military organization had not yet been achieved, set in motion two new studies only ten days after ratification of the 1953 Reorganization Plan No. 6. A new Commission on Organization of the Executive Branch conducted one study, the Rockefeller Brothers Fund directed the other. Both addressed the same targets as earlier—inefficiency, duplication, and rivalry.

Referring to these studies and to a favorable recommendation by his defense secretary (Neil H. McElroy, in office only three months), the president in 1958 proposed to Congress another series of major accretions in the defense secretary's power. The changes were of such a magnitude that they would alter our concept of how to make war. He recommended that the chain of command for combat operations exclude the Joint Chiefs of Staff and flow from the defense secretary directly to the unified commands in the field. He proposed that the role of the Joint Chiefs of Staff thereafter be "to furnish professional advice and staff assistance to the Secretary of Defense." He recommended that the existing statutory authority of the individual chiefs to present recommendations to Congress be repealed and, to help the defense secretary do his work, that the size of the Joint Staff be increased from 210 to 400.

Additionally, although he had been rebuffed by the Congress before, he asked again that all restrictions be removed from the defense secretary's authority to transfer, reassign, abolish, or consolidate combatant functions of the armed services. Such restrictions had been imposed by the National Security Act as being wholly the prerogative of Congress, and it was the lifting of such restrictions that the Marines greatly feared. He also objected to the idea that the secretary of defense must issue directives to the three military departments through the department secretaries, claiming that it was unduly restrictive on the defense secretary. It was in these two areas—whether the secretary of defense should have the authority to transfer, reassign, or abolish functions and whether he should be authorized to bypass the secretaries of the military departments—that the Congress found its greatest concern, concern shared by the Marine Corps.

At the time, I was director of the Marine Corps Educational Center in Quantico, Virginia, and my immediate superior was Lieutenant General Twining. We recognized the threat to the Corps's function implicit in the plan and, at the invitation of Commandant Randolph McC. Pate (1956–59), prepared for him a draft statement designed to convey the Marine Corps's apprehensions to the House Armed Services Committee. In it we urged that the existing statutory protection for the Marine Corps function be left undisturbed. General Pate said:

The Marine Corps is the only one of the services which is actually affected in any fundamental respect by this proposal to give over to the Secretary of Defense the present Congressional authority to abolish and transfer combatant functions. None of the other services is vitally concerned. I very much doubt, for example, if there is any real prospect of anyone wanting to take away from the Air Force the tasks you have given it—conducting warfare in the air; and the same goes for the Navy in the matter of naval warfare; and the same with the Army regarding its important responsibilities for combat on land.

It is the Marines alone—an organization brought into being to meet a strategic situation which is peculiar to this insular nation—an organization designed specifically for the short notice expeditionary tasks which have confronted us so often in the past and will exist in the future—that stands in jeopardy from this proposal.*

Some thirteen hundred pages of both the House and Senate testimony revealed a sincere determination on the legislators' part to give the defense secretary what he required to discharge his duties, while at the same time there was a strong apprehension that granting all the president wanted would be an abrogation of congressional authority.

Witnesses favoring the president's reorganization plan, largely administration officials, made a timorous case, leaning heavily on generalities. Defense Secretary McElroy referred to "the increased tempo of warfare . . . reduction of needless argument and misunderstanding . . . to provide modest flexibility in the handling of defense funds . . . to remove some of the present tendencies toward confusion and overlapping of effort. . . ."[20]

Opponents made an equally frail case, ironically focusing on overconcentration of power in the military and growth of power in the JCS chairman. William H. Harrison, Jr., president of the National Guard Association of the United

---

* Drafts available in Archives, Marine Corps Historical Foundation, Washington, D.C.

States, said, "We find extreme danger in the delegation of decision-making power to a powerful general staff and an extremely powerful chairman or chief of that general staff."[21] While there was something in this, clearly a far greater issue was the burgeoning power of the secretary of defense.

In contrast to the witnesses' generalizations, Congress was not loath to penetrate to the heart of the problem. The report of the House Armed Services Committee summarized the congressional apprehensions. Among other points, the committee made these comments:

- On the scope of activity of the Office of the Secretary of Defense:

  It was never intended, and is not now intended, that the Office of the Secretary of Defense would become a fourth department within the Department of Defense, delving into operational details on a daily basis.

- On the president's desire to eliminate the requirement that the defense secretary deal with the military departments through their secretaries:

  If the military secretaries are to be something more than branch managers, they must be responsible for execution of the directives issued by the Secretary of Defense. If the [requirement] is eliminated the separate identity of the services, the decentralization of the military departments, would become a myth. . . ."[22]

- On the president's desire to authorize the secretary of defense to reassign, abolish, or consolidate combatant functions of the armed services—an action prohibited by the National Security Act:

  Congress must exercise its constitutional responsibility in this area. . . . Such a grant of authority to the Executive Branch would constitute a complete surrender of Constitutional authority. . . ."[23]

Similar apprehensions surfaced in the hearings in the Senate Armed Services Committee. Yet, despite widespread congressional misgivings, the vote proceeded along party lines and gave the president much of what he asked for. A compromise in the critical area of transfer, consolidation, or abolishment of combatant functions obliged the executive to go through two successive periods of congressional scrutiny before any such move could take place.

Congress agreed to an increase in the size of the Joint Staff and to eliminate the authority of service chiefs to present recommendations to Congress. And, in a sobering concession that would have far-reaching effects, it complied with the president's wishes concerning operational authority. Under existing Executive Order, flowing from the Key West Agreement of March 1940, one of the military departments served as the executive agent for each of the unified or specified commands. The chief of staff of that service supervised the execution of plans developed by the Joint Chiefs. The president wanted this procedure changed and the change codified in law. Specifically, he asked that henceforward the chain of authority concerning the unified combatant commands go directly from the commander in chief through the secretary of defense to the several fighting commands. Congress gave the president exactly what he asked for, excluding the Joint Chiefs of Staff from any executive function in the assignment of military missions. "Such combatant commands are responsible to the President and Secretary of Defense for such military missions as may be assigned to them by the Secretary of Defense. . . ."[24] The Joint Chiefs of Staff, from that moment forward, would bear little similarity to the war-fighting institution of 1945. They would function as an advisory committee, providing staff support to the secretary of defense, who would thereafter be, by law, the nation's principal military executive.

These 1958 changes, although threatening to the Marine Corps, went far beyond our parochial apprehensions. Without question, the sensitive balance achieved by the National Security Act was largely destroyed. The assurance that civilian matters related to defense would be handled by a broad base of civilian officialdom was gone. The military departments and their secretaries were excluded from the decision-making process and the president and Congress would receive one consolidated budget from the secretary of defense.

The assurance that purely military matters would be handled by a broad base of military professionals was also largely gone. The secretary of defense was now, by law, the official who created the nation's combatant commands and assigned them their military missions.

The assurance that the commander in chief would receive broadbased, unfiltered military counsel was seriously degraded. He would rarely see the Joint Chiefs of Staff. His military advisors would be the secretary of defense and, on occasion, the JCS chairman. We had witnessed the very trend against which General Edson had cautioned—a steady growth in the defense bureaucracy along with a steady expansion of the Office of Secretary of Defense into professional military areas.

The trend has continued without halt to the present day. Defense Secretaries Gates, McNamara, Clifford, Laird, Richardson, Rumsfeld, and Brown, each in his own way, undertook to enlarge the scope of his office and its capability to influence—if not direct—the detailed activities of the military establishment.

Thus, by 1986, the "Office of the Secretary of Defense" had grown, through changes in the law and creation of nonstatutory agencies, to a massive, complex matrix. A deputy secretary, two under secretaries, two deputy under secretaries, and seven assistant secretaries formed the basic framework, overseeing agencies—(still technically in the Office of the Secretary)—for legislation, public affairs, policy, international security, program analysis, manpower, logistics, intelligence, research, nuclear affairs, communications, finance, civil defense, and even legislation. The total complex embraces more than eighty thousand persons. Quite a change from Secretary Forrestal's 1947 staff of one hundred, which was never contemplated to be an operating entity. At some moment in the ensuing three decades, it achieved a critical mass, exploding into every operational and administrative sector of our military system. The original architects of the National Security Act, one may be sure, never contemplated the moment-to-moment involvement of the office in combat operations that was common-place in the Vietnam War. Nor would they have believed that the office would ever be involved in details so small as debating, in 1982, whether the military necktie should be fifty-two inches long, as preferred by the Air Force, or fifty-six inches long, as preferred by the Army.

Like the other services, the Marine Corps has felt the burden of the massive secretary of defense superstructure, but its position has actually grown stronger since 1947. The McDonough incident resulted in codification of the com-batant structure of the Corps and gave the commandant something more than standing room at the Joint Chiefs table. The General Order No. 5 triumph was another major event, solidifying the Corps's position in the Department of the Navy.

A final step was taken in late 1978 when the commandant was accorded full membership in the Joint Chiefs of Staff. The action had its origin during the final year of the commandantcy of Louis Wilson (1975–79). Wilson, with three years of JCS experience behind him, concluded that the interests of the Corps and national security would be best served if his successors were full JCS members, rather than members only for matters of direct concern to the Marine Corps. He consulted Congressman Bob Wilson, who recommended that the commandant seek to have an appro-priate clause included in the Defense Authorization Bill as it was considered by the Senate.

General Wilson did exactly that, obtaining the bipartisan support of Senators John Stennis and Dewey Bartlett as well as House members Melvin Price and Sam Stratton. When the matter came before the Senate Armed Services Commit-tee, and mainly because of Senator Stennis's leadership, the bill was reported favorably and, ultimately, was passed by the Senate without a dissenting vote. Subsequently, a con-ference with the House accepted the provision, all to the Marines' great satisfaction.

Then the bottom fell out. President Carter vetoed the bill! Not because of the clause relating to the Marines but because the bill included funds for a nuclear aircraft carrier, which he opposed. The bill was returned to conference and the carrier deleted. Anyone minded to oppose the Marine provision during the conference session was probably discouraged by the overwhelming manner in which it had been approved earlier. The legislation sailed through, was signed by the president, and became law, a tribute to the resourceful courage of Commandant Wilson.

Throughout the two hundred years of our country's history, Congress has acted repeatedly to preserve and strengthen the Marines' fighting effectiveness. This congressional determination, while enhanced by lobbying or jawboning, is primarily a product of one thing: confidence in the Corps's performance. Without steady, reliable performance, year in and year out, Congress would never have so consistently stood by the Marines in their times of trial. Performance is what it is all about.

PART
II

THE INNOVATORS

War is a grave concern of the State;
it must be thoroughly studied.

The Art of War
Sun Tzu, 500 B.C.

H. L. Mencken, never an admirer of America's soldiery, once said, "It is a documented fact that the U.S. military has never invented anything remotely warlike save the ramrod."

The pundit was wrong on all counts. The ramrod, as best as can be determined, was invented about 1450 in France, and the U.S. military has in fact a record of significant innovations, to which the Marine Corps has contributed its full share. Hardly storied as studious or contemplative, the Marines have nevertheless thought up or caused to come into being some of the most exciting—and useful—developments in modern operational concepts, weaponry, and equipment.

It came naturally. The Marines' combatant function was and is unique. Nobody has ever been interested in providing the necessary operating techniques or hardware for them, so they have had to do it themselves. Sometimes, their efforts turned out to be failures. Many Marines shudder at the mention of the Marmon-Harrington tank, a five-ton pre-World War II Tinker Toy with a .50 caliber machine gun as its main armament and an engine and suspension system that defied the most conscientious maintenance. Then there was the Reising sub-machine gun, a caliber .45 automatic weapon, made largely of stampings, remembered mostly for its predisposition to rust and malfunction. Or the Mighty Mite Vehicle, a poor man's mini-Jeep—too small, too light, too fragile, and ultimately rejected by its users. And, finally, the amphibian cargo trailer, a watertight trailer intended to be towed from ship to shore by amphibian tractors. It leaked, and it was almost impossible to marry up the trailer with the towing amphibian tractor in a rolling sea. I confess that it was my idea, created in 1943 when I was head of the Logistic Section at Marine Corps Headquarters. We built six hundred; never used one. How I escaped crucifixion for this disaster I will never know.

But it was not all bad. Other Marine innovations have literally changed the character of a war. The precise utilization of naval gunfire in support of landing forces is one example. During the years immediately preceding World War II, under the stimulus of the Marines, the naval gun came into its own as a substitute for landing force artillery until those weapons were ashore. Behind the energetic Marine effort to capitalize on the power of naval armament was Major (later Major General) Donald M. Weller, who made the undertaking a personal crusade. In no other Marine Corps development does a single personality stand out so vividly. Weller's interests extended to every aspect of the problem: the design of ammunition; the development of fire control procedures; the design of communication equipment; the training of naval officers as shore fire control parties and naval gunfire liaison officers; and the establishment of standard procedures for operational planning. The techniques that grew from his effort had a major impact on the conduct of World War II amphibious operations in both oceans.

Another enduring innovation—the art of dive bombing in close support of ground forces—had its beginning in the Marines' Central American "banana war" experience following World War I. The technique, weaponry, and related communications were slowly perfected until World War II found Marine aviators confident of their ability to deliver their ordnance in close proximity to their brothers on the ground, and the ground Marine equally confident that in the air/ground team the Corps had something nobody else enjoyed.

Then there was the whole panoply of modern amphibious developments—with their companion equipments. For example, the tactical employment of helicopters in the ship-to-shore movement, all-weather close air support—combined with the necessary distinctive hardware, such as expeditionary airfields—have "USMC" prominently etched on their nameplate. These sunbursts of creativity in operational techniques and material development are the manifestation of the intellectual efforts of a long line of Marine Corps dreamers—corporals, captains, and generals. They were sometimes misunderstood, but they were men who, as Eric Hoffer said, tried to "think beyond the moment; live beyond the day."

They were the Innovators.

CHAPTER 4

The Amphibious Assault and How It Grew

The military world seems to be particularly prone to use cliché—thoughts and statements that do not bear the trial of proof. Classic among these is General Dwight D. Eisenhower's pronouncement in 1950 that "an amphibious landing is not a particularly difficult thing. . . . You put your men in boats and as long as you get well-trained crews to take the boats in, it is the simplest deployment in the world—the men can go nowhere else except the beach."[1] As if getting to the beach were the whole game instead of just the beginning. Another classic is General Omar Bradley's untimely rumination, "I am wondering whether we shall ever have another large-scale amphibious operation."[2] This only eleven months before the dramatic amphibious assault by the 1st Marine Division and 1st Marine Aircraft Wing at Inchon, Korea.

Also questionable is the frequently heard generalization that man has conducted amphibious attacks since the beginning of history. It is not altogether true. Man has indeed gone to war in ships, boats, or battle canoes since history began. He has undertaken innumerable expeditions overseas, using the oceans as a bridge to the enemy's homeland. From time to time, he has been able to put his forces ashore from the sea in the vicinity of the enemy's principal strength.

But a true amphibious assault against an opponent who has organized the beaches and sea approaches for defense with entrenched infantry and an array of mutually supporting arms is quite another thing. And if the enemy is on an island or a peninsula, where the attacker is limited in his choice of landing site and where the crisis is likely to occur near the beachline, then it is even more difficult. The techniques for bringing off such an undertaking are a relatively modern development, going back in concept to only the nineteenth century. Probably the earliest significant rationalization of this sort of amphibious assault was *Precis de l'Art de la Guerre* in 1838, by Antoine H. Jomini, who addressed many of the critical issues which still confront us. The *Precis* has to rank among the most visionary documents relating to amphibious war. Until the British landing at Gallipoli in 1915, the concept of an amphibious assault against determined resistance had little test, and then the British violated so many basic principles that the test was deceptive.

After Gallipoli, the amphibious assault, never taken too seriously, was largely discounted. Offshore mines, beach obstacles, heavy artillery in fortified emplacements, integrated air defense, aircraft for both observation and attack were all seen as favoring the defense—so much as to make such an assault "difficult, indeed almost impossible," according to British military historian B. H. Liddell Hart.

It is at this point that the Marine usually enters the historical scene. In truth, however, both before and after Gallipoli only a very few Marines were convinced of the feasibility of amphibious assault operations—or even interested in them. Ironically, there were visionary officers in the Navy who many years before Gallipoli—and before the Marines themselves—saw a future for the amphibious assault and, more important, identified that future with the Marine Corps. In 1861 Rear Admirals S. P. Lee and S. F. DuPont recommended that the Marines form expeditionary regiments to serve with the Union Navy in the seizure of

Confederate coastal positions. The idea got nowhere, mainly because of failure by both the Navy and the Marines to grasp the wisdom of the proposal. Later, in 1896, Lieutenant Commander William F. Fullam, USN, with great vision, proposed that the Corps be organized in six battalions for expeditionary duty in support of the fleet. However, until the 1920s, there was no real institutional dedication in the Corps to the idea of an assault landing attack against organized defenses.

Probably a minority of Marines were interested in seeing the Corps involved in the establishment and defense of naval base facilities—overseas—a wholly defensive mission related to the needs of the U.S. Fleet. Many more, whose professional life had been consecrated primarily to expeditionary duty in the colonial infantry role—Haiti, China, Santo Domingo, Nicaragua—remained so oriented. Others who were convinced, before the Great War, that the Corps' future lay primarily in service aboard ship and at naval stations, favored expanding that important relationship with the Navy.

Only a few, a very few, visionaries were willing to attack the formidable conceptual, tactical, and material problems associated with the modern amphibious assault landing: how to get heavy equipment and weapons ashore through surf and across reefs; how to exercise command authority during the sensitive transition period; how to communicate effectively with ships and aircraft; how to cope with mines and beach obstacles; how to provide accurate, timely, and concentrated fire support for the assault forces; how to ensure that essential supplies were delivered ashore where and when needed; how to manage the evacuation of casualties to seaward; and how to persuade the Navy to share its very limited resources in solving these problems. There was a hard core of Marines who saw a future, despite the problems, for amphibious assault. They were resolute men, true pioneers. By no means military intellectuals in the image of Sun Tzu, Frederick the Great, Jomini, or Mahan, they were nevertheless capable of seeing the close relationship between the total exercise of sea power and the narrow issue of seizing a lodgment on a hostile shore against sophisticated opposition.

Among these was John A. Lejeune, a compassionate gentleman, fearless fighter, skilled diplomat, and sensitive military thinker. As early as 1900, Lejeune, with a few other Marines and some visionary Navy colleagues, perceived the necessity of securing base facilities in the vast Pacific. He had been disappointed with the inability of Commandants Heywood (1891–1903) and Elliott (1903–10) to grasp the relationship between the global needs of the Navy and the creation and defense of overseas naval bases. Their view was that the century-old Marine Corps role of providing ships' guards and security for naval stations should still be foremost, that to commit Marine resources to advanced base force duty was an imprudent diffusion of effort. In other words, they were the proponents of a retrospective philosophy that went back a hundred years. Lejeune, in contrast, saw the Navy's need for advanced bases for coal and other logistical purposes as a cardinal factor in preparing to face the challenge of an imperialist Japan, and he was determined to get the Marines involved. He realized further that someday, somebody might have the unenviable task of capturing those logistic bases from a well-prepared enemy, and defending them, once captured. What would be a more logical organization to do the job than the Marines, with their traditional maritime orientation?

Lejeune may not have been the first to say it, but nobody of that era said it any better. With the prescience of a true pioneer, he declared, in a 1915 lecture at the Naval War College, that the ability not just to defend but to seize those bases was a logical and critical Marine function in light of the Navy's growing strategic responsibilities. He saw the Corps as

the first to set foot on hostile soil in order to seize, fortify and hold . . . a base.

Later, after he became commandant, he stated it affirmatively and clearly,

the maintenance, equipping and training of its expeditionary force so that it will be in instant readiness to

support the Fleet in time of war I deem to be . . .
the most important Marine Corps duty in time of
peace.[3]

Finally, in 1927, he procured a significant inclusion in the
governing document entitled *Joint Action, Army-Navy:*

Marines, because of their constant association with
Navy units, will be given special preparation in the
conduct of landing operations.

Specifically, they should be responsible for

land operations in support of the Fleet for the initial
seizure and defense of advanced bases and for such
limited auxiliary land operations as are essential to
prosecution of a naval campaign.[4]

Lejeune's understanding of the Navy's needs, which
stemmed largely from his years at Annapolis and his continuing friendship with many prominent Navy officers, was of
great value to the Corps. His views were mirrored by
another Annapolis graduate, George Barnett, who preceded
Lejeune as Commandant. Their views were shared by
another Annapolis man, John H. Russell (later also to
become commandant).

Russell, Annapolis, '92, may well have exerted greater
influence in rationalizing and regularizing the amphibious
assault than any other single individual in the Corps. In
1910 he made the illuminating observation that when the
fleet was operating at a distance from permanent bases it
should carry with it "a sufficient force and material for
seizing and defending" an advanced base in the theater of
operations."[5]

Later in 1916, he made, in the first edition of the *Marine
Corps Gazette,* an eloquent—and almost heretical—case
for both the base defense and amphibious assault tasks as
Marine Corps missions. Subsequently, as assistant commandant, he persuaded Commandant Fuller and Navy
leaders in Washington to accept as official his view that

the amphibious assault function should be primary Marine Corps business and to adopt his conceptual creation, the Fleet Marine Force, as a Type Command of the Naval Operating Forces.

These developments, which took place over a quarter of a century, were the results of unusual and brave actions. Among those few who both understood and believed in them was one of the most extraordinary men ever to appear in a Corps that has always been generously populated with unusual personalities.

Earl H. Ellis became a Marine private in 1900 after graduating from high school. He was bright—bright enough to be commissioned within a year after his enlistment— and his unusual character surfaced almost at once. Unmarried, he quickly became devoted to the Corps and earned the reputation for studying and working long hours without rest in the Corps's behalf. As early as 1912, still a lieutenant, he began a messianic exploration of the strategic confrontation between the United States and Japan, with whom he was convinced we would eventually go to war. He predicted that the Japanese would initiate hostilities and that the United States would have to fight its way back across the Pacific in a series of hard amphibious assaults to capture the necessary bases. In some cases, the amphibious attacks of 1942–45 took place exactly as he had presaged.

Ellis's brilliance as a planner was widely recognized, both in the Navy and in the Marines. During the First World War, where he served in France as a staff officer, and the five years thereafter, he inspired great confidence on the part of his superiors despite what was already perceived to be a gravely flawed personality. He was moody, often contentious, and impatient with slow thinkers. He had a firecracker temper. He sometimes disappeared for days without explanation. And he drank. He drank a great deal—more and more as years passed. His alcoholism caused him to move in and out of hospitals continually, usually receiving such euphemistic diagnoses as "nephritis," "neurasthenia," "psychasthenia," and "exhaustion." His superiors, including the ascetic General Lejeune, always protected him because of his sheer ability and his total loyalty to the Corps. The bottle finally killed him at Koror, in the Palaus in 1923, during a secret reconnaissance of Micronesia, the area where he was convinced critical battles would be fought in the war with Japan. What he learned in his extensive exploration of the southern islands was not that the Japanese had fortified the area, as was suspected, but that they had done very little— at that time—in the way of fortification, and it was their weakness they were striving to keep secret, not evidences of strength.*

Ellis left behind a precious legacy in the form of an extraordinary thirty-thousand-word study entitled *Advanced Base Operations in Micronesia.*[6] Written in 1920–21, and based on lectures he had prepared in 1916, it was less a true study than a portrait of the future—the fruit of an incredible prescience. It turned out to be an uncannily accurate forecast of things to come. Outlining the step-by-step drive westward across the Pacific to meet the need, as he saw it, for "bases to support the Fleet, both during its projection and afterward," he traced the route through the Marshall and Caroline Islands much as it actually happened. The Ellis study was in fact the framework for the American strategy for a Pacific war, adopted by the Joint Board of the Army and Navy in 1924 as the "Orange Plan."

Even so, Ellis's essay went far beyond strategy. He addressed the full range of tactical, technical, and practical problems that would ultimately confront our forces as they drove across the Pacific from island to island. He warned of the difficulties that would be created by reefs and man-made obstacles. He foresaw the coordinated use of naval gunfire and air support; the technique of combat unit loading of equipment and supplies in specially designed transport ships; the logistical organization of landing beaches; the use of underwater demolition teams ("frogmen"); the tactical use of smoke and darkness; and the utility of amphibious reconnaissance, raids, and feints. In short, Ellis not only

---

* Ellis is memorialized in Ellis Hall, the instructional auditorium at the Marine Command and Staff College in Quantico, Virginia.

contributed to the philosophical "what" of the Marines' amphibious assault future, he clearly identified the more troublesome "how," opening the way for others to address the details.

Contemporary with Ellis, and one of the few Marines who foresaw the future of amphibious warfare, was Dion Williams, an 1891 Naval Academy graduate who had been thinking about the amphibious problem since the turn of the century. Warm, engaging, and proud, he had a respectful relationship with the Navy that flourished when he served in the USS *Baltimore* under Admiral George Dewey at Manila Bay. Williams is credited with persuading Dewey, in 1907, to assert before the Congress that "a force of 5,000 Marines with the Fleet" would have prevented the Philippine insurrection that ensued following the Spanish defeat. Williams's concept of such a "force" was probably the first tiny beginning of the doctrinal sequence that became the "Base Defense Force," the "Expeditionary Force," and, finally, the "Fleet Marine Force."

By the 1920s Williams had become convinced that the assault function, as described by Russell, Ellis, and Lejeune was indeed the Marines' future role. Upon taking over command of the 4th Marine Brigade of the Marine Corps Expeditionary Force at the Quantico Marine Base in 1923, he aimed to prepare it to function as an assault landing force. This was at no small hazard to his own professional career. He had found that, while officially preparing for colonial infantry employment in the manner of Santo Domingo, Nicaragua, or Haiti, the unit was actually training in World War I infantry tactics, as well as reenacting Civil War battles on the nearby Virginia battlefields. This last project was especially valued by the Quantico Base commander, Major General Smedley D. Butler, because he believed its publicity value enhanced his chances of being named commandant.*

---

* He invited President Harding to a reenactment of the Battle of Chancellorsville in the spring of 1921. The president spent the night under canvas with the troops, the first president to do so since Lincoln.

As described by retired General Merrill B. Twining,* Williams proceeded to lecture his troops instead on the history of amphibious warfare and to exercise them in practice landings on the Potomac River. It is ironic that Williams, a vocal exponent of the landing attack, was charged, in the Fleet Exercise of 1923–24, with installing and commanding the defense of the island of Culebra in the West Indies, as a naval base. The bulk of the brigade he had trained was the assault landing force and, using the techniques he had taught them, made landings against the defense force on Culebra.

The commander of the landing force was Eli Kelley Cole, an 1887 Annapolis graduate. Although studious and dedicated, he was not highly renowned in the Corps because of an imperious, irascible personality and a lackluster World War I record.† Convinced that Russell's plea for a Marine Corps amphibious mission was valid, Cole had become intensely interested in Gallipoli—what went wrong there, and why. With the assistance of another thoughtful Marine officer, Robert Henry Dunlap, he developed a series of lectures propounding the idea that Gallipoli need not have been a disaster had it been done right.

That view, in itself, is interesting but not remarkable. What is remarkable is what Cole did with his research. He invited, but did not order, his officers to attend his Gallipoli lectures. He delivered the talks in the Post Chapel at Quantico, during the noon hour so that those leaders who still had little use for amphibious operations—led mainly by the base commander, Smedley Butler—could not criticize him for diverting his officers from their regular duties for frivolous purposes. Yet that was exactly the criticism

---

* General Twining's extensive recollections of this period contributed much to my portraits of Williams, Ellis, Generals Cole and Lejeune, and Colonel E. B. Miller.

† He spent the bulk of the war in Haiti and Parris Island, South Carolina, arriving in France only six weeks before the armistice. His sole World War I decoration was "for his cordial cooperation with and support of the Provisional Government of Haiti and efficient efforts for improvement of the educational and social conditions of the Haitian people." (From official records, Headquarters, Marine Corps.)

leveled against him, giving further evidence of the deep schisms that existed among the Lejeune/Russell school of amphibious thought and those who still held, with former commandants Heywood and Elliot, that the Marines' future lay in ships' detachments and still others like Butler, who wanted an independent Marine Corps of colonial infantry, unfettered by the Navy.

Undismayed by the opposition, Cole proceeded to take his landing force, schooled under Dion Williams, into the 1924 Fleet exercises in Panama and the Caribbean. Cole's forces (some 1,781 men) landed against Williams' defenders (about 1,600 men) at Culebra. Tiny though the exercise now appears, it was accurately described by Williams as being of "a scale of magnitude never before undertaken by our country in peacetime."[7]

The maneuver was awkward to say the least. Ships were improperly loaded. Urgently needed material was inaccessibly stowed under low priority cargo. Loading of boats—such few inadequate craft as the Fleet was able to produce—was confused and badly planned. Navy personnel were uninformed and poorly trained. Boats were landed on the wrong beaches at the wrong time and in the wrong order. There was not enough naval gunfire or air support and it was directed at the wrong targets.

Despite the manifold frustrations, Cole's thoughtful and optimistic report to the commandant put the array of shortcomings into perspective and made sensitive, positive, and specific recommendations for correcting the deficiencies. After pleading for more specialized equipment, boats primarily, and for the codification of an amphibious doctrine in official policy, he ended his report with the poignant observation, "I suppose we must convince the Navy."

Lamentably, there was little progress in the next eight years. The Corps was stretched thin in order to meet its heavy expeditionary obligations in Nicaragua and China. However much they may have desired otherwise, both the Navy and the Marine proponents of amphibious warfare were denied the resources to pursue the "how" of the specialty.

In 1933, General Douglas MacArthur, who was chief of

staff of the Army and openly antagonistic to the Marine Corps on the ground that the Corps constituted an economic affront to the Army, proposed to the president and to several members of the Congress that the Marines—air and ground, people and functions—be transferred to the Army. Failing in that, MacArthur proposed that at least the bulk of the Corps be transferred to the Army, leaving Marines with only base defense and seagoing detachment functions.

The substantial influence wielded by MacArthur impressed Commandant Ben H. Fuller (1930–34) with the gravity of the threat, and gave his assistant, General Russell, the opportunity he sought to drive the amphibious subject to the surface. Russell had help from wise friends on the Navy General Board who, for the first time, stated officially that the Marines' primary job should be "the seizure and defense of advanced bases." With this Navy declaration, he persuaded the commandant that a formalized, written body of amphibious doctrine was needed. It should be prepared by the Marines themselves, it should be in great detail, and should exhibit that they possessed a unique capability not shared by anybody, particularly not by the Army.

Some work had already been done on the subject as early as 1931. Russell's idea was to take these preliminary fragments, mass the total talent of the Marine Corps Schools in Quantico, Virginia*—staff and students alike—and direct them to produce, in a single volume, a full exposure of everything involved in the amphibious assault that in any way affected the landing force. Russell's proposal was carried out. Marine Corps Schools classes were halted and the total resources of the institution were directed toward developing the formal doctrine.

In charge of the project was Brigadier General James C. Breckinridge, commandant of the Marines' officers' school system. But the driving force was Colonel Ellis Bell Miller, one more of the family of unusual Marine Corps personalities.

---

* In 1933 the Schools comprised a Field Officers' School for officers in the rank of major and lieutenant colonel, some fifteen students, and a Company Officers' School, thirty students, in the rank of first lieutenant and captain. The staff aggregated about thirty-five officers.

Commissioned in 1903, with service in Panama, Mexico, China, and the Philippines, Miller was intelligent, intellectual, perceptive, diligent, and thoroughly professional, with all of the essential qualifications for the pioneering job. Unfortunately, he had a few more characteristics that were not so essential. He was demanding, intolerant of any dissent, and impatient with those who could not maintain his pace. These traits, which may have kept him from advancing beyond the rank of colonel, did not keep him from producing a milestone document in the amphibious field.

The Marine officers were first thoroughly oriented on the errors of Gallipoli and given what little information there was on assault landing operations. Then each one was obliged to set down his own thoughts concerning the sequence of events in an amphibious attack, from preembarkation through completion of the landing assault. The individual submissions were organized into topical categories by an intermediate committee and further reviewed by a steering committee, headed by Miller, which, in turn, created a chapter outline for the book. After a critical review by a group of Fleet Marine Force officers, the chapter assignments were farmed out to writing committees, which based the content on the meager practical experience available and, probably more so, on their own reasoning and convictions.

Miller drove the group with apostolic fervor. He set deadlines and was merciless in his criticism. When it was done—the writing took seven months—he had a respectable product. He called it *Tentative Manual for Landing Operations, 1934*. It was not too well written, it was not handsomely printed, and it was bound with shoestring, but it was there, some 127,000 words of it—more hard, doctrinal pronouncement on the seizure of an objective by amphibious assault than had ever been assembled in one place in all of history. For the first time the issues of air and naval gunfire support were addressed in detail. Likewise principles of transport loading, debarkation procedures, guidance for the ship-to-shore movement, and the management of logistics at the beachline were treated in what still must be regarded as great detail.

Miller was not content with the *Tentative Manual,* but it was seized enthusiastically by the Fleet Marine Force for use in training, and it was adopted immediately as a tentative text in the Marine Corps Schools for its 1934–35 term. Furthermore, it was published by the Navy Department as the *Manual for Naval Overseas Operations.*

The Corps set immediately to work to revise, update, and perfect the *Manual.* Over the next two years a series of boards at Quantico prepared revisions, notably a group headed by Lieutenant Colonel Charles D. Barrett, whose scholarly efforts and patient attention to detail resulted in a stronger and much more articulate document.

The *Tentative Manual* was ground-breaking of the purest sort, and it excited enthusiasm in the Navy, which adopted it with minor alterations in 1938 as Fleet Training Publication No. 167, *Landing Operations Doctrine, U.S. Navy."* Three years later, the Army, whose interest in amphibious operations had theretofore been minimal, copied the *Manual,* lock, stock, and barrel, and published it as *Field Manual 31-5.* The *Manual* guided the bulk of amphibious training in the immediate pre-World War II period. More important, it governed every amphibious operation during that war. And it persists today, in its essential parts, as the U.S. joint directive for amphibious operations.

It remained for the Navy and Marines, using their new doctrine, to exercise the practical details of the amphibious specialty and, not just incidentally, to provide training for those Army units which were to take part in the first Army amphibious operations of World War II. In Fleet Landing Exercises 3, 4, and 5, from 1936 to 1939, the *Tentative Manual*—not yet officially binding on the Navy—was nonetheless a powerful influence on Navy-Marine training, in the Caribbean and in Southern California.

The most significant prewar rehearsals, however, took place in 1940 and 1941 after Fleet Training Publication No. 167 had become an official Navy document. It was fortuitous that the Marines in those exercises were led by a dynamic, no-nonsense, war-oriented man, Brigadier General Holland M. Smith.

Commissioned in 1905 after graduation from Auburn and the University of Alabama Law School, Smith had followed the then-standard Marine pattern—service in the Philippines (where, incidentally, he led a company in the regiment commanded by Colonel Eli Kelley Cole), Nicaragua, Panama, China, Santo Domingo, and Cuba. Staff assignments in France in World War I were followed by a course at the Naval War College where, for the first time, the vigorous, straight-talking temperament appeared that later earned him the sobriquet "Howling Mad." He advanced his views regarding the importance of amphibious assault operations—and particularly the need for heavy naval gunfire and air support—with such logic and style as to acquire a reputation as a thinker and an eloquent speaker. Later, at the Field Officers' course at the Quantico Marine Corps Schools, he told his superiors that their curriculum was retrospective and gave them hard examples to prove his point. His renown as an outspoken pioneer was further burnished by his letters in 1935 and 1936 to Commandant Russell, whom he admired, complaining that since war with Japan was clearly approaching, too little was being done in the Marines' amphibious training to meet the inevitable challenge.

Later, in 1939, when given the responsibility for leading and training the 1st Marine Brigade, the deep resolution in Smith's character was plainly visible. While he had the appearance of a country schoolmaster—steel-rimmed glasses, thinning hair, and a slightly spreading waistline—and while he was tender and compassionate with those around him, Smith was fierce in his impatient determination that the Marines whose training was entrusted to him should want for nothing in preparation for the war he was sure was coming. Nor was he restrained in voicing his dissatisfaction with those whom he saw as deficient or derelict. I was on his staff at the time and more than once heard him quote the Chinese philosopher T'sao T'sao, "War cannot be run according to the rules of etiquette."

He took the Marines of the East Coast Fleet Marine Force—about three thousand of them, air and ground—to the Caribbean in the autumn of 1940 and drove them mercilessly in landing exercises at Culebra, grinding the rough edges off their performance. He exposed equipment and supply shortages—both in the Marines and the Navy—

and was bitterly eloquent in underscoring the adverse impact on his force's combat capability resulting from these shortages. He made few friends in the Navy with his critical assessment that the landing craft and troop transport available for the 1940 exercises were wholly inadequate. The troops were carried in the demilitarized battleship *Wyoming,* a supply ship and a converted World War I destroyer and, except for a dozen experimental landing craft, they were transported ashore in standard ships' boats. The Marine Corps, it was plain, was just as impoverished as the Navy. Smith railed at his Marine superiors for widespread deficiencies—trucks, tanks, aircraft, air-ground communications, antiaircraft weapons, ammunition, and combat uniforms. He argued that the Marine who was going to do the fighting deserved the best of everything, and he constantly called attention to the shortages, reminding us that in shortest supply of all was time.

Despite the inadequacies, everyone learned. And the next spring he did it again, this time with a much larger force—an understrength Marine Division and about half of an Army Division.* The Navy, for its part, had made much progress in a year, being able to provide four converted merchantmen as troop transports and a few more acceptable landing boats, but the shortage of floating equipment and its limited quality was still so acute as to move Smith to new heights of rhetoric in behalf of the troops who were destined to do the fighting. When he heard that the crew of the converted transport USS *Harry Lee* was bathing in fresh water while the embarked Marines were using salt water, he sent me aboard the ship to determine whether the rumor was true. "If it is," he said, "I want you to go see the commanding officer. Tell him I said we are all going to the same war and we had all better bathe in the same kind of water—fresh or salt."

The rumor turned out to be true and I made the call as

---

* Army elements included were from the 1st Infantry Division of Ft. Devens, Mass., commanded by Major General James Cubbison. The division brought its share of characters into the Marine environment, including Brigadier General James G. Ord, who attended our first planning conference in a self-designed uniform, including cuffed trousers, spats, a cane, and pince nez.

directed, albeit uncomfortably as I was still only a captain. The commanding officer gave my speech a frigid reception. By the time I returned to the flagship, however, General Smith had received a message from the *Harry Lee's* commander, "Everyone will bathe in fresh water as long as it lasts."

Smith complained to his immediate superior, Fleet Commander Admiral E. J. King, both officially and privately about the state of equipment in the fleet. King was a serious man, not given to humor. He did not take kindly to criticism from anybody and, on the day Smith sent him his written bill of particulars, the general told me (at that time I was his aide) that he expected to be fired for his outspoken complaints. As it turned out, King reacted in exactly the opposite manner, exhibiting respect and trust in Smith because of his candor and his no-frills approach to his job.* His report to the chief of naval operations on the 1940–1941 winter exercises borrowed heavily from Smith's complaints. The report laid out the Navy's material problems in cold detail and concluded with the assertion

> . . . it cannot be too strongly emphasized that until this floating equipment is placed in the hands of the Fleet and brought to a suitable state of combat efficiency, *the mobility and tactical efficiency of Marine troops will remain vitally curtailed.*[8]

Admiral King underscored the entire passage with his own pencil, double underscoring the final section on mobility and tactical efficiency.

Smith took no comfort in King's supportive letter. His simple comment to several of us on the staff was: "I hope to God it isn't too late."

Taking his force back to the United States, Smith continued to drive them unceasingly. He tasked them with perfecting the techniques of their trade, developing and codifying

---

* King's confidence in Smith was transferred to the Marines at large. I was present at a July 1942 Navy discussion of the pros and cons of the shoestring operation at Guadalcanal and was proud to hear King concur in the enterprise at least in part because, as he put it, "Holland Smith says it will work."

procedures for coordination of Marine air and ground operations, training in naval gunfire support,* and conducting schools in embarkation and transport loading. I organized the first such school, at Smith's headquarters in Quantico. Subsequent courses were conducted under Captain S. C. Tracy, USMCR, giving both Marine and Army students a complete package of all the essential embarkation and loading documents—practical standardization at the operating level for the first time.

Smith required us to commit to directive form everything involved with the landing assault, from beginning to end, to the extent that one member of the staff, Marine Major P. P. Schrider, said, "Instead of 'H. M.' his initials ought to be 'S. O. P.' (Standing Operating Procedure)."

Smith's final major effort to make his troops ready for amphibious war took place at New River, North Carolina, in August 1941. By contemporary standards the exercise was large—some seventeen thousand men—the better part of two peace-strength divisions—one Marine and one Army†—a Marine Aircraft Group, some eighteen assorted transport vessels, and a sprinkling of modern landing craft. It was more complex than anything that had gone before, involving night landings, parachute operations, and heavy emphasis on close air support and on landing large quantities of equipment and supplies across the beaches.

Smith's report was detailed and direct. Sparing in praise, it underscored a multitude of shortcomings and concluded

---

* At this time Major Donald M. Weller (mentioned in the introduction to this Part) was also on General Smith's staff. The general gave him free rein in all of his efforts to formalize and codify the naval gunfire field. It must be said that Weller's sincere and engaging personality contributed greatly to his success in dealing with the Navy gunnery people upon whom we ultimately depended.

† The Army learned a lot under Smith's leadership after their decades of uninterest in anything related to amphibious operations. Between May 1941 and July 1942 Smith's headquarters conducted thirteen amphibious training exercises for Army troops, a total of 31,900 men. It was ironic, in this regard, to hear General Jacob Devers tell the Senate Military Affairs Committee in 1945 that "the Army received no amphibious training worthy of the name prior to World War II due to a lack of cooperation."

with some thirty-eight major recommendations regarding the "how" of the amphibious assault. We were finally beginning to reach bone marrow.

Even so, Smith, in his characteristic fashion, underscored "the futility of conducting a forced landing against a well-conducted defense by first-class troops" until the attacking force was not only equipped with the best in weaponry but thoroughly trained as well.[9]. Smith was correct. Much did, indeed, still need to be done before we could feel fully ready for the test soon to come. In his impatience to see that state of readiness achieved, however, Smith—and those around him, too—tended to forget the long, tortuous, obstacle-strewn road the early apostles of amphibious warfare had trod. Others, in retrospect, recognized the magnitude of their innovative triumph. J.F.C. Fuller, a respected British military scholar, described the amphibious assault as perfected and practiced by the U.S. Marines as "in all probability . . . the most far reaching tactical innovation of the war."[10]

A few months after the final Smith-generated exercise in 1941, as the first Marines were wading ashore at Guadalcanal and Tulagi and as the first soldiers touched the North African beaches, the spirits of the Marine pioneers who made it all happen hovered over them. The dreams of Williams, Ellis, Russell, and other visionaries had become a reality—a major part of the strategy for World War II, a principal ingredient in the design for victory.

CHAPTER 5

Ideas but No Boats

The innovative brilliance of those Marines who nourished the idea of the amphibious assault is in no way dimmed by the fact that their wonderful dream would not have become a reality had it not been for an unusual man named Andy Higgins. He was living proof of the adage, "One man with courage is a majority."

There was something about Andrew Jackson Higgins that endeared him to the Marine Corps. A bluff, outspoken, hard-driving, self-made man, Higgins had made and lost three fortunes in his fifty-five years. He owned a large boat works in New Orleans, as well as the largest mahogany veneer plant in America. With the help of his four sons, he ran his businesses in an unconventional and altogether informal fashion. His philosophy was: "Never mind how; just get the job done."

A disciple of good bourbon, a champion of the underdog, and a patriot, Higgins possessed a fighting heart. He was intolerant of bureaucracy, resourceful, courageous, and energetic, in short, the Marines' kind of man. Besides that, he had something that Marines wanted, something they had wanted for a long time.

As far back as 1900, when the concept of the Advanced Base Force was born, the Marines were obliged to face the problem of moving their heavy equipment and supplies ashore over undeveloped, often surf-pounded beaches. Progress toward solving the problem was almost negligible. By 1913 the Navy had developed and built six unpowered artillery lighters, each capable of transporting a single heavy artillery piece, but they were rudimentary and of limited usefulness. They had to be towed to the surf line, then turned around and eased onto the beach on an anchor line. It could not have been more awkward.

Then, as the regimes of Generals Lejeune and Russell hammered on the need for the Navy and Marines together to develop an offensive amphibious capability, a corresponding need for assault landing craft grew. Progress was disappointingly slow.

By 1923, in addition to the half dozen towed artillery lighters of 1913 vintage, there was exactly one additional experimental craft designed specifically for amphibious operations. It was a fifty-five foot, twin-engine wooden boat with a steel canopy, dubbed "Troop Barge A," "Beetle Boat," or "Kelly Cole" after Marine Colonel Eli K. Cole, who led the campaign to persuade the Navy to build it. The boat's steel canopy, intended to protect the passengers from small arms fire, was more likely to prevent a hundred Marines or so from getting out if the boat capsized or sank. It had no surf capability at all, was extremely hard to control, and had no provision whatever for carrying motor vehicles.

For the next ten precious years, essentially nothing happened in the resource-starved Navy to move the ship-to-shore operation from an idea to a reality. The money was not there, nor was there widespread acceptance in either the Navy or the Marines that the idea was sound in the first place.

Nevertheless, the Marines, at Headquarters in Washington and at their Equipment Board in Quantico,* kept pressure on an impoverished Navy somehow to find the means to get vehicles and heavy weapons into the battle. But

---

* The Equipment Board was created in 1933.

as late as the winter maneuvers of 1936–37, where the whole of the Fleet Marine Force (two brigades) exercised together at San Clemente Island off southern California, there still was no practical way to move the power of a landing force from ship to shore. There was no powered boat that could carry a vehicle, no boat that could manage the surf. The only purely amphibious craft programmed for the exercise was the old experimental 1923 "Beetle Boat," which never got to the exercise. In an act of final ignominy, it capsized and sank while being towed from San Diego to San Clemente. The ensuing board of investigation disclosed that the boat had been loaded with kerosene tent stoves which may have contributed to its instability. I was responsible for the old boat during the maneuver and narrowly escaped censure for the loss through the fortunate fact that I had protested in writing the loading of the cargo of stoves. Lady Luck again.

The exercise underscored the melancholy fact that our landing craft had not advanced far beyond what it was during the Revolutionary War. It was still a matter of manhandling what could be manhandled over the sides of conventional Navy ships' boats—whose hull design had not changed materially for more than forty years—or just doing without until a harbor became available. The amphibious assault, with its early need for heavy weapons, vehicles, and equipment, could never come into its own until the need for ship-to-shore transportation was met.*

The first big break came in September of 1937. I was a lieutenant serving as assistant intelligence officer in the 4th Marines in Shanghai at the time fighting erupted between the Chinese and Japanese. I got permission, first from the Marines, then from the Navy, and then from the Japanese, to observe a Japanese amphibious assault on Chinese positions defending the Liuho area, at the mouth of the Yangtze River. I was fortunate to fall in with George R. Phelan, USNA '25, the assistant fleet intelligence officer, who was enthusiastic about my idea of seeing the war at close hand.

---

* On-going pressures, culminating with the San Clemente maneuvers, caused the secretary of the navy to create a Continuing Board for the Development of Landing Craft in 1937. The Marine Corps provided one member. I was the Marine Corps member in 1941.

He arranged a U.S. Navy tug for our transportation and the services of a Navy photographer's mate. The Japanese paid us little attention. We watched troops debarking into boats from transports. We watched destroyers deliver naval gunfire on the beach prior to the landing and in support of the advancing troops afterwards. Most important, we got near enough to take close-up photographs of the Japanese assault landing craft. And there we saw, in action, exactly what the Marines had been looking for—sturdy, ramp-bow-type boats capable of transporting heavy vehicles and depositing them directly on the beaches. What we saw was that the Japanese were light years ahead of us in landing craft design.

I was excited by what I had seen and wrote an enthusiastic report on the various landing craft types the Japanese were using. The report, complete with photographs and sketches, went off to Washington, and I was confident that we would soon see a profusion of equally useful American ramp-bow landing craft.

Alas, two years later, in July 1939, upon returning to the United States, I spent a day hunting for my report in the files of the Navy's Bureau of Ships. Finally unearthed, I was chagrined to read a marginal comment from some bureau skeptic that the report was the work of "some nut out in China."

Somewhat crestfallen, I nevertheless built a foot-long model of the boat similar to those I had seen in China and took it, along with my 1937 China report, to Brigadier General H. M. Smith, then commanding the 1st Marine Brigade in Quantico, Virginia. He was excited about it, and took the model and me to Washington and showed it to Commandant Holcomb. The commandant was equally interested and said he would like to keep the boat and my report to show the secretary of the navy. I would be proud to say that my model was the stimulus for the beginning of the modern American landing craft program. Maybe it was, but the truth is I never saw or heard of the model again.

Despite the overpowering austerity of the period, there had been some activity in the landing craft field. In 1935 the Marines, with Navy help, designed a device to fit into a Navy fifty-foot motor launch to make it possible to carry a heavy vehicle or light tractor. Tested in fleet exercises at

Culebra in 1936 and at San Clemente in 1937, it was so top-heavy that it struck fear into observers' hearts. I was responsible for the San Clemente test. We waited for a calm day—no more than one or two feet of surf. The way the loaded boat rolled was so terrifying as to cause us to cancel all further tests. Concurrently, and responding to constant Marine prodding, the Navy had built one self-propelled, tank-carrying lighter of its own design in 1938, and two more in 1939, all capable of carrying a sixteen-ton tank. All were underpowered, top-heavy, and at a serious disadvantage in the surf. Indeed, one overturned in the 1940 maneuvers. Meanwhile, the Navy Continuing Board for Development of Landing Craft was involved in testing four kinds of New England fishing boats and a privately designed surf boat to ascertain their adaptability for transporting troops in amphibious operations. They had none.

Finally, and by far most important, Brigadier General E. P. Moses and Major E. E. Linsert of the Marine Corps Equipment Board met Andrew Jackson Higgins of New Orleans. They struck up a warm relationship from the start.*

In 1924 Higgins had designed a powerful shallow draft thirty-six-foot boat with a novel underwater hull, for use by rum-runners in the Mississippi Delta during Prohibition. The design was ideal for beach landings because it protected the propeller from striking the bottom and facilitated retraction from the beach. He offered this boat, called the "Eureka," to the Navy in 1926 and every year thereafter to meet the need for a landing craft to carry personnel and light equipment.

The Marines first saw the Eureka design in 1934 and perceived it to be a big step toward what they were seeking. They quickly formed a pact with Higgins, an alliance fertilized by their mutual impatience with the Navy's Bureau of Construction and Repair (later Bureau of Ships) for what they saw as its dilatory approach to the landing craft

---

* Moses was the ideal man for the occasion. A thoughtful, conscientious professional, he had a great interest in landing craft. He had commanded the 2d Marine Brigade in the 1936-37 Fleet Landing Exercise No. 3 at San Clemente and was painfully aware that the lack of suitable boats overshadowed everything else in the exercise.

problem. Pressure generated by that alliance resulted in the Navy's cautious purchase, in late 1937, of just one of Higgins's boats. They stipulated, however, that it be thirty feet in length rather than thirty-six feet, in order to match the davit spacing on Navy transports.*

It was tested, in conjunction with three Bureau of Ships-designed boats, in a 1939 exercise in the Caribbean but, despite great Marine enthusiasm, it received only qualified Navy approval. Five more Eurekas were purchased in time to take part, along with twelve Bureau of Ships-designed boats, in a major amphibious exercise in the Caribbean in 1940, where the Higgins craft performed extremely well. With war on the horizon, Major General Holland M. Smith, in command of the Marines in the exercise, assessed the boat situation with his usual candor. He said that field test of the Bureau of Ships–designed boats disclosed them to be "without merit." The Higgins boats, on the other hand, added "a new dimension." "If we had 300 of those boats and the ships to carry them, we'd be in business."[1]

Higgins, meanwhile, was having his problems with the Navy, in no small measure a product of his own impatient personality. The more dissatisfaction he exhibited for what he considered to be Navy bureaucratic inefficiency, the closer he came to the Marines, who saw Higgins, his ideas, and his energy as their salvation.

In March 1941, with the prospect of war growing by the hour, there were rumblings that we might have to seize Martinique from the Vichy French to preclude its use by the Axis. This was all General Smith and Higgins needed. Smith sent me to New Orleans along with Major Linsert of the Equipment Board to explain our needs. First, we asked Higgins to redesign his Eureka boat to incorporate a ramp for landing small vehicles. I illustrated this with pictures taken of the Japanese craft in Shanghai in 1937 as well as pictures of the model I had built in 1939. Second, we asked

---

* Later, in 1940, Higgins told me that he reduced the length from thirty-six to thirty feet only under protest and that he sold the boat to the Navy for $5,200, considerably less than his cost of $12,500, because that was all that was available in the Navy's landing craft budget.

him to design a steel tank-carrying lighter capable of carrying an eighteen-ton tank.

Higgins, in his characteristic forthright manner, took both ideas aboard at once and proceeded, at his own expense, to rebuild two of his Eureka boats—lengthened from thirty to thirty-six feet, with Navy concurrence—to incorporate a bow ramp.* In addition, in the space of sixty-one hours, he quickly converted a forty-five-foot steel lighter, which he had built for the Colombian government, into a ramp-bow craft capable of carrying an eighteen-ton tank.

Both ideas worked. The Marines were ecstatic. The Navy, however, was more hesitant, opting in April 1941 to buy only five more of the Higgins thirty-six-foot ramp-type boats for further testing and evaluation. This time the evaluation was conducted by a board of Marine Corps and Navy officers, headed by General Moses of the Equipment Board, who was already well acquainted with what the craft could do. Not unexpectedly, the board report was overwhelmingly favorable. The Navy then ordered two hundred of the Higgins ramp-type boats and, at long last, the LCVP (Landing Craft, Vehicle and Personnel)—workhorse of World War II—was a reality. General Smith declared, in what may be a forgivable overstatement, that it "contributed more to our common victory than any other single piece of equipment used in the war."[2]

At the same time, however, the Bureau of Ships declined to invest any money in a Higgins-designed tank-carrying lighter since they had a design for a steel tank carrier of their own.† Despite unfavorable reports on its performance in

---

* The issue of the thirty-six- versus thirty-foot boat is told in an interesting and altogether accurate way by General Holland M. Smith in his *Coral and Brass,* Charles Scribner's Sons, 1949. Higgins, in a stormy meeting at the Bureau of Ships, which I attended, declared that the thirty-six-foot boat had almost twice the capacity of the thirty-foot version and demanded that the davit spacing on the new Navy transports be designed to fit the landing craft, rather than the reverse.

† The Navy design had evolved from a 1935 thirty-eight-foot model, capable of handling a five-ton tank, to a 1938 forty-foot model designed for a fifteen-ton tank, to a forty-five-, forty-seven- and, finally, fifty-foot model designed to handle the thirty-ton tank.

exercises in the Caribbean ("slow, difficult to control, difficult to retract and equipped with an unpredictable power plant" according to General Smith), the bureau had six months earlier awarded the first increment of a 1,100-unit contract (96 lighters) of this design to the American Car and Foundry Company (ACF).

In June 1941 a major exercise, involving the 1st Marine Division and the 1st Infantry Division at New River, North Carolina, exposed the grim depth of our landing craft shortcomings. Delivery of the fifty-foot tank-carrying lighters designed by the Bureau of Ships was months behind schedule; none had yet appeared and none would be available for the exercise. The need for a tank carrier was so great that indefatigable General Smith, buttressed by the support of Commandant Holcomb, persuaded the Bureau of Ships to order one experimental fifty-foot craft from Higgins. It was a success, resulting in an order for nine more. They gave him fourteen days to build them—just time to make the craft available for the New River exercise.

Higgins took the proposition in stride, as if it were the sort of thing he did every day. He had no plans, but said he would do the job if someone would tell him exactly what we wanted. Major Linsert and I went to New Orleans again and were there on the spot to answer Higgins's questions even as he proceeded with the project. He had no space in his plant to accommodate the construction, so he persuaded the city of New Orleans to block off City Park Avenue adjacent to his plant so that he could set up a production line. He had the requisite steel, engines, and transmissions but needed brass propeller shafting. He located some in the hands of an oil company in Texas, but the company declined to release it to him. Later he told me that one of his four sons and two employees went to Texas and came back with the shafting. Just how they got it is not clear, but Higgins told me that he ultimately paid for the material.

Despite all the problems, Higgins managed to turn out the nine lighters in twelve days and to ship them off by rail to Norfolk, where they were embarked to take part in the New River maneuvers.

The craft were a triumphant success, but Higgins still got no more orders. ACF, who had yet to deliver one tank carrier, still had the contract for 96 of the required 1,100 craft. As explained by the Bureau of Ships, the craft designed by the bureau, with modifications developed during tests, would be superior to the Higgins product because the tanks would be carried above the waterline and the boat, accordingly, could not be swamped. The point was quite correct, although the higher center of gravity diminished the boat's stability. In the Higgins craft the tank rode below the waterline, making the boat more stable, although susceptible to swamping, which created a need for a powerful bilge pump capacity for emergencies.

All of this was too much for the acidulous Higgins and his impatient Marine friends. They went at once to powerful Senator Harry Truman, chairman of the Senate Committee on Preparedness. Influenced by their story and by two illuminating meetings with the colorful Higgins, the Senator laid a hard demand on the Navy: "Produce one of your boats. Put it in a head-to-head operational test in competition with Higgins's product, and see what happens.[3]

By early March of 1942, the ACF tank carrier of the Bureau of Ships design, enlarged to handle the Army's thirty-ton Sherman tanks, made its appearance. Higgins had also enlarged his tank carrier to handle the new tank. The scene was set for the much heralded competition, to take place on the beach at Camp Pendleton, south of Norfolk, Virginia. It was an excellent site for the test. The beach is open to the sea and often experiences high surf.

As the saying goes, everyone who was anyone was there— senior representatives from the Navy Department, the Bureau of Ships, and the Marine Corps, as well as the Army, which was greatly interested because of emerging plans for the North African amphibious landings. Higgins was there, along with his voluble Marine cheering section, in which I was included. With some political foresight, he had also brought with him an administrative assistant from Senator Truman's office. The whole group embarked in one large Navy boat to go out and watch the drama unfold.

It was a chill gray day. A brisk wind covered the sea with white caps and angry eight-foot waves were breaking on the Camp Pendleton beach. Everyone's binoculars were focused to pick up the contestants as they rounded Cape Henry light and came into the open sea. Presently the two craft hove into sight, each loaded with thirty tons of dead weight, ploughing and splashing, side by side, through the dark Atlantic seas. Then, as they began to turn south and head for the Camp Pendleton beach, the trouble began. Caught in the trough of the big ocean swells, the Bureau of Ships-designed craft, with its higher center of gravity, began to roll. It rolled more and more until we all feared it might capsize. The coxswain, realizing the craft was in extremis, cut back his power and, after wallowing uncertainly for a few moments, turned slowly around and headed back for the shelter of Norfolk harbor.

The contest was over before it began. The Higgins craft drove ahead through the rough seas, landed handily through the heavy surf, and retracted without difficulty. Then, almost as an act of defiance, it did it twice more.

That was it. The proposals for subsequent tank carrier construction were all based on Higgins's design.

Although Andy Higgins and his Marine allies were rejoicing over the triumph, we could not of course be fully aware that this was a watershed day for America. Our dreams of the true amphibious assault were, until then, just dreams. Now they had become a reality. For the first time there was a reliable way to make tanks, trucks, tractors, artillery, anti-aircraft weapons, and heavy engineer equipment a part of the beach assault.*

Thenceforward, America's amphibious march across the Pacific would be, as far as boats were concerned, Andy Higgins's war. His landing craft, built not just by Higgins but, with his permission, by anyone who wanted to borrow his plans, were a living ship-to-shore bridge that bore much

---

* That it had been a long hard road was obvious; that it was little understood and less appreciated was ironic. As late as 1945 General Eisenhower, in testimony before the Senate Military Affairs Committee, complained that "before World War II it was hard to get anyone interested in the design and production of landing craft," ignoring the fact that the Army was aware, at every step, of what the Navy and Marines were doing in this area in the 1920s and 1930s by virtue of their observers at fleet landing exercise. The truth is, the Army was not interested.

of the weight of American amphibious power from Pearl Harbor and Guadalcanal to Tokyo Bay, from North Africa and Italy to Normandy.

A tribute to Higgins it certainly is. Equally, it is a testimonial to the persistence of Marines of three generations, a fact that Higgins himself understood. He wrote to General Smith, ". . . my contact with the Marine Corps is the bright spot in my recollections of those intense and hectic days . . . I believe the things we foresaw and did had a profound effect on the winning of the war."[4]

CHAPTER 6

Breaching the Coral Wall

One of the many problems examined by Major Earl Ellis in his 1920 forecast of the Great Pacific War was that of the coral reef. Most of the islands which we would have to conquer were fringed with coral, a big obstacle to any amphibious attack. The water over the coral reef was often too shallow to be negotiated by boats. Other times the existence of coral was complicated by heavy surf breaking on the reef's edge. While Ellis had no answers to the coral reef problem, he did his successors a favor by illuminating its magnitude. And students of Gallipoli perceived another problem—a need for some certain means of moving supplies quickly through the beach area, in order to avoid the nightmarish congestion and carnage at the beachline that characterized the Gallipoli disaster.

Although Andy Higgins and his boats solved many problems, they did nothing to meet either of these two issues. Yet if we were to fight our way across the Pacific, solutions would have to be found. And they were. This time the answers came from another unusual civilian, a man as different from Higgins as anyone could be, different, that is, in every way but one. Both of them were instinctive and unselfish patriots.

Donald Roebling gave no indication, by background or appearance, that he was likely to have any great ability to contribute to our military affairs. Large, overweight, gentle, quiet, slow-moving, and serious, he was interested in peaceful pursuits. He wanted, for instance, to create a device that could be used to rescue people lost in the Everglades or isolated there by tropical storms. As he saw it, what was needed was a rugged vehicle, equally at home in the water and on the land, one capable of crawling over forbidding Everglade terrain—over mangrove and irregular coral, through mud and shoal water—and one with a respectable cargo capacity.

He designed and hand-built such a machine in 1935, with the financial help of his father, John A. Roebling, the steel and wire rope magnate. Of riveted all-aluminum construction, Roebling's first product was seriously defective. It was underpowered and its continuous track, whose cleats gave it both land and water propulsion, was both fragile and inefficient. Still, with all its defects, the machine gave promise of being able one day to do what its designer wanted it to do. Subsequent modifications—greater power and a more efficient track design—gave Roebling, by 1937, the rescue vehicle he had been seeking. Its performance was impressive and the resulting nationwide publicity brought the machine to the attention of the Navy and the Marine Corps.

One visit to Roebling at his Florida home by representatives of the Navy's Bureau of Ships and the Marine Corps Equipment Board created visions of what a similar machine could do for the Corps in the broad reaches of the Pacific. In mid-1938 Commandant Holcomb formally requested the Navy to pursue the development of an experimental military version of the Roebling machine.[1]

The road was not altogether smooth. Some Marines were dubious of the machine because of its slow water speed, its lack of water maneuverability, and the prospects of problems ashore with such a large unsprung weight. Then, too, there were problems with the Navy. Very little money was available for experimentation, and there was a basic jurisdictional issue of whether the Navy should be involved with the development of the machine at all, since it was certainly not a boat. And Roebling himself was not enthusiastic about becoming involved in a military project. It took ten months to solve these problems, to find the funds in the very limited Navy development purse, and to persuade Mr. Roebling that he was the one to do the job. But once started, the project moved ahead rapidly. By the spring of 1940, the first version of a military amphibian tractor, built by hand in Roebling's shop in Dunedin, Florida, was completed.

The significant point is that there was no great bureaucratic delay in the process. The Marines saw something they believed would help them fight the upcoming war. They persisted in their effort to get it. Donald Roebling, once he was convinced the idea was important, willingly gave his time and later his design. The Navy cooperated and, in twelve months from decision to launch, it all happened.

One must sense the great contrast between the course of this developmental effort which resulted in the rapid creation of a machine crucial to winning the war, and the bureaucracy that today burdens military material development. In late 1985, for instance, our Defense Department research and engineering function embodied a defense under secretary, six deputy under secretaries, seven assistant under secretaries, fifty-eight directors, and seventy-eight other senior individuals. And the development process itself—the so-called program planning and justification sequence—now embraces fifty-two separate sequential steps. Had the same procedure been in effect in 1939, it is doubtful there would have been an amphibian tractor available in time to take up its important role in the march across the Pacific.

The Marines received the first prototype model of the military amphibian in September 1940. They held a series of generally encouraging tests at Quantico, Virginia, which culminated with a demonstration for Marine Commandant Holcomb.* Thereafter, the vehicle was sent to the 1st

---

* The tractor hung up on a mud bank in Chopawamsic Swamp, near Quantico, marooning four of the Washington observers for an hour, but the incident did not greatly diminish the enthusiasm of the Marine and Navy officers who witnessed the tests.

Marine Brigade in Cuba with instructions to subject it to a comprehensive series of service tests in connection with landing exercises soon to take place on the island of Culebra.

At the time I was serving in the staff of the brigade commander, Brigadier General H. M. Smith, and he placed me in charge of the test program. Among my problems was the fact that every Marine who saw the machine was fascinated with it. They all wanted a demonstration—to ride in the tractor, to see what it could do, and to offer ideas concerning its design. I remember one demonstration vividly. After the Culebra exercises began, General Smith, who was greatly excited over the machine, directed me to put it through its paces for Admiral Ernest J. King, who had just assumed command of the Atlantic Fleet.

Following General Smith's instructions, I brought the amphibian alongside the flagship, the old battleship *Wyoming,* where General Smith had his headquarters, went on board, and explained the machine's capabilities to the admiral. He did not seem particularly interested, but when General Smith offered him a ride he agreed, more as a courtesy than anything else. He specified, however, that his time was limited and that the ride must be brief. Along with an aide he boarded the amphibian and observed its operation as we cruised about the flagship.

Then, on an impulse, I headed the craft toward the nearby coral reef that fringed the harbor and told the admiral that I intended to show him how it behaved in crossing the rough coral surface. He did not want to go, saying that time was short, that he was due back in the flagship. I assured him that the demonstration would take only a few moments, a statement that turned out to be greatly in error.

We were in a protected harbor. The water was quite calm with no waves over the reef, which was under about three feet of water. I was confident that we could negotiate the rough coral, having done it several times before.

But not this time.

A coral head knocked off one of the tracks. There we were, helplessly immobilized some fifty to one hundred yards from dry land, unable to go one way or another, inaccessible by boat. My experience with previous track problems assured me that its repair would be at least a two-hour job.

Admiral King, at his best, was not an easygoing man. When he understood the situation it took him only a moment to address a few plain words to me—words not intended to contribute to my long-term peace of mind. Then, without hesitation, he clambered over the side—starched white uniform and all—followed by his aide, who was not happy either. They waded ashore to the accompaniment of the admiral's cursing, thumbed a ride to the dock two miles away, and finally made their way back to the *Wyoming*. Members of the staff told me later that the admiral was still enraged when he boarded the ship, making his feelings known to General Smith loudly and without restraint. The general, in a living disclaimer of his nickname, "Howling Mad," never reproved me.

As the Culebra exercises came to an end and our test program was completed, the commandant of the Marine Corps sent a member of his staff, Colonel W. W. Rogers, to Cuba in December 1940 to go over our criticisms of and recommendations for the new machine. The list was long. Deficiencies related to the hull, power, track, suspension, controls, communications, and visibility, but there was nothing whatever on our list that condemned the basic idea. Rogers took the critique, returned to Washington and, in conjunction with the Navy Bureau of Ships and Mr. Roebling, quickly established the design criteria for the production model of what came to be known as the LVT (1) (Landing Vehicle, Tracked Model No. 1).*

Two prototype production models were built in the spring of 1941 and tested in Florida on a high-priority basis. Further design changes were made and two hundred more were quickly built. Delivery began in July 1941, only six months after the decision to go into production—an incredibly brief time.

The LVT(1) came off the production line rapidly. The vehicles were organized into 100-unit battalions and manned by Marines trained in a school set up by the Marine Corps in Dunedin, Florida, near the factory. The battalions

---

* There was some debate in the Bureau of Ships as to the designations. Was it a boat or a vehicle? Finally, because it was moved through the water by a track rather than by a propeller, it was called a vehicle.

were assigned to the Marine combat forces as they became ready. That turned out to be soon enough for one battalion to take part in the Guadalcanal offensive in August 1942, where they were found to be most useful in moving supplies directly from ships to supply dumps ashore.

Despite all the testing, little was known about the true capabilities and limitations of the machine in action. Sometimes it was necessary to learn on the job. I became involved in one such learning experience without knowing why.

In May 1943 I was in New Caledonia, commanding the 2d Parachute Battalion. One day I received a message to report at once to Corps Headquarters at Noumea, thirty-five miles away. When I arrived the chief of staff showed me a message that had originated in the Joint Chiefs of Staff. As I recalled it later that day, it said: "Desire exhaustive test of loaded LVT crossing coral reef under heavy surf conditions. You are authorized to expend two vehicles for the purpose if necessary. Request test be conducted ASAP [as soon as possible] and message report submitted."[2] The corps chief of staff, who had been on General Smith's staff in the Caribbean when I ran the tests on the first prototype, notified me that I would be in charge of the experiment. Two LVTs had been removed from depot storage, tested to ensure that they were in good condition, and loaded with five thousand pounds of dead weight. Along with crews they were ready to go.

I called my battalion, told the executive officer I might not be back for several days, and asked him to send me some clothes. Then I checked the condition of the two LVTs and satisfied myself that the crews were competent. The following morning, I told them, "We are going to take these two machines out to the reef, find a place where there is a heavy surf, bring one of the LVTs through the surf from seaward, and see what happens when the tractor hits the reef." As far as I knew, no one had yet tried to ride an LVT through both coral and heavy surf, and the picture of what might happen to a fifteen-thousand-pound unsprung iron box when a wave brought it crashing down on a coral ledge was not encouraging to any of us.

Early the next morning we crossed the ten-mile-wide lagoon, finding a forbidding surf of between six and ten feet pounding over a rough reef submerged under one to three feet of water. I had one LVT remain on the calm lagoon side of the reef with instructions to stand by while we took the other LVT out into the open sea for the test. I felt that we might upset during the surf run when we struck the reef, and the second machine would be in a position to pick us up.

Apart from getting wet, we had no problem getting out into the ocean through the surf. We then turned around, waited for a good-sized roller, and put the LVT on it at full speed. It was my hope that we could hold the craft square to the wave so that we would not hit the reef at an angle, in which event I was sure we would upset.

We managed to maintain our heading. As the wave broke over the reef edge, we came down nose-first with a great crash, while the wave rolled into the cargo compartment of the tractor. We all expected the track to collapse. It didn't. We also expected the hull to crack open. It didn't. In fact, we were all surprised to find, once we got the excess water out of the cargo compartment, that the machine was still able to operate.

We checked the machine over carefully, ran it around in the lagoon and, when sure that it would still function satisfactorily, went back and took it through the surf again. The result was the same—a shattering crash, a lot of water, but the LVT held together.

We did the surf run four more times. After the third time the hull began to leak a little. On the fourth run, we came in at an angle, almost upset when we struck the reef, and knocked off one track. The sequence of test runs convinced us that a loaded LVT could negotiate a heavy surf—six feet or more—on a coral reef and probably survive.

I wrote my report, turned it in, and thought nothing more of it. It was a year before I learned the reason for the crash test. In planning for the November 1943 landing on Tarawa, it was not known, for sure, whether there was enough water over the reef to accommodate conventional landing craft. Furthermore, a strong surf sometimes pounded at the reef's edge. LVTs would be a logical answer, if they had the capability to handle both the surf and the reef problems. And it seemed that nobody knew for sure.

As a result of the report of our test in New Caledonia, it

was decided to plan for the use of LVTs in the Tarawa operation. A similar surf and coral reef test conducted in the Fiji Islands in October 1943 corroborated the results we had obtained in New Caledonia. As a result, a final decision was made to employ the 125 LVTs available for the Tarawa attack in an altogether new role—as a conveyance for troops in the initial assault. Before this, because of its thin skin and slow speed, it had been regarded as a logistic vehicle.

The chronicles of the bitter thirty-hour Tarawa battle are replete with testimonials to the decisive contribution of the LVT to the victory. Troops were disembarked from transport ships into landing craft and then transferred to LVTs for the final run across the reef to the beach. It was a bloody time for the LVT crews and their passengers. Some sixty-one tractors were disabled by enemy defensive fire either at sea or as they repeatedly crossed the reef with successive loads of men and supplies. The remainder of the tractors succeeded in making numerous trips with their precious cargo of assault troops intact. At the shoreline, eleven more were knocked out by direct fire weapons or land mines. All things considered, however, they served their purpose well. The assault force had been brought face-to-face with the enemy, albeit at great cost; some 60 percent of the personnel of the 2d Amphibian Tractor Battalion were killed, wounded, or missing in action.[3]

Tarawa validated the LVT as an assault conveyance. General H. M. Smith, who had always been high on the vehicles, applauded its performance but urged that it be fitted with a ramp to facilitate unloading and that it be given more armor, more speed, and better communications.[4] Only a month later it was again employed in the assault role in the landings at Cape Gloucester, a role in which it performed for the remainder of the war. In the final operation at Okinawa in June 1945, more than eight hundred of the craft—faster, more heavily armored, and embodying a ramp—were employed to land the sixteen assault battalions.

At the time of the Tarawa operation some of the basic LVT hulls had been modified to mount a 37-millimeter gun. While not available in time for Tarawa, the so-called ar-

mored LVT led the assault at Cape Gloucester, in the
Marshall Islands, and at Guam. Other versions, armed with
a 75-millimeter howitzer, were in the van of the attack at
Saipan, Tinian, Iwo Jima, and Okinawa. In the last operation, once ashore, the LVT weapons were integrated into the
structure of Marine division artillery and fired in close
support of the advancing forces.[5]

Before the global conflict ended, more than fifteen thousand LVTs had been built and had served in every theater of
war. Like Andrew Higgins, Donald Roebling neither asked
for nor received any emolument for his contribution to the
victory, his total reward being a citation from the U.S.
Government and the gratitude of a legion of admiring
Marines and soldiers.

Speaking of Higgins, it is interesting to recall his initial
reaction to the LVT. The first time he saw one he derided it,
declaring that its design was flawed. There had to be a better
solution than a machine that depended on a track, he said,
with all of its moving parts continually exposed to the
corrosive effect of salt water and the erosive effect of sand.
He later built, at his own expense, an amphibian that
eliminated the track, depending for its land and water
mobility on three large drumlike cleated wheels on each
side.

The machine worked well. Higgins had a series of impressive demonstrations in the Louisiana bayous for both Navy
and Marine representatives in mid-1942. As far as could be
discerned, his trackless machine equaled or exceeded the
performance of the LVT, but it was too late. We were
proceeding, flat out, to build LVTs of the accepted Roebling
design. There was no time to make a major change in design
philosophy. Higgins's design disappeared—although the
prototype machine did not. I saw it again, sitting in his
boatyard, in 1946.

The tale of Roebling and his LVT, as well as the account of
Andy Higgins and his landing craft, tells an eloquent story
about the Marines themselves. In both cases, in the face of
apathy and sometimes opposition from within their own
ranks, the Marines were determined that there must be a
family of mechanisms that would be able to carry them,
their weapons, and their equipment through the seas and

the surf and deliver them face-to-face with the enemy on his own shore. That those mechanisms materialized was a product of stubborn faith. Indeed, faith—in themselves and in their purposes—has been the prime ingredient in the innovative quality that has become such a vital part of the Marine personality.

PART
III

THE IMPROVISERS

The world reserves its great rewards
for one thing—initiative.

Elbert Hubbard

The space separating defeat and victory is often very small, and the more powerful assailant does not always prevail. "The battle, sir," said Patrick Henry, "is not to the strong alone; it is to the vigilant, the active, the brave." Most often, the ingredients of victory are initiative, resourcefulness, adroitness, and improvisation.

The Greeks before the walls of Troy were the weaker by far. But they created the Horse, which erased the difference between weak and strong, and Greece triumphed.

The American colonists at Princeton had little hope of matching, much less exceeding, the British strength. Yet they won by improvisation. Leaving campfires to flicker in the night, the Americans in fact broke camp and surprised and routed the more powerful British.

At Cannae, Chancellorsville, the Plains of Abraham, and Stony Point, one of the contestants made his tactical or strategic point by deception and improvisation.

Improvisation has been a way of life for the Marines.

Examples extend all the way from conversion of native Central American livestock and canoes into military transportation to use of a home window air conditioner in Vietnam to keep the electronics systems in a complex aircraft operational. But few improvisations are more impressive than their figuring out how to drop bombs accurately in the dark or their contriving to land at Inchon, Korea, in 1950 without the forces, means, or time to do the job.

CHAPTER 7

The Marines' Push Button

A constant lament of soldiers throughout history has been, "If only I could see in the dark. If only I could see in the dark and the enemy could not, everything would be different." Despite other great strides in military technology, it is a hunger that is still largely unsatisfied.

In one area, however, we have breached the cloak of night. We can drop a bomb from an aircraft at high altitude in closet darkness or in the worst of weather and be reasonably sure of its hitting very near the target on the first try. We can do this, although neither the pilot nor friendly forces on the ground can see the target. This is a monumental breakthrough, and one that has killed many an enemy at greatly reduced risk to our own pilots.

And the Marine aviators did it. Combining vision, improvisation, and resolution, they managed to do it. It all began in the closing days of World War II. Among the prizes that fell into American hands was a stockpile of about eight hundred German V-1 buzz bombs. This was a small pilotless airplane powered by a crude pulse-jet rocket engine with four hundred pounds of fuel and a thousand-pound warhead. It was designed to do no more than fly across the English Channel and, with luck, to hit Greater London. A simple, ground-controlled radio guidance mechanism influenced the early part of the rocket's flight; as the weapon descended it was nothing more than a ballistic missile, wholly unguided and hence quite inaccurate.

A few of the rockets were sent to the Navy missile test center at Point Mugu, California, where the first idea was to adapt the V-1 (which engineers there had renamed "the Loon") to operate from a submarine. The rocket, housed in a watertight compartment, would be rolled out and launched after the submarine had surfaced. Guidance was crude, not unlike the radio control for today's model airplanes. The submarine's small radar would follow the bird after it was launched, sending signals to a computer in the ship's control room. The computer would then tell a command control radio what signal to send to the missile to alter its course to left or right, pointing it in the general direction of the target. When the rocket motor burned out, the small wings would automatically blow off and the weapon would become a simple free-falling bomb.

It was, to say the least, an inaccurate system, affected by the submarine's own navigation limitations and by the inaccuracies of the controlling radar, which grew progressively less trustworthy as the distance between the rocket and the submarine increased. In tests, if the bomb flew twenty-five miles and landed within three or four miles of the target, the project managers congratulated themselves.

Enter the marines, four officers and eleven enlisted men, all with extensive World War II combat experience in infantry artillery and aviation, all with high I.Q.s, most with prior scientific or engineering training in college or at the Army guided missile school at Fort Bliss. Each received orders in the spring of 1948 to report to Point Mugu for "on-the-job-training in guided missiles."

There was no intention on the part of the Marine Corps to constitute them as a Marine unit. So far as Marine Corps Headquarters was concerned, they were at Point Mugu for training—to study under the Navy as individuals. But Captain Marian Cranford Dalby saw it differently. Dalby, the senior Marine and a fighter pilot, was quiet, persistent, thorough, and immensely curious. He had an affection for hard work and a zest for achievement. He was the right man for the job and, as it turned out, he made history.

Dalby was the first to arrive at Point Mugu, and he chose to interpret the term "on-the-job-training" in a manner reminiscent of the White Queen who, when asked the meaning of a word, responded, "What does it mean? It means what I mean it to mean, no more and no less." He captured the incoming Marines ("through a combination of personal charm and threat of court martial," he says) and organized them into a tight little command which he named "Marine Guided Missile Unit."* He immediately set about farming them out, throughout the various projects on the base, wherever he saw an opportunity for them to learn something about the missile business that he felt might benefit the Corps.

One day, the director of technical activities at Point Mugu, Commander Grayson Merrill, USNA '34, lamenting the immense control problems in the Loon submarine project, asked Dalby what he thought about involving a team of Marines in the control of a Loon flight. As Merrill visualized it, the submarine would surface and fire the rocket. The Marine detachment, which had landed clandestinely ahead of time from another submarine with their own radar and computer, would then take over radio guidance of the bird and steer it on to the point where it would become a free-falling bomb. Being much closer to the scene, the Marines' guidance efforts would, presumably, result in greater accuracy.†

Dalby jumped at the chance to have a project with a Marine Corps imprimatur on it. Never mind that there was neither a computer nor a radar in existence that could be landed from a submarine, it still provided an opportunity for his little Marine group to strike off into an uncharted area, and he seized it.

---

* Dalby and I discussed his activities at Pt. Mugu in personal meetings and, more important, he committed some of his reminiscences to writing—a significant archive, now at the Marine Corps Historical Center, Washington, D.C.

† Recollections of Merrill, now a captain, USN (Ret.), who describes Dalby as "a tiger who just wouldn't quit."

He shared the news with his troops, who received it with enthusiasm. Two technically talented members of the group, Master Sergeants William L. Holtz and Floyd A. Dickover, set to work building a computer that would be portable enough to land from a submarine and still do the job. Within a few weeks they had one, a product of their own hands, made completely from hardware provided by the Navy. It was not handsome, but it worked.

As to radar, there was no good answer in sight. The only one available that met the technical requirement was the SCR 584,* an Army antiaircraft artillery item housed in two motor home–size vans, quite unsuited for amphibious employment. Nevertheless, because there was nothing else, the Marines worked it into their system. Then other problems began to surface. It was almost impossible to procure the precious Loon to shoot for practice. There were too few of them, and there were too many competitive experiments of higher priority. Also, it was difficult to arrange for a submarine, for firing range clearance, and for the mountain of logistic preparations needed before a missile could be fired.

After only two such firings using their improvised equipment—hard to arrange but, incidentally, quite successful—the Marines concluded that there had to be some easier way to test and perfect their equipment and to train with it. Master Sergeant Clark D. Hayden had an idea. He designed a device that would permit the automatic pilot in a Marine fighter aircraft to accept radio commands from their control system just as if the plane itself were the Loon missile in the controlled part of its flight.† A bomb carried by the plane then performed as the Loon in the free-fall part of its flight. It worked. The radar on the ground tracked the plane, the homemade computer generated control commands for the radio which told the plane's automatic pilot what to do and gave the pilot the signal to drop the bomb. Then Hayden devised a scheme to permit the radio equip-

---

* The abbreviation "SCR" derives from the words "Signal Corps Radio."

† Dalby says, "This was particularly impressive on Hayden's part because he had never seen a fighter plane up close before he tackled the job."

ment on the ground to send a signal to release the bomb. Thus the aircraft accurately simulated the flight of the Loon during its controlled phase, while the bomb, released by radio, simulated the Loon in its free-fall phase. Because the procedure eliminated the need for both submarines and the precious Loon rockets, the entire testing system was much simpler to organize. Soon, training runs became very accurate, with errors measured in yards rather than in miles, as had been the case with the submarine-launched Loon. Altogether, it was an impressive and successful improvisation, and the more the Marines exercised the system the better it worked.

At this point, there came a sudden flash of perception, the sort of thing of which history is made. One day Dalby and one of his assistants, Captain Samuel A. Dressin, simultaneously hit upon the same idea. Dalby recalls that they asked each other, "Why in hell are we fooling around trying to simulate submarines and clumsy Loon rockets? With the equipment at hand, that combination is not going to work anyhow. Why not just work on guiding the airplane by radar, computer, and radio and getting conventional bombs on the target instead of a Loon? That's really what we are playing with now, and that's Marine business." Here was serendipity. Looking for a small island of a solution to the Navy's guided missile program, Dalby's little group had stumbled onto a new continent in the world of Marine all-weather close air support. Improvisation had reaped dividends.

The impact of this idea on the rest of Dalby's Marine group was electric. Here, in their hands—the fruit of their own resolve and genius—was a system that, once perfected, would be able to drop bombs accurately in the dark and in bad weather. The realization of what that could mean—to pilots used to being frustrated by the elements or to Marines on the ground who needed close air support in daylight and dark, in fair weather and foul—drove the pioneers to new heights in their determination to make their scheme a practical reality. With the help of the Navy's Point Mugu engineers, the Marines incorporated new characteristics into their homemade computer that would give the system greater accuracy and would make it compatible with rough handling on the battlefield. When the redesign was complete, they hand-built two computers and replaced an unwieldy five-by-six-foot plotting board with an ingenious little tracing device no larger than a shoebox.

The massive and impractical SCR 584 radar was still their major problem. Then Dalby heard of a new and more compact radar, still in development for Army antiaircraft artillery, the SCR 784. He had to have one and sent off one of his officers, First Lieutenant Robert G. Harris—a Marine artilleryman and University of Michigan engineer—to Fort Bliss to see what he could do. By some legerdemain, Harris returned with two of them!

By early 1950, the equipment was still an awkward-looking jungle of wires and breadboard-style panels. Even so, Dalby concluded that it was sufficiently reliable to risk exposing it to the using Marine Corps. In April, he took the contraption to the Marine Corps Base at Camp Pendleton in southern California, where he demonstrated it for a group of ground and air Marines, including representatives of the 5th Marines, which I commanded at the time. We went to the demonstration because we were told to go. We had no idea what to expect.

In his orientation Dalby told us that he had two aircraft, flying at 18,000 feet, and said, if everything worked, that his device would direct the course of the aircraft and release the bombs, which would fall within one hundred and fifty yards of a target. He reemphasized that all of this would happen without the pilot ever seeing the target and that the equipment on the ground—not the pilot—would drop the bomb!

We were incredulous. Dalby invited me to select the first bombing target. I chose a terrain feature that was clearly visible and we waited, with little confidence that the bombs would fall anywhere near it.

On the first run, two bombs landed within fifty yards of the target. We were shocked but still unbelieving. Someone else chose another target, and on this run the bombs made a direct hit! After three more runs, all with similar results, there was no doubt: all-weather bombing had arrived in the Marine Corps.

On that day, Dalby earned a chorus of supporters. The support was not, however, universal. In the audience was a brigadier general from Washington. After the demonstration, he examined the equipment and was repelled by its obvious tentative condition. He commented that it had no real combat application, that "rain would short out this maze of wires in nothing flat." I heard Dalby declare that he would "never let a general behind the scenes again until I have it packaged up like a box of candy."

This was only the first of many demonstrations and, as time passed, the system, named AN-MPQ-14,* gradually became more solid, more combat-compatible, and more efficient. The choir of enthusiastic supporters—air and ground—who were convinced that the idea was worthwhile grew accordingly. Support from Marine Corps Headquarters was willingly forthcoming and effective. Requests made, whether for people or equipment, were quickly met. The assistance was largely due to the efforts of Lieutenant Colonel Homer G. Hutchinson, a perceptive aviator who, as Dalby put it, "really knew his way around the Washington jungle . . . Without Hutchinson's help, the whole MPQ-14 project would probably have died." Through Hutchinson's efforts, Dalby even ended up with two new Corsair night-fighter aircraft, complete with pilots, for use in training.†

Thus, as the Korean conflict approached, the little group of pioneers had abundant proof of its ability to put bombs within fifty yards of an unseen target from an altitude of 20,000 feet. Some of us from the 1st Marine Division who had been so impressed by Dalby's April demonstration would find ourselves in Korea in only a few months. We did not forget what we had seen.

By July 1951, the team was ready to go to war. The equipment had been finally hardened to meet the strains of combat. It had been tested a hundred times over. And its operators were as skilled as only those who have invented, built, and tested a machine can be.

I was in Korea, serving as chief of staff of the 1st Marine

---

* AN-MPQ-14 means (A)Army-(N)Navy-(M)Mobile-(P)Radar-(Q) Combination purpose-(14)14th model or modification.

† Hutchinson recalls having to field a complaint from the quartermaster general who, having received a requisition from Dalby for artillery survey equipment, wanted to know what possible use an aviation unit could have for transits and levels.

Division, and as soon as we learned from Dalby that the unit was ready to move, I urged its deployment. Marine Corps Headquarters reacted favorably. When the unit arrived in Korea, the commanding general of the 1st Marine Aircraft Wing agreed to position it with the 1st Marine Division, which, at that time, was involved in heavy fighting with the North Koreans a few miles south of the 38th Parallel. After establishing itself with the division, the group quickly made converts everywhere.

It found its first new friends among the aviators. The morale of the 1st Marine Aircraft Wing's Corsair night-fighter squadron, VMF-513, was low because, in providing night support for the ground Marines, the pilots had to fly at low levels up dark Korean valleys, trying to find their targets under flares. They were suffering heavy casualties in the process. They quickly saw the great benefit of flying at altitudes of 15,000 to 20,000 feet, far above the enemy antiaircraft fire, and having greater success hitting the target.

The approval of ground forces followed shortly. Suddenly close air support was available around the clock and in the worst of weather. Enemy artillery that had taken refuge in caves at the first sight of a low-flying aircraft were repeatedly caught unawares and destroyed by bombs falling from 20,000 feet. In truth, a new era had dawned. The Marines on the ground, the direct beneficiaries of the night and all-weather bombing, were enthusiastic in their praise and vocal in their calls for more systems of the same type.

There were still many problems to be solved, of course, but the idea was validated over and over throughout the remainder of the Korean War and, later, in Vietnam. Now organized in Air Support Radar Teams and using a new generation of the original device—designated AN-TPQ-10*—the all-weather close air support was integrated into the Marines' daily operations. During the siege at Khe Sanh, because of the unfavorable weather, the AN-TPQ-10 was a major factor in meeting the needs for round-the-clock fire support for the base. Reliably putting bombs within fifty

---

* Meaning (A)Army-(N)Navy-(T)Ground Transportable-(P)Radar-(Q)Combination purpose-(10)10th version or modification.

yards of a target, the versatile system handled as many as 105 missions in a single day. Colonel David M. Lownds, in command of the Khe Sanh defense said, "Anything but the highest praise would not be enough."[1] Air Force Major Milton G. Hartenbower, an Air Force liaison officer at Khe Sanh said, "These skilled specialists could bring strikes within 50 meters of Marine positions in an emergency."[2]

It is plain, in retrospect, that AN-MPQ-14 and its successor, AN-TPQ-10 stand as shining monuments to the innovative drive of Dalby and his associates and give powerful testimony to a quality that distinguishes the entire Marine Corps air/ground combat system. It is one of professional independence, a conviction that the Marines' job, being different, is certain to have many different needs. It has long been understood that fulfilling those needs demands a willingness to acknowledge that nobody else is going to do it for us, coupled with a determination to find a way ourselves. It was in that tradition of proud and stubborn independence that MPQ-14 was born. Today's overbearing atmosphere of military standardization certainly makes resourceful improvisations such as MPQ-14 far more difficult. But, one way or another, the Marines are going to have to keep the pioneering spirit alive because it is very near to the heart of what the Corps is all about.

CHAPTER 8

You Can't Get There from Here:
The Inchon Story

The 28th of March 1949 was a melancholy day in the history of the Marine Corps—and no cause for rejoicing by the other services either. On that day Louis A. Johnson was sworn in as secretary of defense. The Corps had not been altogether pleased with James Forrestal, his predecessor, but it came to regard the Forrestal regime with nostalgia compared with the stewardship of Johnson.

An attorney who had been moderately successful in West Virginia politics, Johnson had formed a friendship with President Truman when the latter was in the Senate, based on their Army service in France in World War I and their association with the American Legion. Later he served as finance chairman for the Democratic National Committee. He was appointed to the Defense position with the understanding that *economy* was to be his watchword. At the time Truman was surfeited with the Navy and Marines,* and Johnson's appointment was preceded by a general understanding that the president wanted the two maritime ser-

---

* Part I chronicles Mr. Truman's growing disenchantment with the Navy and Marine Corps during the unification period and the years immediately following.

vices brought to heel. Johnson's attitude is characterized by a conversation he had with Admiral Richard L. Connally shortly after his appointment:

> Admiral [he said], the Navy is on its way out. There's no reason for having a Navy and a Marine Corps. General Bradley tells me amphibious operations are a thing of the past. We'll never have any more amphibious operations. That does away with the Marine Corps. And the Air Force can do anything the Navy can do, so that does away with the Navy.[1]

President Truman was dissatisfied with the provisions of the National Security Act of 1947. Even with the 1949 amendments that created a JCS chairman and enlarged the functions of the secretary of defense, the modified law had still not gone far enough in concentrating military authority at the top, certainly not far enough to please Truman's most trusted military advisor, General Marshall. On the basis of the 1949 changes, the president undertook to curb the Navy and Marine Corps through administrative and fiscal actions. This was what the new defense secretary was busy doing until war and Congress intervened.

The secretary had starved all of the services—and very nearly had killed the Marines—by a program of severe budget cuts. When he took office, Johnson found a very austere Marine Corps, which included eleven infantry battalions and twenty-three aircraft squadrons. He decreed that in fiscal year 1950 the Corps's fighting forces would be reduced to eight understrength battalions and twelve aircraft squadrons. For the fiscal year beginning in July 1951 he directed that the number of battalions be reduced yet again, to six. His aspirations were plain. He intended to diminish progressively the fighting units of the Corps and, ultimately, to transfer what remained to the Army and the Air Force.

Johnson's plan, where Marine Corps aviation was concerned, was far advanced. In an off-the-record speech at the Waldorf-Astoria Hotel in New York, he declared that he was taking action to do away with Marine aviation and that papers to accomplish the Marines' transfer to the Air Force were on his desk.[2]

This was too much. Major General C. C. Jerome, a respected Marine aviator, alerted Representative Carl Vinson, chairman of the House Armed Services Committee, a staunch Navy/Marine supporter, and a firm believer in the National Security Act in its original form. Vinson made short work of the heavy-handed secretary. He called Johnson to his office and delivered a lecture on those provisions of the National Security Act that expressly forbade such transfers of major combat functions. Then he obliged the secretary to write him a memorandum saying (albeit untruthfully) that no such step as transfer of Marine aviation to the Air Force was under contemplation and, in any event, that he would consult with the appropriate congressional committees before even considering an act of this sort.

Johnson worked his will on the Marines in other ways, however: in curtailment of appropriations for equipment, ammunition, supplies, and people, and through a policy of exclusion in various aspects of tactical training and planning. He approved the action of Admiral Forrest Sherman, the chief of naval operations, in assigning the bulk of the Navy's amphibious ships to train the Army, thus precluding the Corps from practicing at its statutory specialty. And in strategic planning by the Joint Chiefs of Staff, the Marines were allowed no part at all. Commandant Cates persuaded Navy Secretary John L. Sullivan to intercede, asking that the Marines be permitted to take part in JCS discussions when their interests or operational employment were involved. Sullivan, for his pains, received a rebuke from Johnson:

> I cannot see any justification for giving the Commandant of the Marine Corps a special role not accorded to the chiefs of various other arms and services which are integral parts of the Army, Navy and Air Force.

This is another way of saying that Johnson saw the Marines on a par with the Army Nurse Corps or the Navy Bureau of Supplies and Accounts.

These were major matters, but the secretary was not above some pettiness too. He crossed the Marine commandant off the list of those Washington officials authorized a chauffeur and a limousine and off the list of service chiefs for whom a special gun salute was prescribed on ceremonial occasions. He forbade celebration of the Marine Corps Birthday.* Small things, all, in the context of national security but a measure of the man nevertheless.

Taken all together, Johnson's erosive actions where the Marines were concerned had an effect for which he has never really been brought to account. Largely through his actions, at the outset of the Korean conflict, the Fleet Marine Force, the expeditionary element of the Corps, was pitifully anemic, having shrunk from its World War II peak of more than 300,000 men to only 27,656. Of these, some 8,000 were serving in a greatly attenuated 1st Marine Division (war strength 22,000) at Camp Pendleton in California. Its companion 1st Marine Aircraft Wing, at only 3,700 men (war strength about 12,000) was at El Toro, forty miles away. Things were little better on the East Coast. The 2d Marine Division at Camp Lejeune, North Carolina, had 9,000 men and its companion 2d Marine Aircraft Wing at Cherry Point a few miles distant had only 5,300.

In the basic combat units this pitifully small figure equated to three infantry battalions and three tactical aircraft squadrons on the West Coast and three infantry battalions and four tactical aircraft squadrons on the East Coast. All of these formations, plus units of supporting artillery, engineers, tanks, air control, and supply were gravely understrength. Despite the Johnson austerities, however, the Marines had managed to attain a respectable state of training. The officers and noncommissioned officers were professionals—many with World War II experience. Their air and ground equipment—almost all of World War II vintage—was often threadbare, but they had kept it in good repair.

At the time (1949–1950), I was in command of the 5th Marine Regiment at Camp Pendleton, California, the only

---

* In all fairness, he also abolished Navy Day and Army Day. He learned, however, that it is very difficult to prevent an institution from having a birthday. Following Johnson's action the Marines celebrated 10 November with even greater vigor—if that is possible.

infantry regiment in the 1st Marine Division. We felt the dead hand of starvation everywhere. War strength for the regiment was 3,900 men. We suffered along with 1,800. Each infantry battalion was short one of its three rifle companies, each of which had two instead of the prescribed three platoons. Artillery and other supporting elements were correspondingly reduced, and service troops had been even more severely curtailed. Training presented a real challenge because of the limitations on ammunition, repair parts, and gasoline. But there was nothing Louis Johnson could do to prevent us from maneuvering up and down the brown hills of the 120,000-acre Camp Pendleton reservation. Supported by 1st Marine Aircraft Wing planes (to the extent that they had fuel to fly), we trained at length and with much intensity. Indeed, we spent so much time in the field that the wife of one of my men reproved me, "My kids have forgotten what their father looks like."

While training ashore presented few problems, training in landing operations was a different matter, because the Navy's meager amphibious shipping resources had been assigned mainly to work with the Army.

One stroke of fortune came in early 1950 in a directive for the 5th Marines to stage an amphibious demonstration at Camp Pendleton for the Army Command and General Staff College. We were given an array of precious resources, most important, sufficient amphibious shipping to embark the regiment. With the understanding assistance of the Navy commander involved, Rear Admiral James H. Doyle (later to distinguish himself at Inchon), we were able to parlay our programmed one-day demonstration into three rehearsal landings and a five-day amphibious exercise. But that was our only taste of saltwater in a twelve-month period, and the same unhappy situation prevailed on the East Coast.

Put in other terms, on 25 June when the North Korean blitz of some 75,000 men drove south across the 38th Parallel, the Marines' existing air/ground expeditionary force was tiny and emaciated. But what there was of it was ready to go.

The Korean crisis became a reality for the Marines just

five days later. On 30 June, the Fleet Marine Force Pacific headquarters in Hawaii* received a cryptic message query from the chief of naval operations. Prompted, we later learned, by Commandant Cates, it asked:

> How soon can you sail for combat employment in the Far East: (a) A reinforced battalion: (b) A reinforced regiment?

I had reported for duty as force operations officer only two days before, having relinquished command of the 5th Marines on 15 June. After studying the message for a moment, I drafted a reply and took it to the chief of staff. Referring to the JCS message, it read:

> (a) 48 hours. (b) Five days, including a Marine aircraft group.

The chief of staff read the proposed reply and said, "How do you know we can do that?" I answered, "I don't, but if we can't, we're dead."[3] He released the message.

To do (b)—provide a reinforced regiment and a Marine aircraft group at anything approaching full war strength—would take the bulk of the Fleet Marine Force resources on the West Coast. Only bits and pieces would be left of the 1st Marine Division and 1st Marine Aircraft Wing. Realistically, however, that is what they were there for.

We immediately alerted the troops on the West Coast to the possibility of imminent expeditionary deployment. The commandant of the Marine Corps, almost simultaneously, did the same thing. Two days later, on the morning of 2 July, we received a message directive to prepare an air-ground Marine brigade for combat employment overseas. Preparations went forward by word of mouth, being confirmed by messages on 6 and 7 July. The

---

* Lieutenant General T. E. Watson, the incumbent commander, had departed for a new duty station. Lieutenant General L. C. Shepherd, Jr., the new commander, had not arrived. Colonel Gregon Williams, the chief of staff, was in charge.

preliminary orders we issued to the forces involved said,

> Take whatever is required and available in troops and equipment from the 1st Marine Division and 1st Marine Aircraft Wing, plus what Marine Corps Headquarters provides from other sources, make a provisional brigade consisting of the 5th Marine Regiment Reinforced and Marine Aircraft Group 33, both at reduced strength, embark them in ships the Navy will provide and set sail for the Far East.

It was not easy but within four days of the initiating directive, units of the brigade, designated First Provisional Marine Brigade, had begun loading. The ground elements embarked in San Diego, the air elements in Long Beach, where the two attack squadrons went aboard the small escort carrier *Badoeng Strait*. By 14 July they were loaded and gone—a 6,500-man air/ground brigade—and they could have departed a day or two earlier had ships been available. Commandant Cates came from Washington to tell them goodbye. "Clean this up in a couple of months or I will be over to see you," he said.

The steady performance of the 1st Provisional Marine Brigade in Korea under Brigadier General Edward A. Craig and the contribution of its air/ground team to the defense of the Pusan Perimeter are the substance of another story. It is important here to reflect only on the brigade's validation of the Marine dictum—"Be ready to go with whatever you have."

The departure of the brigade left the remaining Marine Corps fragments on the West Coast, both air and ground, in disarray—mainly sick, short-timers, and men in a disciplinary status. Unhappy as it was, the condition would not have been crucial had it not been for events taking place in Tokyo.

Lieutenant General Lemuel C. Shepherd, Jr., had assumed command of Fleet Marine Force Pacific on 2 July. With the encouragement of Commandant Cates and Admiral Arthur Radford, commander-in-chief, Pacific, he went to the Far East on 7 July to get a sense of the state of affairs on the Korean peninsula. Independently, he had two other aims: first, to ensure that the 1st Provisional Marine Brigade would be employed as a unified air/ground formation; and, second, to investigate the prospects for committing additional Marine forces. He hitched a ride to Tokyo with Vice Admiral Thomas Sprague, taking an aide and me with him.

We went first to Yokosuka, the headquarters of Naval Forces Far East. Until 25 June it had been a sleepy little eddy in the backwash of postwar retrenchment. Now it had suddenly become a beehive of frenzied effort to do in emergency all the things that Johnson's economies had made so difficult to do as a matter of routine. There General Shepherd made his plea that our air/ground brigade be employed as a unit and received a favorable response from the Naval Forces Far East commander, Vice Admiral C. Turner Joy, including assurance that the two fighter/attack squadrons from Marine Aircraft Group 33 would be able to support the ground units of the brigade from the escort carriers *Badoeng Strait* and *Sicily*.*

The next day, 10 July, General Shepherd went to Tokyo to see General MacArthur. MacArthur was just entering the Dai Ichi Building as we pulled up. After a brief visit to the daily staff conference, we went to MacArthur's office, where he saw us almost at once. He described the bad situation on the Korean peninsula in unvarnished terms but voiced confidence that the North Korean blow would be absorbed by General Walton Walker's Eighth Army forces, not, however, without hard fighting and heavy casualties. Then, he spoke eloquently of the need for an early counteroffensive and, with a few positive remarks about the conduct of the 1st Marine Division when it served under him at Cape Gloucester in World War II, he walked over to a map of Korea and said,

---

* Another air element, a light observation squadron, was ultimately landed at Kobe, Japan. The aircraft were assembled on the dock and then took off from one of the main streets of the city.

If I had the 1st Marine Division now, I could stabilize my front [he didn't even have a front] and make an amphibious envelopment here—at Inchon on the west coast.

General Shepherd encouraged him to ask the Joint Chiefs for the division and for an accompanying Marine aircraft wing too. MacArthur responded enthusiastically, "You draw me up an appropriate message to the JCS," he said, "and I will send it."[4]

We left MacArthur and went into an adjoining office, where I borrowed the desk of an Army major, one of MacArthur's aides, and assembled a simple message covering points outlined by General Shepherd. He took it in to MacArthur and was back in a minute or so with the word that the message was approved and would soon be on its way. When MacArthur put his signature on the message he set in motion a series of crash improvisations that have rarely been equaled in the Corps's history.

The real significance of the moment emerges when one realizes that General Shepherd knew, without a long exchange of messages, just about what the Marine Corps could produce. Even more important, he knew if he generated a request for a division/wing team to go to war that Marines all the way up the line would support it. And they did. Later, on 14 August in a meeting at Camp Pendleton, Commandant Cates was eloquent—even stern—in impressing on General Shepherd how the Inchon undertaking was consuming the total resources of the Corps—but he never faltered in his support.

The Marines assumed, in advance of a national decision, that MacArthur's 10 July request to the JCS would be granted, and they set about trying to reestablish some military capability in the 1st Division and 1st Wing. Since there were not enough men in the 1st entire Fleet Marine Force to make one division/wing team, Commandant Cates on 13 July took the first hard step. Through the chief of naval operations, he urged immediate mobilization of the Marine Corps Reserve, both air and ground.

President Truman was a realist. He was aware of the grave

situation facing Army forces in Korea and perceived that without the reserves MacArthur's crisis demand for Marines could not be met. He did not hesitate. Approval for mobilization of the Marine Corps Reserve ground elements came on the 19th and on the 22d for aviation units. On the 20th, twenty-two ground units were ordered to active duty and given only ten days to get to Camp Pendleton. Within the next fifteen days the whole of the Marine Corps Ground Reserve—138 units, more than 33,000 men—were ordered to active duty.

Concurrently, on the 23rd, three Marine Corps Reserve fighter squadrons and six ground control intercept squadrons were ordered to active duty. In little more than a week, most of them had arrived in El Toro and were shaking down in Major General Field Harris's 1st Marine Aircraft Wing. Many had left good civilian jobs behind and were now contemplating how they were going to support a wife and possibly children on a corporal's pay.

The 25th of July was a watershed date. On that day, just a month after the conflict began, the Joint Chiefs of Staff formally announced approval of MacArthur's request for a Marine division and wing and approved their expansion to war strength, less the elements of the 1st Brigade then enroute to Korea.* This meant that two infantry regiments had to be created, since the 5th Marines—enroute to Korea—was the only infantry unit in the division.

In the wake of the 25 July decision a series of intra-Marine Corps crash actions began. On that day all Marine Security Forces (mainly detachments at naval stations) were reduced in strength by 50 percent. The 3,630 men thus produced were started on the way to Camp Pendleton and El Toro and all of them had arrived within ten days.

The reaction of the reserves to the sudden call made, to me, an interesting portrait of the American society itself. A minority made every conceivable effort to obtain a

---

* The magnitude of the expansion was great. A war strength reinforced division numbered about 22,000; at peace strength only 10,000.

deferment—telephone calls, hardship affidavits, congressional influence, even spurious medical certificates. But the great majority of those called up responded promptly and enthusiastically. Others who were not called went to the nearest Marine Corps training center and pleaded to be included. In the end, the greatest problem was to determine those whose burning desire to go concealed a lack of essential training.

Concurrently, a directive was issued for a major cross-country transfer of 7,182 men from the Second Marine Division in Camp Lejeune to the 1st Division, all to report in two weeks, and individuals were ordered to Camp Pendleton from any location in the Corps they could be found. Finally, Congress passed legislation authorizing the president to extend enlistments for one year, thus making about 1,500 short-timers in Camp Pendleton and El Toro eligible to deploy.

Also on 25 July, amid all of the turmoil, a new division commander, Major General O. P. Smith, arrived in Camp Pendleton. If it were necessary to describe the tall, thin, white-haired Smith in a word, it would have to be *calm,* a quality he would greatly need in the days ahead. Smith found waiting a directive from the commandant of the Marine Corps to recreate the 1st Marine Division from the cascade of Marine reserves coming from civilian life and from regular Marines coming from a dozen directions within the Corps. He had to determine their individual state of training, to arm them, equip them, assign them to units—some of which had to be constituted from scratch—and to exploit the few precious hours available to give them some training. Weapons and combat supplies had to be provided for the greatly enlarged division, hardware in storage since World War II had to be depreserved, issued, and tested. The embarkation of the entire force had to be planned, including coordination with the 1st Marine Aircraft Wing, which was to embark at Long Beach.

Had General Smith's peace-strength staff been twice its authorized war strength, it would have been overworked. As it was, about one-third of it was already enroute to Korea with the 1st Marine Brigade and, it turned out, the division staff was not to be united until the members joined on the beach at Inchon the day of the landing.

The directive received by General Smith provided that two infantry regiments would be formed. The 1st Marines, to be commanded by the legendary Colonel Lewis B. "Chesty" Puller, would consist mainly of men from Camp Lejeune on the East Coast plus men picked up locally at Camp Pendleton, and a few reservists. The last major infantry unit of the division to be formed would be the 7th Marines, under Colonel Homer L. Litzenberg. The organization was a classic example of barrel scraping. It comprised approximately equal numbers of reserves and men from the 2d Division in Camp Lejeune, except that the regiment's third infantry battalion was to be the 3d Battalion, 6th Marines, currently deployed in the Mediterranean, halfway around the world. The battalion was ordered to sail directly to the Far East, via Suez. The unit's first sight of the 7th Marines was when they joined up on the beach at Inchon.

Colonel A. L. Bowser, whom I had relieved as operations officer of Fleet Marine Force Pacific on 28 June, had gone directly to Camp Pendleton, where he doubled as 1st Marine Division operations officer and chief of staff. He was mindful of the immense short-term job involved in planning and executing the embarkation and of the limited capacity of the staff. He hit on the idea of borrowing the Embarkation Section from the Landing Force Training Unit attached to the Navy's Amphibious Training Command in San Diego. With the Navy's concurrence, the unit stopped its training function and took over the entire division embarkation project. As Bowser put it, "They didn't just advise us—they put the division and its equipment to sea from San Diego."[5]

Loading of both the division and the wing began on 8 August, even as the influx of personnel continued. The ships provided were largely of civilian origin, only six of the nineteen being regular U.S. Navy amphibious types. The nineteen ships had to be loaded in four different places with supplies and equipment coming from five different sources, and there were only ten days allocated to plan the embarkation, to assemble the people and material—both air and ground—and get the force aboard.

There was not enough of anything—dock space, marshaling areas, transportation—but, especially, there was not enough time. The plan provided that the ships were to sail to Japan, where everything would be unloaded, sorted out, and reloaded in combatant shipping. While this sounded reasonable, little did those involved realize the brief time they would have in Japan or the procession of hurdles they would face when they got there.

When the embarkation in San Diego and Long Beach was completed, we would have in or enroute to the Far East a Marine division/aircraft wing team of more than thirty thousand men, fully a quarter of whom had been peacefully pursuing their civilian careers three weeks before.

Meanwhile, everything that happened, it seemed, was an enemy of the clock. The City of San Diego would not permit ammunition to be loaded at its municipal piers, so every ship had to be moved to the North Island Naval Air Station to take on ammunition. Since most of the ships were civilian-owned and manned, they had to be loaded by civilian stevedores. But between Long Beach, where aviation units were loading, and San Diego, only sixty stevedore gangs could be mustered, against a minimum need for ninety. A proposal that they be augmented by Marines generated a threat by the stevedores' union to call a strike. Despite the most determined efforts by the Navy, three of the civilian ships were late in arriving, and one Navy amphibious cargo ship, the *Titania,* developed a bad boiler. Already loaded, it had to be unloaded and its cargo moved into other ships, while the Navy set about getting a replacement.

Despite these and other impediments, it all came together —not smoothly, not neatly, but it came together—Marines from everywhere merged into combat units, the hardware of war moved into ships. The embarkation was a product of experience, improvisation, corner-cutting, risk-taking, and refusal to accept no for an answer.

Then, at the height of the embarkation, General Mac-Arthur asked for the immediate dispatch of a planning

group from the 1st Division headquarters. The already attenuated staff was split in half, with one group of twelve officers
and six enlisted men flying out to Japan, arriving on 18
August. When they arrived they learned, for the first time,
that a landing at Inchon (Operation Chromite) was definitely on, that D-day was 15 September, less than a month away,
and that the date could not be slipped because the 15th was
the only day for a month when the tide at Inchon would be
high enough to permit the beaching of landing ships.

The remainder of the staff—eleven officers and four
enlisted men—arrived two days later, and it was this group
of only twenty-three officers and ten enlisted men that faced
a planning task for which a team three times the size would
not have been excessive. Subtracting time required for
movement to the objective and time required for distribution of the plans, once made, General Smith and his little
group had just ten days to do a thirty- or forty-day planning
job.

Their first problem was an inexplicable state of mind on
the part of MacArthur and his staff. Never mind that the
hydrography and the topography united to make Inchon an
immensely complex problem, never mind that the thirty-
foot tides dictated that the assault take place in late afternoon, the party line was that the Inchon landing was a piece
of cake. And no contrary thoughts were tolerated. General
Smith provides some of the flavor of what they were up
against:

General Almond dismissed the whole matter by stating
that there was no organized enemy anyway, that our
difficulties were purely mechanical.[6]

General Shepherd adds:

MacArthur stated that he did not believe Inchon was
defended, that the people would rise up and welcome
the invasion.[7]

The people who were faced with having to do the job—
Admiral Doyle and General Smith—did not share these

sanguine sentiments. Put plainly, they did not want to go to Inchon. While they saw the virtue of an enveloping attack that severed the lifeline of the North Korean forces besieging the Pusan Perimeter, they believed it could be done more surely and effectively by landing at some point less forbidding than Inchon.

In early August, as General Shepherd became acquainted with the unusual problems involved with the Inchon area, he asked me to study the region and to try and find another landing area nearby that offered less formidable obstacles. I prepared a terrain study and an estimate of the situation which concluded that a landing at Anjung (also called Posung Myon), about thirty miles south of Inchon, was to be preferred. The current intelligence disclosed no enemy there. We would avoid landing in the heart of a large city, and we would not have to land at a specific time (at Inchon in late afternoon) during the only day on which a tide high enough for beaching the LSTs (landing ships) occurred in more than a month.

The alternate landing site would avoid the forbidding hydrography of Inchon harbor, yet it would not sacrifice the benefits of an envelopment and would still be near enough to Inchon and Seoul to permit their early capture. We took the study and accompanying maps with us on a trip to the Far East on 21 August. Upon arriving there, General Shepherd found that he had a determined ally, not only in General Smith but in Rear Admiral Doyle.

Doyle was a gaunt, Lincolnesque figure with a pink complexion, a Boston Irish accent, a hot temper, and a cool sense of humor that surfaced at times of great tension. He had, and deserved, the reputation for being the Navy's preeminent amphibious admiral. As the attack force commander for the Inchon landing, he had the task of taking the landing force to the objective, putting it ashore, and then providing the successive increments of logistic support that would keep it there. He was dissatisfied with the Inchon idea for many of the same reasons as the Marines—perilous navigation, the tide problem that required an evening landing, unfavorable hydrography, and the difficulty of landing in a large city which, despite careful precautions, might well be burning. As the one responsible for surmounting the naval aspects of these problems, Doyle was strongly opposed to the Inchon site and he stood up and said so. At a meeting of Navy and Marine commanders at Yokosuka on 21 August he laid the problem out in great detail in a manner so clear and persuasive that everyone present was convinced that a landing somewhere to the south of Inchon —at Anjung (Posung Myon), for instance—was to be preferred. Among those present was Admiral Forrest Sherman, the chief of naval operations, who had come to the Far East with Army Chief of Staff Collins to examine the concept on behalf of the Joint Chiefs of Staff. They were to see MacArthur in about two hours, and we were happy to hear that at the meeting he would support Doyle in his opposition to Inchon and his proposal to land in a more practical area farther south.

They went to the meeting. Doyle made his presentation— "Magnificently put on," according to Sherman—but it served only as a trigger for a forty-five-minute Churchillian oration by MacArthur on the importance of the capture of Seoul and the consequent rewards assured by success at Inchon, ending with the words—quoted to me the next day by Doyle: "We will land at Inchon and I shall crush them."*

According to Doyle, Sherman gave him no support in his counterproposal. Sherman did declare later, however, that MacArthur was fearful that coordinated opposition by Collins and Sherman to the Inchon attack might prevent the approval by the Joint Chiefs of Staff of an early amphibious envelopment, and so,

> When it was proposed that the landing take place some thirty miles to the southward MacArthur jumped at the idea, stating if such an area could be found it would be acceptable to him.[8]

---

* In *MacArthur in Korea, The Naked Emperor*, Robert Smith recounts an amusing sidelight. Doyle had been reciting the serious hydrographic problems to be encountered in Flying Fish Channel, near Inchon, along with the added hazards presented by shore batteries. Sherman is quoted as saying, "I would not hesitate to take a ship there," to which MacArthur responded, "Spoken like a Farragut," whereupon Doyle said to those around him, "Spoken like a John Wayne."

The next day, enroute from Japan to Korea, General Shepherd and I outlined to Sherman in greater detail, with the help of a map, the multiple advantages of the Anjung landing. Sherman listened. Both General Shepherd and I were sure we had convinced him. But in the end it all amounted to nothing. Two days later (24 August), in Tokyo, General Shepherd laid out the Anjung concept for Lieutenant General Edward M. Almond, MacArthur's chief of staff, who was also to command the landing. After the meeting General Shepherd told me that Almond dismissed the idea summarily, saying that Inchon had been decided upon and that was where it would be, that Seoul was the real objective.[9] So, with only a little more than two weeks remaining before sailing, the people who knew better were obliged to abandon their convictions and settle in on making and issuing plans for a landing at Inchon.

Generals Smith and Harris, the Marine ground and air commanders, faced a procession of brutal problems, paced to the inexorable march of the clock. To complicate matters, the two commanders were not working out of the same location. Smith was in Kobe and Harris was at an air base at Itami, some forty miles away. They needed to know the effects of tides and currents, the consistency of the Inchon mud flats, height and character of the Inchon seawall, the nature and location of enemy defenses—data that took time to obtain. The tasks of composing, reproducing, and distributing the tactical plans were straightforward functions and well understood by the planning staffs, but it all took time, and time was a fast disappearing commodity.

To cope with the possibility of boats and amphibians grounding in the mud flats, the planners hit on the idea of putting two planks in each to support men walking across the mud. To surmount the stone seawalls fronting Inchon harbor, they decided to build and install a scaling ladder in each boat and LVT. Again, a simple improvisation, but it consumed precious time.

The few days and hours still remaining were further invaded by problems with the Army and Navy. Both General Almond's X Corps staff and Admiral Struble, the overall Joint Task Force Commander, were opposed to a pre-D-day naval bombardment, hoping, thereby, to maintain the element of surprise. Admiral Doyle and General Smith were convinced that there were enough enemy targets in the area to warrant an aggressive naval gunfire program. It took three time-consuming meetings, on 1, 3, and 8 September, to get the matter settled on terms agreeable to Doyle and Smith.

This problem, important as it was, nevertheless was eclipsed by difficulties with MacArthur's staff and most particularly Lieutenant General Almond, who had by now assumed overall command of the landing force. In a military anomaly, he still retained his position as chief of staff of GHQ and was thus able to issue orders to himself. Lieutenant General Shepherd was the logical landing force commander. The bulk of the forces, air and ground, came from his command, Fleet Marine Force, Pacific, and he had the requisite depth of amphibious experience. MacArthur recognized this and told General Shepherd on 24 August that had he not already promised the command to Almond he would have given it to Shepherd.[10]

As detailed planning proceeded, it became increasingly clear that the forces and equipment the Marines were bringing represented the bulk of the Inchon investment. At one of Almond's planning meetings where the crossing of the Han River was discussed, for example, it turned out that the quantity of bridging equipment shown by the briefing officer as available was exactly the amount being brought with the 1st Marine Division. Without it there would be no bridging in X Corps at all. The Marine force included two photographic aircraft, which had gone to the Far East to provide aerial photographic coverage for the 1st Marine Brigade. X Corps appropriated the little detachment as its sole photographic resource.

The 1st Marine Division is what MacArthur asked for as the ground force to do the Inchon job. It was what the JCS authorized and what the Marine Corps was in the process of providing. Of the division's three infantry regiments, one, the 5th Marines, was busy fighting as part of the 1st Provisional Marine Brigade in the Pusan Perimeter. Another, the 1st Marines, was enroute from the United States to Kobe and due to arrive between 28 August and 3 September. The remaining one, the 7th Marines, was due to arrive in the

Far East about 15 September. Thus, General Smith was obliged to plan his 15 September landing around only two regiments, one of which was already fighting near Pusan.

Smith began asking Almond to release the 1st Brigade from the Pusan Perimeter on 23 August. Almond's response, in his capacity as GHQ chief of staff, was that the release of the brigade ". . . would be bad for the morale of the Eighth Army and, in any case, would be dependent on the tactical situation . . ."[11] Smith repeated his request to Almond on 30 August and was put off again with the excuse that MacArthur's headquarters was unwilling to direct the release of the brigade because of the tenuous situation in the Pusan area. The brigade commander himself, Smith was told, should negotiate his release directly with the Eighth Army commander. Smith refused to accept this and on 1 September sent an official dispatch requesting release of the brigade to permit it to plan, load, and embark for the operation. A dispatch releasing the brigade was finally issued on 4 September.

More precious time had been lost in haggling. The division sent a liaison officer to the brigade on 2 September to acquaint the units with the tactical plan and to give them data from which they could develop their own detailed plans. The liaison officer arrived to find that the brigade had been committed to action again to meet a North Korean threat. Lieutenant Colonel (later Major General) Raymond L. Murray, commanding the 5th Marine Regiment, said,

> I received first news of the operation via a liaison officer while we were heavily engaged in the Second Battle of the Naktong. I was given an aerial photo of Inchon and told we would land on Red Beach over the seawall.[12]

Twenty-four hours later, even as the brigade was moving heavy equipment to Pusan in preparation for embarkation, and as ships to transport the unit to Inchon had been dispatched from Japan, the order for its release was revoked. General Smith was notified that the 5th Marines would be replaced in the assault landing task organization by the 32d Infantry of the 7th Infantry Division—a unit that had no amphibious training whatever and included 40 percent Korean conscripts. Usually a taciturn man, General Smith lost his composure. With the help of Admirals Doyle and Joy, he arranged a showdown meeting with Almond. It took place the next morning (3 September). Smith was clear in his position. He would not employ the mixed U.S./Korean unit in an amphibious assault role. He would land on one rather than two beaches and he advised Almond that removal of the 5th Marines would go beyond the point of acceptable risk. Almond responded that, "GHQ would take the risk and that General MacArthur would be present for the landing and would take the responsibility for calling it off if necessary."[13] As if calling off an amphibious operation, once begun, is analogous to turning off a light.

In an ensuing heated discussion, they finally agreed that the 7th Infantry Division unit would be embarked to serve as a floating reserve for General Walker in the Pusan Perimeter, and that the 5th Marines would be released for the Inchon operation—but not until midnight, 5 September!

Smith had prevailed but another day had been expended in debate that need not have taken place, and there were not many days left. Where the 1st Marine Brigade was concerned, there would be only six days from the hour of their withdrawal from heavy combat until they had to be embarked and on their way to the Inchon battle. During that time they would march eight miles, truck fifty miles to the port of Pusan, prepare and distribute plans for the landing, receive and absorb replacements for combat losses (some 30 percent of the infantry strength), replenish supplies, build scaling ladders, receive and integrate the third rifle company for each infantry battalion (just arrived from the United States to bring the unit to full war strength), embark and sail around the Korean peninsula to join the Inchon attack force. In addition to all this, the brigade was made responsible for getting the Korean Marine Corps Regiment to Inchon, only to find, on 6 September, that one of its battalions had no weapons! The Marines procured the necessary arms from Army stock and, as General Murray recalls, "We even found time to conduct some basic weapons training for the Korean Marines."[14] They did it all and were aboard and under way on 12 September. The amphibious ships were crowded and hot but they provided a bath, hot food, and a bunk—pure luxury to the Marines who were exhausted by the Pusan Perimeter combat.

There were other assaults on the Marines' time, such as notification, in the midst of planning, that General Almond wanted to have a war game of the Inchon-Seoul operation. A liaison officer delivered the directive for the war game to the overworked 1st Division operations officer, Colonel A. L. Bowser. Bowser says,

> I took the directive, folded it several times, tucked it into the liaison officer's pocket and told him to take it back to GHQ.[15]

Another hair shirt was tried on for size on 7 September, when General Almond's X Corps headquarters notified General Smith that a detachment of 100 Marines was desired to operate as raiders along with a detachment of Army Rangers and British Commandos. The concept was that they would paddle ashore from a ship at night in rubber boats, move ten miles over land on foot, and capture Kimpo Airfield, northeast of Inchon. How the two- or three-knot rubberboats were to operate against tidal currents that reached six knots and how the small, lightly armed infantry group was to cope with even moderate resistance ashore was never explained. In any case, after several frustrating exchanges, Smith simply sent a message saying the Marine raiders were not available.[16] He heard nothing more about it.

It seemed that everyone had a part in invading the precious hours standing between the Marines and D-day. On 6 September the secretary of the navy issued an order that all Marines who had not reached their eighteenth birthday must be withdrawn from the troop list. All records in both the division and wing had to be researched. It turned out that some six hundred men fell under the age restriction. They were everywhere—enroute, aboard ship, ashore in four different places—and they had to be assembled and provision made for their care in Japan, once the division and wing units were gone.

And fate added to the Marines' torment, too. On 3 September, at the height of the 1st Marine Division's reloading process, Typhoon Jane, 75 knots, struck Kobe. Several ships broke their moorings, breakers rolled across the piers, cargo in the process of being resorted was damaged by seawater and torrential rain, vehicles were flooded, and all loading operations were suspended for more than twenty-four hours.

One of the last ships to arrive from the United States, the SS *Noonday,* carrying general cargo and ammunition, caught fire as she was approaching Kobe. By the time the fire tugs had extinguished the blaze and the soaked cargo had been unloaded, refurbished, and reloaded, more valuable time had disappeared.

On 10 September warning was received that Typhoon Kezia, 85 knots, was approaching Kobe. Admiral Doyle directed that all of the large transports and cargo ships, thirteen of them, scheduled to sail on 12 September, get under way on the 11th. After they had been at sea for twenty-four hours, suffering greatly because of the high winds and mountainous seas, the thirteen ships reversed course, assuming they could not get around or through the typhoon. When Doyle, whose flagship had departed shortly after the transports, learned of this he issued a simple order: "Reverse course and follow me." Had the resolute admiral not taken that timely and courageous action, the critical 15 September D-day would not have been met.

And finally, on the 13th, Admiral Doyle was notified that a landing ship carrying the headquarters of the 2d Battalion, 1st Marines had broken down. It had only one engine operating and could make only six knots, which would not get the ship to Inchon on time. A tug was provided and with its help the ship could manage eight knots, which was just enough to get her to Inchon for the landing.

That was the final crisis. From that point on, everything that could be done had been done. The force was on its way. Now MacArthur's "10,000 to one gamble" was in the hands of fate.

In the final hours, several incidents occurred that provide

an interesting look backstage before the lifting of the curtain on the battle. General Shepherd and I accompanied General MacArthur in his aircraft from Tokyo to Itazuke on 13 September and from there some eighty miles to Sasebo to join up with the *Mt. McKinley.** Waiting for the ship to arrive, the party passed about three hours in a Navy Petty Officers' Club, eating sandwiches, drinking coffee, and talking. During the entire period, in which MacArthur took the conversational lead himself, the discussion never once touched on Inchon, the challenge involved, or the series of unusual actions that had brought the task force together. The conversation, which included primarily MacArthur, Major General Courtney Whitney, and MacArthur's more intimate associates, was confined to one subject—their pre–World War II days in the Philippines. In the space of three hours, Inchon was never mentioned. It seemed to me that they still did not sense either the fragility or the complexity of the operation facing us.

The next day, enroute to the objective, we received some surprising news. President Truman, under heavy fire for the lack of preparedness of American forces in Japan at the war's beginning and tired of Louis Johnson's squabbling with Secretary of State Dean Acheson, marched his defense secretary down the plank. Johnson was fired, and there was genuine rejoicing about *Mt. McKinley,* from MacArthur down. There seemed in this to be some just retribution. Although he was not the only reason for all our high-pressure scrambling of the past few weeks, Johnson was certainly the cutting edge of the imprudent economy movement that had made the preparation for Inchon such a nightmare.

Next, there was an incident on the flag bridge of the ship on the afternoon of D–1. Rear Admiral Doyle, the steadfast Amphibious Task Force commander, Major General E. K.

---

* MacArthur properly belonged with Admiral Struble, the overall commander of the force, in his flagship, USS *Rochester.* However, the general insisted on embarking in *Mt. McKinley* with the landing force. So, with his staff, Admiral Doyle's staff, General Almond's staff and General Smith's staff there were thirteen flag and general officers in one ship—hardly a prudent distribution.

Wright, MacArthur's operations officer, and I were talking of the parade of problems that had characterized the preceding few weeks. Wright said, "I sometimes felt we'd never make it."

Doyle, who had endured more than his share of problems, and who could be testy when he felt like it, said,

> Get this straight. We wouldn't have made it; we wouldn't be here today, if the operation hadn't been in the hands of Navy and Marine professionals who knew exactly what they were doing.[17]

Wright didn't say anything, and I didn't have to.

A final prebattle incident occurred early on the morning of D-day. *Mt. McKinley* had anchored near the transport area where an LSD of the attack force was to launch assault forces of the 3d Battalion, 5th Marines in amphibian tractors (LVTs) for their attack on the offshore island of Wolmi-do. Along with others, I was on the boat deck as the dawn broke, watching the air and naval gunfire preparation by planes of the 1st Marine Aircraft Wing and ships of the task force. As the first LVTs began to emerge from the mother ship, I commented to Lieutenant General Almond, who was standing nearby, "That LVT is certainly a versatile machine."

Apparently not aware that I was referring to the ship-to-shore conveyance we were watching, he responded, "Yes. Tell me, can it float?" I was nonplussed. Here was the leader, bearing the immediate responsibility for the entire landing force in a critical amphibious operation, and he wanted to know if an LVT would float! The Marines had been concerned about Almond during the planning phase when he seemed to have his mind only on the big picture—the capture of Seoul or "making an anvil for the Eighth Army's hammer." Yet the landing force—his landing force—was confronted with immense and immediate problems. A race with darkness, getting over mud flats, across sea walls, through a big Oriental city, seizing an airfield, initiating a major logistic system, establishing a beachhead—these were the essential precursors of any hammer and anvil, and they were Almond's direct responsibility. It seemed, from the first, that he did not understand these things. That apprehension was now heightened in my mind as we stood there watching LVTs bearing the 3d Battalion, 5th Marines plough through the waves toward Wolmi-do.

The preliminaries to Inchon were unusual in many ways, and there will be many judgments as to the identity of the catalyst or catalysts that brought it all together. A fair case can be made that Inchon would never have happened were it not for three things.

First, it would never have happened had General MacArthur, with a keen strategic sense, not expressed his desire on 10 July for the 1st Marine Division to make an amphibious envelopment and had not Lieutenant General Shepherd volunteered, then and there, to help him procure the division and the 1st Marine Aircraft Wing.

Second, it would never have happened had Commandant Cates not thrown his total support behind the project and urged mobilization of the Marine Corps Reserve, and had President Truman, in the face of strong political opposition, not approved the Reserve mobilization.

Finally, it would never have happened were it not for the ingenious and altogether professional actions of the Marines and Navy people involved. The piecing together of the thirty-thousand-man air/ground force in the space of three weeks, the succession of improvisations in embarkation and in planning, the steadfast poise with which General Smith, Admiral Doyle, and their staffs fought off the meddling of General Almond as they pursued their affairs, the ingenious adaptations to the unusual nature of the mandated landing area—these were the indispensable lubricants that oiled the gears of strategy, these were the things that converted Inchon from a dream to a reality.

PART
IV

THE PENNY PINCHERS

Waste Not, Want Not

Poor Richard's Almanac

The American public sees the Marines as fighters—trained, equipped, and conditioned to be the first into battle. The other U.S. armed services are likely to portray them as fiercely defensive, competitive, and sometimes boastful. Our country's enemies view them as formidable and resourceful antagonists.

But the United States Congress sees the Marines as a frugal and altogether reliable investment, dedicated, like nineteenth-century British general Sir John Moore, to "fighting on the cheap." And this Marine Corps characteristic has deep roots. As far back as 1798 Commandant Burrows (1798–1804), anxious to attract musicians to the Marines' ranks and unable to find any appropriations to fund a bounty for their enlistment, had no compunction about leaning on his officers to contribute $10.00 each for the musician's bounty fund (at a time when an officer's pay averaged about $35.00 per month). To preserve further the Corps's meager appropriated funds, Burrows also decreed that recruiting officers pay from their own pockets all expenses incurred in enlisting a man who turned out to be physically unfit.

During his generation-long commandantcy (1820–59), Archibald Henderson made much official use of the Marines' ability to do more for less. He managed to get his troops into the Seminole War mainly on the claim that they could do the job more cheaply than the Army. Then, by making the same pinch-penny appeal to President Polk, he got a Marine battalion involved in the attack on Mexico City in the Mexican War (thus, "From the Halls of Montezuma"). Henderson set the tune in establishing institutional frugality as a Marine Corps principle. He cashiered officers for extravagance. He railed at his quartermaster for what he perceived to be costly and wasteful practices, finally firing him, for which act Henderson himself was court-martialed (he was acquitted). He boasted unceasingly to Congress that the Marines were habitually the most thrifty of all the services, doing more work for less pay than anyone else.

Henderson declared, moreover, that a piece of equipment might wear out but as long as it worked, it was never wholly outmoded—a concept that persisted for generations. This may account for the Civil War equipment that was still in the Marines' inventory in the War with Spain and for the solid-tire trucks, obsolescent in 1917, that Marine heavy artillery units were still driving at the beginning of World War II. Nor can I forget that my regimental commander in Shanghai in 1938 rode around the city in an antique Cadillac sedan that had seen hard service in France in the First World War.

Henderson's precepts of military thrift were reflected in the behavior of his successors, mainly Commandant John A. Lejeune (1920–29). The Coolidge and Hoover administrations were anything but generous to the military at large, and the Marines were certainly no exception. It is told— probably apocryphally—that in reviewing the Marines' 1928 budget, which sought funds for the purchase of sixteen aircraft, President Coolidge said, "Why don't they buy just one airplane and take turns flying it?" The same story is told about the Army Air Corps.

Lejeune reacted to this form of stimulus by demanding

economies wherever they could be found. It was his intention, at the end of the budget year, to actually return dollars to the Treasury. And he usually did, with predictably favorable effects on Congress. The impact on individuals in the Corps, however, was sometimes burdensome. Take, for example, Captain Lemuel Shepherd (later, from 1952 to 1955, commandant of the Marine Corps) on an expedition to China in 1927. He had been ordered to join the 3d Marine Brigade in Tientsin on short notice, leaving his family in quarters at the Marine Barracks, Norfolk Navy Yard. When they came to China to join him some months later, he had to pay their way himself. Moreover, he was required by Marine Corps Headquarters to continue to pay rent for the quarters in Norfolk, even though they were vacant, because nobody else was available to move in.

In the same vein, an individual moving from a duty station on one coast to the other during the 1920s was likely to be ordered to travel in a Navy transport, via Panama. That it would take him away from useful employment for six weeks or so seemed to make no difference. It was cheap. If he owned a car, he had no way of getting it across the continent unless he paid someone to drive it. He could, of course, elect to drive the car himself, understanding that there would be no reimbursement from Headquarters.

Frugality was, in short, the Corps's way of life, at least until the onset of World War II. Of course, it was a terrible hair shirt to the rank and file, but it was a hair shirt that kept them warm.

CHAPTER 9

Do It on the Cheap

For the better part of two centuries a central figure in the Marines' philosophy of string-saving was the Quartermaster General. His office was the guardian of the warehouse, keeper of the exchequer, and bete noir of the working Corps. It was seen by all as a faceless, penurious, intractable institution that rarely had on hand what was needed and was unwilling to dispense what it had. It was the common claim that the Quartermaster always procured the cheapest and least desirable article, whatever its purpose might be, through his stranglehold on the purse. And it was universally believed that he exercised far too much influence on decisions about what the Corps needed to do its fighting.

Marines of the 1920s and 1930s recall, with revulsion, the issue brass polish that wouldn't polish, the green paint that wouldn't dry, the flimsy khaki shirts that wouldn't fit anybody, the flannel shirts that shrank with every washing, the necktie that had the consistency of a wet noodle, the belts, cap visors, and shoes made of belly leather that would have been disowned by any self-respecting cow. They would grimace at the tight-fitting khaki trousers from which hip pockets had been omitted to save money; the green uniforms, poorly cut from an incredible kersey material that defied pressing; the coat and trousers from dye lots so different that the outfit appeared more a yachting costume than a uniform.*

They would laugh at the story—probably inaccurate—that, while cotton underdrawers varied greatly in the waist, they were all exactly the same in the crotch, and, while the Army and Navy issued their enlisted men underdrawers with three buttons, the Marines' version, manufactured at their Quartermaster Depot in Philadelphia, had only two because it was said to be a penny cheaper.

They viewed with humorous resignation the Quartermaster's cautious action in 1933, when the old World War I 3-inch trench mortar was supplanted in the Army with the new 81-millimeter Stokes-Brandt design. He purchased a total of three. One went to the East Coast Fleet Marine Force, one to the West Coast Fleet Marine Force, and one to the Philadelphia Depot of Supplies for stock!

In the image of Archibald Henderson, the quartermaster of the 1900–1940 era pursued the concept that waste is obscene, that, as Juvenal declared, "luxury is more to be feared than war." He decreed that nothing could ever be lost without corresponding pecuniary responsibility on somebody's part. There was no such thing as an unexplained loss for which nobody paid the piper. Many a hapless Marine thus found his meager pay checked and his record sullied because of the imprudent loss of a compass, a canteen, or a bayonet. And for the loss of a pistol there were no questions asked, just an automatic court-martial.

While onerous in the extreme, the effect of the continuous policy of thrift was to imbue every Marine with a sharp

---

* Until 1880 the Marine Corps purchased their uniforms on contract but constant complaints of low quality caused Commandant McCawley to direct creation of a clothing factory at the Philadelphia Depot of Supplies. It made little difference. The uniforms still lacked both quality and fit. General G. C. Thomas recalls a visit to the clothing factory in the 1920s. "They were proud to show me a new process by which 100 coats were cut out at a time. When they were sewed up they looked to me exactly like they had been cut out 100 at a time!"

sense of property value and an instinctive determination to husband resources of whatever sort. This quality certainly helped to preserve the Corps in lean times and, for that, a long line of Quartermasters—villified and often misunderstood—deserve much credit.

The classic representative of the Quartermaster's tradition of fierce frugality was William P. T. Hill (1895–1965), from Oklahoma. Part Indian, World War I aviator, competent geologist, world authority on coral, writer, Gobi Desert explorer, and anthropologist, he began his association with the Quartermaster's Department in 1929 and served as Quartermaster General from 1944 to 1955. He rose to be a major general, insisting on the occasion of each promotion that he be administered the oath of office on his Indian Bible.

Hill was no ordinary man. He was proud, intelligent, eloquent, stubborn, and possessed of an immense memory. *Thrift* was his watchword and, to him, burnishing the image of the Corps with Congress transcended just about everything else. His mind was anything but orderly but from it he could draw an immense array of facts.

His office mirrored his personality. It was austere; the floor was bare, and the furniture included only straight, hard-backed chairs. There was no art to relieve the severity, and one wall was all glass, so that he could have a good view of his subordinates. There were few places to sit, since most of the office chairs were cluttered with papers as was the scarred oak conference table and the corners of the room, as well. His desk was a mountain of documents, file folders, ledgers, Congressional Records, charts, and books. There was no space for work. But it made no difference because he had no intention of working at his desk. Rather, it was his habit to work standing up at a chest-high worktable, itself only slightly less cluttered than the rest of the furniture in the office. His telephone was on the floor beside the stand-up desk, there being no other place to keep it.

When asked for a document that ought to have been safely sequestered in a secretary's file cabinet, Hill would raise his hand, wrinkle his high forehead, squint over his Ben Franklin glasses, and say, "I have it right here—somewhere."

After a few moments he would miraculously unearth the paper from one of his various pyramids.

His memory was legendary. He kept no file of telephone numbers because he needed none; he remembered them all. His recall for the details of his work was so incredible that it is unlikely that he would have given much consideration to using a computer had they been available. His computer was his own mind, buttressed by the memories of a small number of trusted associates—officers, enlisted men, civilians. Together they had a hammerlock on the material and fiscal affairs of the Corps. On one occasion Hill told the commandant (General Vandegrift) exactly how many pairs of combat boots the Marine Corps had in storage. The commandant challenged him: how could he possibly remember such a detail? Hill sent for the stock records, which validated his memory almost exactly.

A burden to his associates and his subordinates, a terror to those who opposed him, he was nevertheless respected by the Appropriations Committee members of both the House and Senate. They enjoyed his ready answers to their questions and his invariable emphasis on Marine frugality. They were abundantly aware of the examples of his parsimony, which they knew to be genuine. And they trusted him totally, to the immense benefit of the Corps. If Hill said the Marines needed it, that was enough for them.

Stories of Hill's behavior are legion. He required that all officers in the Quartermaster's Department who were formally accountable for funds be bonded. And then, in an act of extreme frugality, he required each one to pay $10.00 a year for his own bond.

Never impressed with ostentation, Hill enjoyed deflating the pompous and self-important. He was fond of leading anyone overly impressed with himself to the window, pointing out the white crosses in Arlington Cemetery across the road and saying, "There lies a large group of indispensable people."

My own Hill story dates from 1941, when I was on Major General H. M. Smith's staff. We were anxious to find a way to waterproof our vehicles to make it possible for them to ford deep water between the landing craft ramp and the beach. I signed up for a jeep, on which we did our experimentation and which we ultimately destroyed by repeatedly immersing it in saltwater. The Quartermaster had me on the hook for a jeep ($2,700), and it took a major effort by General Smith to get me off.

In the wake of World War II's first offensive campaign at Guadalcanal, the people doing the fighting expressed a need for jungle hammocks (a hammock with a built-in mosquito net) and for a sheath knife for each Marine. Hill opposed both requests. Quickly calculating the cost in his head (quite accurately), he declared that they cost too much for the good they would do and, to him, that was reason enough. Creating his own scenario, he said that a midnight emergency might find the sleeping Marine entrapped in his own mosquito net. Where the knife was concerned he warned that it was just too dangerous. The Marines would be found injuring themselves or their associates. It made no difference that the troops in the field wanted them. He was against the idea, and it took a decision by the commandant himself to set the procurement in motion.

In 1954 Lieutenant Colonel William Hunt, serving with the Central Intelligence Agency, visited Hill with a modest request. There were, in Marine Corps storage, several hundred old Springfield rifles, standardized in 1903. An excellent weapon in 1903 and useful even in World War I, it had been superseded by the M-1 semiautomatic rifle before World War II. The Central Intelligence Agency wanted the old rifles to distribute to indigenous forces in underdeveloped countries.

After hearing Hunt's request for the Marines' "excess and obsolete Springfield rifles," Hill responded in the true tradition of Archibald Henderson: "If we have the rifles, they're not excess and if they will shoot, they're not obsolete. Try the Army. They'll give anything away." And that ended it.

In 1954 the Department of Defense was engaged in a massive standardization program. Everything possible, from socks to nightsticks, was to be of a standard Defense Department design, and contracting and manufacture were to be consolidated. In this atmosphere the Marine Corps was directed to make plans to discontinue manufacturing clothing, tent poles, helmet covers, and so forth at its Philadelphia Depot of Supplies. Henceforward the items would be procured on contract.

Upon receiving the directive, General Hill made one visit to Capitol Hill. It was followed promptly by a telephone call from powerful Carl Vinson, chairman of the House Armed Services Committee, to the Secretary of Defense, Charles E. Wilson. "Look a here, Mr. Secretary," Vinson said, "Those Marines give us more fight for the dollar than anybody else, and I'd appreciate it if you'd leave their Supply Depot alone." Wilson did not know exactly what Vinson was talking about, but he knew enough to call his standardization crew off the Marines.

The Supply Depot is still there, and so is the lesson. Hill was trusted by people of great influence, and not just because of his own knowledge and diligence or because of his colorful personality. Instead, people trusted him because he represented the solid record of frugality earned by the Marines over several generations.

CHAPTER 10

The Honorable Art of Institutional Theft

Military units have stolen from one another throughout history, but the Marines have probably brought institutional theft to a higher state of development than anyone else. Partly because of the exhilaration of the chase, but far more because of poverty, the Marines—particularly those of the 1920s and 1930s—strove to outwit and steal from one another and from others, just to make the supply books balance.

The Quartermaster issued toilet paper to units on the basis of sheets per man per day, not rolls. It was thus not uncommon for the police sergeant from one Marine organization to conduct midnight foraging raids on the sanitary facilities of a companion unit to capture a few rolls of the low-quality product.

Similarly, as motor vehicles became a major military item in the 1920s, there was a continuing round of gasoline siphoning, one unit's vehicles being fair game for another. And the same held true for tires—a moonlight exchange of old tires for new ones, captured from an unsuspecting unit's vehicles,

In field exercises, such things as cots, tent pins, mosquito nets, and shovels were always at risk. The very first step, after acquiring the booty, was to obliterate the owning unit's markings and substitute the purloining unit's designation.

Messes and food service were another area of theft. As the end of the month neared, a unit whose mess appeared in danger of being overdrawn against its monthly dollar allowance was likely to require some of its more gluttonous privates to move surreptitiously into the mess line of a neighboring unit. If the second unit happened to be in similar financial straits some of its trenchermen would also be found invading another neighbor's mess line.

The upshot of this peripatetic situation might be a round robin where nobody benefited, but the practice went on, nevertheless.

There were a few unwritten rules. You stole for the outfit, never for yourself. You didn't steal weapons. Some poor fellow was signed up for every one. And, if you knew what was good for you, you didn't steal from the Quartermaster. He was mean, and he was merciless if you were caught. But the rules were more relaxed where the other services and the civilian world were concerned. With them it was pretty much open season, which gave rise to great ingenuity.

Take, for example, the case of Building 131 at the Marine Corps Recruit Depot, San Diego. Every government building has a history, a written record. It is possible, through research, to ascertain exactly when a building was built and exactly how much it cost. But not Building 131. As far as source records are concerned, it was never built. But it obviously was, because it is there today, and that introduces Sergeant Peter Paul Wolkovitz. Wolkovitz was a man of limited education but immense native wisdom and great industry. He was incredibly skillful with his hands and had a quick and resourceful mind. From his enlistment in 1924 to his retirement in 1945, he served as a carpenter. Between Nicaragua, Haiti, China, Alaska, and elsewhere he lived a life where the means and materials at hand were rarely equal to the task. Consequently, he learned the art of midnight entrepreneurship in all of its aspects, earning a reputation for being capable of almost miraculous feats of procurement.

In 1936, Wolkovitz and I were serving in the Second Engineer Company at the Marine Corps Base, San Diego. He had a chance to exhibit his talent when we were put on a long leash by the commanding general, Brigadier General Douglas C. McDougal.*

The general was keenly interested in boats—experimental landing boats, recreation boats, and pulling boats. There were seven boats on the base and I had the misfortune of being in charge of them. The general decided one day that he wanted a boathouse and a marine railway to pull the boats out of the water so that we could repair them ourselves. Being the commanding general, he wanted it right away and told me to "see what I could do." Our small engineer unit had no materials and no way of getting any. We did, however, have Wolkovitz, which turned out to be quite enough.

After a briefing, Wolkovitz required only one Sunday night, the use of a truck, and the help of two privates to assemble the essential materials for the boathouse project. From Consolidated Aircraft, then building an aircraft plant next door, he liberated enough corrugated iron siding, cement, roofing, and structural steel to do the job. From the San Diego Street Railway Company, which was installing some track outside the base, he procured rails for the marine railway. He was sufficiently foresighted to take more rail than he needed, so that he could trade it later to a friend at the neighboring Naval Training Center, for wheels to make a dolly for the marine railway.

There is no record of complaint or question on the part of any donor, and when I commented on this point to Wolkovitz he just said, "They get more generous after dark."

The boathouse—some 30 by 90 feet—grew quickly to maturity, as did the marine railway, to the great satisfaction of the commanding general, who never asked me where the materials came from or how it all happened. I had a feeling that he already knew. Shortly later, in the course of a routine annual inspection, a representative of the adjutant and

---

* General McDougal was himself an unusual man, who had served in the Army, Navy, Marines, and Coast Guard (Revenue Cutter Service).

inspector of the Marine Corps, knowing nothing of the origin of the building, assumed it to be part of the base public works program. He commented favorably on the structure, but noted that it bore no official building numbers.

McDougal, claiming oversight, selected the number 131 arbitrarily and had it painted on the structure. The number and the building are both still there.

Shifting to another scene and another day, we again encounter Gunnery Sergeant (then Sergeant) Walter Holzworth, who opened this book, this time serving as supply sergeant at the Marine Barracks, Guam, in 1924. One night a Japanese freighter was driven on the reef during a violent storm and rapidly broke up. Much of its cargo of lumber was cast up on the reef. The early hours of the morning found both Navy and Marine units searching for the crew of the foundered vessel. But not Holzworth. He was busy in another way—walking up and down the reef with ink and a brass stencil in his hands, industriously stenciling "USMC," "USMC," on every piece of lumber he could find.

In World War II, the Marines had no corner on institutional theft. The New Zealanders were at least their equal in both tenacity and sophistication.

Jeeps were the prime target, and there seemed no way to protect them against the New Zealanders' depredations. They defeated our tactic of padlocking the gearshift lever to the dashboard by using a boltcutter, and they defeated removal of the distributor cap or rotor by carrying a supply of their own. Once they had the vehicle in their possession, they quickly painted it their peculiar gray and perforated the body with ⅛-inch holes forming the letters "NZ."

The Marines finally outmaneuvered the resourceful New Zealanders. They would capture a jeep—or perhaps recapture one—fill up the holes spelling "NZ" with lead, cover it all with a coat of Marine Corps paint, and then spell out "USMC" on the body with welding rod and torch.

In late 1944 Guadalcanal was in the backwash of the war. Many units were preparing to move elsewhere. Some of the departing Army units chose to leave behind items that stimulated the Marines' acquisitive instincts. I was serving as operations officer of the 6th Marine Division, training on Guadalcanal in preparation for the Okinawa operation. One day Captain John E. Dodd, the division air officer, reported that there were three new Army liaison and observation aircraft in a salvage area and that he could have them simply by signing his name.

I told him by all means to go get them. We uncrated the planes, assembled them, and used them freely in our training around Guadalcanal. It was not a matter of needing the aircraft; we already had a full liaison squadron attached to the division. But the mere thought of turning down something of value, and free, was contrary to everything we had been taught and believed.

In the First Battle of the Naktong in the Pusan Perimeter in Korea the 1st Marine Brigade had badly mauled a North Korean division. In their retreat the Koreans left much equipment behind. A few days later, General Shepherd and I were visiting the brigade near the town of Masan, while it was catching its breath. Everywhere we turned we saw Marines carrying Russian pistols, Russian rifles, or Russian field telephones and driving Russian jeeps. It was not that they needed these things—indeed, some of them were liabilities—but to the Marines it was unthinkable to leave anything behind.

This procession of examples portrays something of the extent to which the spirit of thrift, in the image of Henderson and Lejeune, animated the Marine Corps. While theft, institutional or otherwise, is on its face mischievous and wicked, it is not hard to see how it became a way of Marine Corps life given the dedication to making do with very little that, of necessity, had pervaded the Corps for so long.

Alas, it is sadly true that just as much of America has evolved, over the past generation, into an Oliver Twist society, holding out its bowl and saying, "Please, sir, some more," so has the Marine Corps in some respects strayed from its frugal ways of 1800 to 1940.

At Danang, in 1965, it was determined to enlarge the headquarters complex to accommodate an operations center for the principal Marine commands in the area. The Seabees came in with their trucks and bulldozers, their cranes and tractors, their hand tools, and their supplies.

They delivered an immense pile of plywood sheets to the site in preparation for the job and then left them there, unguarded, for a week. Nobody disturbed the treasure—not one sheet!

It could be said that this was no more than the noble and moral thing to do. I can only say, however, that thirty years earlier the plywood would not have survived a single night. Sergeant Wolkovitz would have managed to take possession of it all, put it quickly to what he saw as a higher and better use, and, in so doing, let it be known that anyone so careless with his property deserved to be taught a lesson!

PART
V

THE BROTHERS

For he who fights with me this day
will be my brother.

Henry V, Act 4, Scene III

Among Marines there is a fierce loyalty to the Corps that persists long after the uniform is in mothballs. There is an intense devotion to the Corps by reservists that seems never to die. Woven through that sense of belonging, like a steel thread, is an elitist spirit. Marines are convinced that, being few in number, they are selective, better, and, above all, different.

This matter of being different has been nourished, over the years, by the Marines' combining of the characteristics of both the sailor and the soldier while not being fairly described as either one or the other. They have always been alert for opportunities to exploit this anomaly to their own benefit, playing the Army and the Navy against each other. As far back as the 1798 Act for Establishing a Marine Corps, Congress had formalized this hybrid condition, prescribing, when the Marines were ashore, that they would be governed by the Articles of War and, when at sea, that they would be subject to the Navy Regulations. This straddling of the other services enabled perceptive Marine leaders to avail themselves of the best of both, thus contributing further to their sense of elitism.

The determination to be different also manifested itself early on in terms of appearance. Turning to Europe for a model, Commandant Wharton created in 1804 a distinctive Marine Corps uniform, using the already traditional Marine colors of blue, red, and white and including a tall leather cap bearing, as today, an eagle and an anchor. (The globe came later.)

The sense of superiority has grown most of all from the fact that every Marine, whether enlisted or officer, goes through the same training experience. Both the training of recruits and the basic education of officers—going back to 1805—have endowed the Corps with a sense of cohesiveness enjoyed by no other American service. In World War II, Commandant Thomas Holcomb (1936–43) directed that all evidence of source of entry—volunteer, reservist, or draftee —be removed from a Marine's record, to emphasize that all were the same in the eyes of the Corps.

Their distinctive characteristics, plus the catalyst of combat, have united Marines of all ranks in a mystical brotherhood that baffles observers and frustrates critics. That brotherhood is more than a state of mind; it is embodied in Marine Corps dogma in a golden paragraph that first appeared in the 1921 Marine Corps Manual. Written by Commandant John A. Lejeune, the paragraph has not been changed in more than half a century. It is as fresh and powerful today as the day it was written:

Relations Between Officers and Enlisted Marines.

a. Comradeship and brotherhood.—The World War wrought a great change in the relations between officers and enlisted men in the military services. A spirit of comradeship and brotherhood in arms came into being in the training camps and on the battlefields. This spirit is too fine a thing to be allowed to die. It must be fostered and kept alive and made the moving force in all Marine Corps organizations.

b. Teacher and scholar.—The relation between officer and enlisted men should in no sense be that of superior and inferior nor that of master and servant, but rather that of teacher and scholar. In fact, it should partake of the nature of the relation between father and son, to the extent that officers, especially commanding officers, are responsible for the physical, mental and moral welfare, as well as the discipline and military training of the young men under their command who are serving the nation in the Corps.

c. The realization of this responsibility on the part of officers is vital to the well-being of the Marine Corps. It is especially so, for the reason that so large a proportion of the men enlisted are under twenty-one years of age. These men are in the formative period of their lives, and officers owe it to them, to their parents, and to the nation, that when discharged from the services they should be far better men physically, mentally and morally than they were when they enlisted.

d. To accomplish this task successfully a constant effort must be made by all officers to fill each day with useful and interesting instruction and wholesome entertainment for the men. This effort must be intelligent and not perfunctory, the object being not only to do away with idleness, but to train and cultivate the bodies, the minds and the spirit of our men.

e. Love of Corps and Country.—To be more specific, it will be necessary for officers not only to devote their close attention to the many questions affecting the comfort, health, military training and discipline of the men under their command, but also actively to promote athletics and to endeavor to enlist the interest of their men in building up and maintaining their bodies in the finest physical condition; to encourage them to enroll in the Marine Corps Institute and to keep up their studies after enrollment; and to make every effort by means of historical education and patriotic address to cultivate in their hearts a deep abiding love of the Corps and Country.

f. Leadership.—Finally, it must be kept in mind that the American soldier responds quickly and readily to the exhibition of qualities of leadership on the part of his officers. Some of these qualities are industry, energy, initiative, determination, enthusiasm, firmness, kindness, justness, self-control, unselfishness, honor and courage. Every officer should endeavor by all means in his power to make himself the possessor of these qualities and thereby to fit himself to be a real leader of men.

This warm and human example of soldierly philosophy, in addition to its enduring wisdom, implies a lesson for anyone who aspires to lead men. In it, General Lejeune used the term *officer* ten times, the term *men* ten times, and *leadership* or *leader* three times, but he never used the more sterile terms *persons, personnel, supervision,* or *management* at all. Lejeune knew he was talking about warm, living human beings. To the extent that that perception pervades the Corps, the Marine brotherhood will continue to flourish.

CHAPTER 11

This Precious Few

In the Marines, recruit training is the genesis of the enduring sense of brotherhood that characterizes the Corps. In that twelve-week period, an almost mystical alchemy occurs. Young adults from diverse areas of the country and backgrounds are immersed in an environment wherein they are able to perceive, understand, and finally accept as dogma the essential Marine Corps virtues.*

New recruits are told, the day they enter recruit training, that "A Marine Believes—in his God, in his Country, in his Corps, in his buddies and in himself." When I commanded the San Diego Recruit Depot in 1960, I had the words painted on a sign at the entrance to the receiving area where the recruits, awaiting processing, had an opportunity to contemplate their meaning. To read those words is easy, but to believe and to follow them is quite a different matter. Nevertheless, the instinct to practice them in fair times and

---

* Women Marines undergo rigorous, inspirational recruit training, too. This chapter, however, addresses specifically the transformation of the male Marine in a few short weeks from young civilian to dedicated warrior—the embodiment of all the Corps stands for.

foul is the bedrock of the Marines' brotherhood, and the way that instinct is created in a few short weeks is a wondrous thing.

If a recruit's parents were to ask him minutes after the graduation ceremony to describe exactly what had happened to him during the three-month training period, the young man would have difficulty putting his experience in words. He would make clear that it had been a hard and awesome thing, quite different from anything he had ever experienced before, and something he would never forget. He would talk of long, hard dawn-to-taps days, of running until he felt his chest would burst, of calisthenics and marching, of obstacle courses and hand grenades, of inspections and parades, and, especially, of shooting. He would exhibit with pride his rifle qualification badge and, if he were one of the distinguished few in his group, his private first class chevron. He would then speak enthusiastically, and with self-conscious professionalism, of where he was going next, what he intended to do there, and why. Throughout the monologue would be woven recurrent references to his buddies, his drill instructors, and "the platoon . . . the platoon . . . the platoon." He would probably insist on his parents meeting some of those buddies and his drill instructors, most particularly his drill instructors. By this time the parents would understand that, somehow, their son had become a part of something important.

There are not many books or articles parents can turn to to get even a rudimentary understanding of what their sons go through in the recruit training experience. While the commandant of the Marine Corps publishes standard operating procedures governing the daily—and hourly—details of recruit training, there is little written about the philosophy underlying the process. The philosophy itself is predicated on a single assumption—that the young men under training may have to fight for their country. It is the Marines' obligation to ensure not just that they win but that they come home alive. In summarizing what he expects recruit indoctrination to achieve, the commandant of the Marine Corps says in his "Program of Instruction for Male Recruit Training" that the overall goal is "to instill in the recruit the skills, knowledge, discipline and self-confidence that make him worthy of recognition as a United States Marine." The same motivation was expressed in somewhat blunter language by Commandant Pate (1956–58), "Recruit training consists in preparing and conditioning mentally, physically and emotionally a group of young and naturally well-disposed youths to meet the experience of violence and bloodshed which is war."[1]

To do all of these things is a major order. During his twelve weeks of sixteen-waking-hour days a recruit will run ninety miles, march two hundred and fifty miles, run the obstacle course ten times, do at least seventy hours of calisthenics, at least sixteen hours of swimming, and spend ninety hours in field training. It is an intensely physical experience, fueled by a daily thirty-three hundred–calorie diet. On an average he will lose eight pounds of fat and gain twelve pounds of muscle. It is also an intensely mental and spiritual experience whose success involves transmitting a great volume and variety of information to the recruit in a brief time. It involves imbuing him with the instinct of swift and total obedience, something with which he may not have been familiar. Most of all, it involves developing in the recruit a sense of commitment.

Commitment is the thing. Soldiers in the ranks have rarely, over the ages, fought for king, country, freedom, or moral principle. More than anything else, men have fought and winners have won because of a commitment—to a leader and to a small brotherhood where the ties that bind are mutual respect and confidence, shared privation, shared hazard, shared triumph, a willingness to obey, and determination to follow.

Historian Richard H. Kohn says it well. "Rather than being motivated by patriotism or political ideology, our soldiers have sustained themselves in the stress of battle by a variety of means, from the network of esteem and interdependence that creates the cohesion of a unit to the will and instinct for survival."[2]

Bravery, as we recognize it and reward it, is far more than anything else a matter of commitment to the hero's leader or peers. The Marine says, "I am going up the hill in the face of that enemy fire because the Gunny says so." Or, "If the other guys can do it, I can." Or, "I have to go. I can't let my buddies down." Marines do not leave their wounded or dead behind, not so much because it is uncivilized but simply because the casualties, living or dead, are still their buddies and to forsake them would be unthinkable.

The entire Marine recruit training process is dedicated to developing this sense of brotherhood, interdependence, and determination to triumph. Marines like to say that it is this almost apostolic approach to recruit training that distinguishes the Corps from most other military formations. As they put it at Parris Island, "This is where the difference begins."

For the young man who aspires to become a member of the Marine fraternity, initiation starts with a reduction of all to a common denominator. Stripped naked in a group for a physical examination, they are bathed together, their heads clipped, civilian clothing and jewelry removed, all dressed exactly the same. From this moment, none is different from any other. None is better than any other. After this egoectomy, they start from an initial zero and they are rebuilt from there.

From the very beginning the recruits' development leans heavily on paternalism, both institutional and individual. They are in a strange environment, understandably lonely, and in need of someone to look after them, to see that their teeth are filled, their hernias repaired, their glasses refitted.* To some this paternalism is a totally new experience, to all it is most welcome, serving to balance the hard reality that recruits' lives are pivoted on stress. The unremitting stress challenges them to achieve, both as individuals and as members of a progressively closer group. It challenges their bodies beyond any previously imagined limit, their abilities to learn and remember, and their instincts of responsibility, propriety, and obedience. How successful each is in meeting these challenges under comprehensively stressful conditions —alone and as a member of the group—is one important

---

* In an average recruit platoon 30 percent will need glasses, and 80 percent will need dental repair, of which over half is of a major nature.

measure of his progress in earning the right to be called a Marine, a title which he will not bear until the day of his graduation. Until then he is addressed only as "Private" or "Recruit."

While stress is central to the entire recruit training process, there is a narrow line between productive stress— either physical or mental—and destructive stress. During my time at a recruit depot, I realized that the line exists, but nobody was ever able to trace it for me or even to define it. I do know, however, that the acceptable level of stress increases as the recruit's capability grows, and the standards he must meet are consequently raised throughout his training.

Evolving from casual civilian to membership in the Marine brotherhood requires a constant iteration of the importance of all standards, not just those related to physical achievement. Standards of appearance, loyalty, technical performance, obedience, and discipline—most of all discipline—are what knits and holds the Marine Corps together.

Commandant Franklin Wharton (1804–18) took the first tiny step in 1805 in building this sense of discipline and in formalizing the evolutionary recruit-training process. Not a particularly soldierly man himself, having had little field experience, Wharton nevertheless had a keen concern for the welfare and the professionalism of his men. He wanted them to know how to march and how to shoot. Those aspirations have not changed in the ensuing century and three quarters.

Wharton created a school for recruits at the Marine Barracks in Washington where, in two months at most, the young men were supposed to be taught the rudiments of discipline, drill, the manual of arms, and marksmanship. Since some were as young as fifteen, most were illiterate, and some had problems with English, two months were hardly enough. Moreover, those who taught them (mainly the adjutant and officer of the day of the barracks) were not too experienced themselves. The adjutant's instructions were to "superintend generally their arms and appearances." The officer of the day was in charge of drilling and was directed "to attend particularly to the wheeling backward and forward of the men, teaching them to count their steps and halt when they are ordered. . . ."[3] Clearly, recruit training in 1800 bore little similarity to the comprehensive experience of today.

The Wharton program did not flourish far beyond the initial rudimentary stage for the usual reasons—not enough men and not enough money. The problem was underscored in the long regime of Commandant Archibald Henderson (1820–59), who tried several times to enhance the quality and scope of recruit indoctrination but with little success. The need for men in the ships of the fleet and in the several barracks took precedence.

Later, at the outset of the Civil War, Commandant Harris (1859–64) persuaded Congress to double the authorized size of the Corps (to three thousand men), but there still was time only for the most perfunctory recruit training because the need for men was so great. Even at that, there were few people available to do the training. Such indoctrination as recruits received came at the barracks nearest their place of enlistment, and this same inadequate pattern continued for the next half century.

In the first years of the twentieth century, however, the Corps's combat renown in China, Nicaragua, Mexico, and the Philippines created dramatic changes. The Marines' high profile so stimulated recruiting that the Corps reached full authorized strength (about eight thousand) in 1907. At last, effective recruit training became a practicable matter.

As one of his first acts, Commandant William P. Biddle (1911–14) directed the creation of recruit training depots at Philadelphia, Norfolk, Virginia (later Port Royal, South Carolina), Puget Sound, Washington, and Mare Island, California. Eventually the entire Marine Corps recruit-training function was concentrated in two places—Parris Island, South Carolina, and San Diego, California.

Physically the depots are very different. Parris Island, in the swampy coastal Carolina lowland, is truly remote. Its six thousand acres, despite extensive marsh areas, provide ample space for all required training activities. The depot came into Marine Corps hands in 1915 after it had served variously as a Union naval base in the Civil War and a naval disciplinary barracks. The thousands of Marines who have since been trained there remember it most for the intensely humid climate and the sand fleas.

San Diego, which has been the West Coast recruit-training center since 1923, came into the Marines' possession in 1917, partly by purchase ($250,000), partly as a gift from the community. In contrast to Parris Island, the San Diego facility is located in the middle of the city and is small—only some 700 acres. San Diego must rely on Camp Pendleton, about forty miles away, for its marksmanship ranges and field training facilities. Despite their differences in size, setting, and facilities, Parris Island and San Diego share the same philosophy about recruit training. Their curricula are essentially identical and, most important, their products are indistinguishable.

Many Marines will challenge this, contending that the training at the two bases is quite different, that the Parris Island experience is harder and that the successful Parris Island graduate tougher. When I commanded the San Diego depot, I tried to find out if this was true. I sent teams to observe the Parris Island training in detail, went there myself, and invited reciprocal visits. Our conclusion? That there was little difference in either the experience or the graduate. Thereafter, I responded to the rumor by quoting Lieutenant Colonel (later Brigadier General) L. E. Fribourg. "Yes," he had said, "there *is* one difference. At San Diego they teach recruits, when jumping off a sinking ship, to hold their nose. At Parris Island they teach them to hold their privates. So, the only way to know for sure where a Marine was trained is to wait until he jumps off a sinking ship."

Back in 1905, in his effort to formalize recruit training, Commandant Biddle had prescribed an eight-week program, to include drill, physical exercise, personal combat, and intensive marksmanship qualification with the new M1903 Sringfield rifle that the corps had recently adopted. He was, in other words, taking up where Commandant Wharton left off a full century earlier. With one big difference—Biddle had more resources. With them he was able to infuse vitality into a formula that has since given upwards of two million Marines a true identity. The formula is built on the concept that from the moment the training begins to the moment of graduation the recruit is in the direct care of a noncommissioned leader, the drill instructor.

The key noncommissioned officer leader is not a new idea. The great military formations of history have all been built on a foundation of competent career small-unit leaders. To these individuals, the imperatives of continued promotion are subordinate to the challenge and exhilaration of directing the efforts and sharing the hazards of their own closely knit groups. British Major Reginald Hargreaves describes the quality clearly, "The vital spark is that single-minded devotion which places duty before all thoughts of self. . . ."[4] The ideal drill instructor is just that kind of professional, one whose obligation is to expose the recruit for the first—and, one hopes, decisive—time to the picture of a small-unit leader who can do anything the recruit is asked to do, and more, and whose total concern is for the welfare, the training, the success, and the survival of those in his charge.

It is incredible to me that it took the Corps a century and a half to awaken to the extraordinary importance of the drill instructor's task. Because of the sensitivity of the position, it would seem immediately obvious that none but the very best noncommissioned officers should be given the job and that candidates should be carefully screened. Until the onset of World War II, the drill instructor was simply designated from men of the command and was handed his great responsibility without special prior indoctrination. Inevitably, inconsistency in standards and treatment resulted, with some recruit units run with casual laxity and others with a heavy hand. The unevenness was finally recognized, and in 1942 special schools and careful screening were instituted at both Parris Island and San Diego to ensure not only that the most skilled noncommissioned officers were involved in recruit training, but also the best suited. The drill instructor schools have continued, with few interruptions, since that time.*

---

* In 1976 a program of preselection screening was instituted for D.I. school candidates and, by 1983, the program had matured into a comprehensive 8.6-week course designed to cover every aspect of the D.I.'s responsibility and to evaluate the students in order to

To be any good—to stimulate the essential Marine sense of patriotism, discipline, loyalty, and brotherhood—recruit training has to be hard and high tempo. Because it is hard and because it involves immature, unskilled, and undisciplined youngsters, the opportunities for trouble are infinite.

Marine recruit training in World War I, an eight- to ten-week program emphasizing drill and marksmanship, was renowned for its intensity. Three drill instructors had essentially full responsibility for the sixty-four-man platoons, demanding much of them in their professional performance and having no compunction about correcting recalcitrants with physical punishment.

Retired Major General Walter Greatsinger Farrell told me of his time at Parris Island, between August and October 1917, with sober emotion. He was a transfer from the Army and had already undergone the Army recruit indoctrination, of which he says, "Beside Parris Island the Army was a garden party." He describes his Marine recruit training as entirely war-oriented, with the greatest emphasis on shooting. Even after more than sixty years, the drill instructors remain fresh in his mind. "We had a sergeant D.I. and two corporals who took care of us day and night. They were tough but fair. They carried swagger sticks made of swab handles, and they used them freely. We felt them across our legs, in the stomach or, worst of all, they would drag the tip across your ribs like rattling a stick on a picket fence. But they always had our welfare at heart. By the time they were finished with me, I knew the meaning of instant obedience and I understood the importance of loyalty up and down."[5]

Retired General Gerald C. Thomas also told me of his time at Parris Island in 1917. "We marched and we marched, we drilled and we drilled, we fired our weapons, we crawled and we ran and then we drilled some more. Even though it was a dawn-to-dark affair my drill instructor, Sergeant Johnny Borden, was there all the time. He got us up in the morning and he put us to bed at night."[6]

---

eliminate those who, for professional or emotional reasons, are not likely to succeed on the drill field. As of 1982 Marine Corps Headquarters said that attrition in the school varied between 20 and 30 percent.

The products of this training acquitted themselves very well in France and gained the respect of the other military forces. American Expeditionary Forces inspectors described the Marine 4th Brigade as "probably the best" American unit in France for appearance and discipline.[7]

During World War II, the recruit-training formula did not vary greatly from World War I, except that the pressure of rapid growth—27,000 to 450,000—initially caused the Corps to cut the training cycle from eight weeks to four weeks, a mistake that generated many problems and was quickly reversed. It took every bit of eight weeks to screen out the misfits who came to the Marines through the Selective Service System, and the pressure on the drill instructor to cope with the functionally illiterate, the physically marginal, and the emotionally unmotivated was immense. As in World War I, there was strong emphasis on the attentive, paternal drill instructor, and there was little aversion to rigorous physical punishment, a practise that gained in seriousness as personnel shortages caused the inclusion of relatively inexperienced privates first class as drill instructors. Despite its faults, the system as a whole was successful. The young man who completed the training had clearly acquired some of the precious virtues of commitment and obedience, and he met the extreme challenge of combat from Guadalcanal to Okinawa with poise and steadiness.

Korea brought the same critical problems—draftees of limited capability, drill instructors of limited experience, a short indoctrination period, and heavy reliance on physical suasion. Yet high standards of performance resulted in a combat-creditable graduate. Fresh replacements, only weeks beyond recruit training, were steady and resolute at Inchon and at Seoul and the annals of the Chosin Reservoir are rich with accounts of loyalty, teamwork, individual sacrifice, and small-unit solidarity.

As the Korean action wound down, the recruit cycle sought a peacetime level—ten weeks of training, and three noncommissioned officer drill instructors per platoon. All D.I.s were prescreened and graduates of a month-long drill instructor indoctrination program. Recruit training was still an intense experience and, because the Marines had proven so eminently effective in combat, the system had really never been subjected to close analytical scrutiny. Commandant Pate had occasion to underscore this point: "There has been a reluctance to alter radically a system which has been as successful in teaching Marines how to fight and win."[8]

That close analytical scrutiny was finally initiated by the events of Sunday night, 8 April 1956, when Staff Sergeant Matthew McKeon, a junior drill instructor at Parris Island, marched his platoon of seventy-four men into Ribbon Creek and came out with only sixty-eight. The others drowned in the black waters of the tidal estuary.

McKeon was a successful graduate of a four-week drill instructor school, respected by his peers, and admired by his recruits. His purpose in ordering the after-hours march was to discipline the entire recruit platoon for what he saw as inadequate performance in training. In his view, they were not good enough, not obedient enough, not trying hard enough to meet the standard set for the platoon, and he was determined to see a change for the better. However laudable its purpose, the nighttime venture into the swampy estuary was a monumentally bad idea. Mass punishment always is. Beyond that, it was expressly prohibited by a 1955 Recruit Depot Parris Island order.

Even so, such punitive marches were not an unknown occurrence, rather they were part and parcel of a drill instructor philosophy that had prevailed for years.* In brief, as the drill instructors saw it, that philosophy said,

> In 2½ months I have to turn these seventy individuals into a team of obedient Marines who believe in their buddies and the Corps, who can survive on the battlefield. And my superiors want no excuses.
>
> The recruits are young and often ignorant.
>
> Many of them have never been a part of anything

---

* What is permitted in terms of punishment is a constantly changing thing. The Articles for the Government of the Navy, edition of 1800, for example, embodied what was perceived as a major step toward moderation of a common contemporary punishment—flogging. It limited the design of the cat-of-nine-tails to rope alone. Wire was forbidden, and the lashes could not be knotted.

meaningful. Many have never been motivated to do anything useful.

Some of them are physically weak.

Some of them have never had to respond to authority and do not know the meaning of obedience.

In short, they are mostly immature kids, and if I am to convert them into proud and competent Marines I am going to have to start out by treating them with the patience required by kids, rewarding them like kids, punishing them like kids.

And I know how to do it. The captains and colonels don't know how. Very few of them have ever been through it.

I have, and I intend to do what is needed so that the recruits will end up as useful members of a team—a credit to me, the Corps and their country.

That very philosophy—doing whatever was needed to produce an effective graduate—was the heart of the defense offered in McKeon's behalf in his court-martial. While ably presented, it did not prevent his conviction. The court-martial, highly publicized, embodied the skillful legal performance of a civilian defense staff headed by Emile Zola Berman, a prominent New York attorney. It met for twenty-five days, resulting in conviction on charges of negligent homicide and drinking and acquittal on charges of manslaughter, oppression, and conduct detrimental to the service. The court sentenced McKeon to a Bad Conduct Discharge, confinement at hard labor for nine months, forfeiture of $270.00, and reduction to the rank of private. The secretary of the navy reduced the sentence to three months' confinement and reduction to private. McKeon's conviction was publicly condemned by the Veterans of Foreign Wars, the Marine Corps League, and the AmVets as threatening the disciplinary fabric of the Corps.

Whether the conviction threatened the disciplinary fabric of the Corps, I don't know. The Ribbon Creek tragedy itself certainly did exhibit a basic flaw in that fabric. Commandant Pate acknowledged the fact in his endorsement to the secretary of the navy on the record of the Ribbon Creek Court of Inquiry, "In a very real sense the Marine Corps is on trial for the tragedy of Ribbon Creek, just as surely as is Sergeant McKeon. I will not blind myself to this fact nor will I seek to disown the responsibility which is mine as Commandant of the Marine Corps." What he should have said in addition was that not only he but everyone in the intervening chain of command shared in the blame.

In the aftermath of Ribbon Creek, some important facts and attitudes came to light. Some drill instructors, motivated to make respectable Marines of their charges, would drive their platoons beyond the limit of the physical endurance of some members. Some would apply senseless and inhumane measures to get a recruit's attention—hit him or force him to run an obstacle course with pockets filled with sand, to smoke a cigarette with his head covered by a bucket, or to perform calisthenics beyond reasonable endurance. These, and other similar measures, reprehensible, indefensible, and unnecessary, were illuminated in the wake of Ribbon Creek.

The question was then, as it is today: just how much a part does this improper conduct play in recruit training? It is hard to quantify with precision the frequency of abusive conduct. Recruits themselves are likely to deny they have been maltreated, perhaps because of fear, peer pressure, or genuine loyalty to the D.I. The same recruits who Sergeant McKeon led into Ribbon Creek, for example, applauded him at his court-martial. Private Hector Serantes: "He was one of the most human sergeants that I have ever served under, sir." Private William McPherson: "I thought he was an excellent D.I.—a man with great patience." Private Walter F. Nehrenz: "Sergeant McKeon had a lot of patience for everybody. He took his time."⁹

Right after Ribbon Creek, at Parris Island, it is likely that very little definable as maltreatment took place because of the intensive effort at supervision.* Some instances still

---

* In the eleven months following the Ribbon Creek incident, four Parris Island D.I.s were court-martialed for mistreating recruits. In 1980, a total of 1,576 NCOs served as drill instructors at both depots. Of those, 124 were disciplined for transgressions involving maltreatment. Thirty-one of the offenses were serious enough to warrant trial by court-martial. During my tenure I awarded seven general courts-martial for maltreatment.

occur, but now they are few. Constant, round-the-clock vigilance goes far to control overzealousness on the part of any D.I. who might be so inclined. The specter of Ribbon Creek was still so visible to me, when I assumed command of the San Diego Recruit Depot in 1959, that I wore my uniform every day but six in two and one-half years and could often be found wandering through the recruit area at midnight or 4:00 A.M. My presence there, I found, guaranteed the unannounced presence also of others in the chain of command.

Certainly, one of the most beneficial results of the Ribbon Creek affair was the reaffirmation of a truth well known in the Corps—that a solid chain of command, with appropriate responsibility at every level, is essential. There had been a widespread perception, among recruits and drill instructors alike, that the recruit platoon was a little world in itself with the drill instructor as supreme and answerable only to God.

That is not true today, where the chain of command is dynamic and visible at every level—depot commanding general, recruit training regiment commander, recruit battalion commander, recruit company commander, and series commander. The last named, the series commander, is a critical element in the command structure, being intimately involved with the hour-by-hour training of his series (four or five platoons). He has an assistant series commander who contributes further to making the chain of command effective around the clock. Today, there is no question, it is a fact and it is clearly understood, the officer is a powerful influence in the recruit's daily life.

While recruits in training usually deny the existence of any brutality, successful recruit graduates themselves tend to exaggerate the physical hardships. Theirs is a normal human disposition to boast of the difficulty of any achievement. Young Marines have emerged successfully from an experience that has posed greater challenges than anything they have encountered before. The tendency to overstate its rigors is understandable. After all, they have passed the initiation into an elect fraternity and they have without knowing it become elitists. They have earned the right to be proud. Under no circumstances would they have anyone believe their experience was easy, and under no circumstances should anyone mistakenly intimate it was.

Brutality, in short, is not a dominant factor in the recruit-training system. Far more important is the influence of the paternal drill instructor, which is to say, most of them. Imbued with high standards, the drill instructor is a dedicated, sensitive Marine—demanding much of his charges while patiently teaching them, among other things, to brush their teeth, wash behind their ears, and make up their bunks properly. He is willing to sacrifice his own limited spare time to help a marginal recruit in danger of falling behind. He is willing to forgo a weekend with his family in order to remain with the platoon. He is instinctively keen to counsel, encourage, and defend an errant recruit just because he is a member of the platoon. In short, he is the essence of the tough, resolute, compassionate, professional leader whose behavior is the mortar that binds every successful military structure together. It is the D.I.'s devotion to his task that catalyzes the whole Marine recruit-training experience and what he does for his charges is likely to influence their behavior for the rest of their lives.

In his *The Kingdom and the Power,* the story of *The New York Times,* Gay Talese writes of publisher Arthur Ochs Sulzberger, Jr.'s, period in the Marine Corps:

> His drill instructor at Parris Island was a tough corporal named Rossides who achieved in a few weeks what a generation of educators and the Times family had failed to do in twelve years. Punch Sulzberger reacted immediately to orders, he kept up with his group. . . . In the Marines the commands were loud and clear and there was no doubt who was the boss. Sulzberger's family connections carried no weight with Rossides. Decades later Punch would remember Rossides with gratitude and affection.

Eugene B. Sledge, a World War II Marine who did not pass beyond the rank of private first class, possessed an eloquence to be envied by all. He drew the portrait of the genuine D.I. in firm brush strokes:

My Drill Instructor (Cpl. T.J. Doherty, Platoon 984, San Diego, 1943) was a small man. He didn't have a big mouth. He was neither cruel nor sadistic. He was not a bully. But he was a strict disciplinarian, a total realist about our future and an absolute perfectionist dedicated to excellence. To him, more than my disciplined home life, a year of college ROTC and months of infantry training I attribute my ability to have withstood the stress of Peleliu.[10]

Commandant Robert H. Barrow (1979–83) applied the capstone:

My Drill Instructors lighted a fire in me 40 years ago. It's still burning and will until I die.[11]

How could it be stated better? As Dr. Sledge implies, the young recruit is being mentally conditioned for combat, and the most reliable measure of the quality of his basic training is his subsequent performance under the stress of battle. In this sense, if the graduate recruit's parents, of whom we spoke at the beginning, could study three related pictures, they would begin to comprehend the meaning of the experience their son had undergone.

The first picture would portray the straggling, unkempt, and bewildered group of new recruits who have just arrived at the depot, still in their civilian clothes, enroute to their first haircut and bath. Stumbling, fumbling, frightened, they know neither where they are nor where they are going. And they certainly look nothing like the stuff of which fighting Marines are made.

The next picture would show the same group, only twelve weeks later, enroute to their graduation ceremony.* Now

---

* Of course, they would not all be there. According to Marine Corps Headquarters, on an average, the attrition from all causes in 1983 was about 12 percent. The greatest single cause is medical disqualification—some 5 percent. Unsuitability adds another 3 percent, training failure only 1 percent. The remainder includes fraudulent and erroneous enlistment, prior narcotics involvement, or discharge for their own convenience.

they are lean, fit, clean, bright-eyed, and straight-backed, they march in perfect unison in their crisp uniforms and respond precisely to the commands of their D.I. They are proud. They know where they are going.

The final scene would portray a half-dozen of the same group, this time in full combat equipment. The unit of fighting Marines crawls methodically up a hill under heavy enemy fire to capture a pillbox. Through the noise, confusion, and smoke of battle it is plain to see that they are behaving as a team. They are visibly calm and confident, professional and purposeful. They move coolly and resolutely, each dependent on the others, each determined to do his share, all determined to win.

There, at the level of the battle, is the payoff. It provides both a rationalization and an explanation. The molten crucible called Marine-recruit training has produced a line of furiously loyal men who have learned that the Marine is the Corps and the Corps is the Marine. They have carried America's colors in four wars with unfailing steadiness, unity, and dependability. And they have returned to the civilian world with a higher sense of commitment to their country. It is all an eloquent testimonial to a system that is one of a kind, and its product is proudly named—A Band of Brothers.

PART
VI

THE FIGHTERS

Come on, you sons of bitches,
do you want to live forever?

Gunnery Sergeant Dan Daly,
USMC

In the autumn of 1941, Gunnery Sergeant Walter Holzworth, whose philosophy introduced this book, wrote to me from his station on the USS *Arizona*.

"They tell me we are headed for war," Holzworth said, "If it comes to a fight I want to be in at the start. That's where the Marines belong."

A few weeks later, Holzworth was swallowed in the black waters and flaming oil of Pearl Harbor. It had come to a fight, and he was in at the start "where the Marines belong."*

Of the various enduring faces that have come to distin-

---

* I was saddened by Holzworth's death. He was more than a fighting man; he was something of a philosopher, too. Once when I asked him the formula for succeding with our captain, he said, "It's simple, lieutenant. Just find out what the old SOB wants and give it to him." I never forgot the advice.

guish the Corps, the first to emerge was the conviction that fighting was its business, conflict its way of life. The Continental Marines had scant chance to exhibit much heroism in the Revolution, but in subsequent years the Marines gradually sketched in their reputation as men who made fighting—any kind of fighting—their business. In the Seminole War, for example, Commandant Henderson forsook Washington, D.C., to lead a regiment (and earn a brevet promotion to brigadier general); in Mexico, Marines with Brigadier General John A. Quitman, USA, made the identification of the "The Halls of the Montezumas" with the Corps a permanent thing. The reputation was enhanced further by the behavior of Marine expeditionary forces: to Cuba in 1898, to the Philippines in 1899, and to China in 1900. Names were appearing to burnish the legendary luster: daring Lieutenant Presley N. O'Bannon at Derna in Tripoli; romantic Lieutenant Archibald H. Gillespie with Fremont in California; flinty Lieutenant Colonel Robert W. Huntington at Guantanamo Bay. Plainly, by the turn of the century, the Marines' combatant image was etched onto the imaginations of the American people. The recruiting posters told the story. In 1907, when Army posters said, "Join the Army and Learn a Trade," and Navy posters said, "Join the Navy and See the World," the Marine posters came to the point with disarming simplicity, "First to Fight."

World War I really established the picture of the Marine as first and foremost a fighter. The triumphs in the meat grinders of Belleau Wood, Soissons, St. Mihiel, Blanc Mont Ridge, and the Meuse-Argonne were reflections of both professional steadiness and personal valor, giving substance to the memorial published by Commandant Lejeune on the Marine Corps Birthday of 1921 when he said, "The term *Marine* has come to signify all that is highest in military efficiency and soldierly virtue."

And so it had, setting the scene for the procession of Marine Corps triumphs of World War II, sagas of violent air/ground combat where resolution and individual heroism predominated. Korea followed, and the same qualities distinguished the performance of the Marines. The Marine was, by this time and because of his indoctrination, not only ready and willing to fight, but determined to win. The many-sided Vietnam conflict added an entirely new dimension to the Marines' combatant character—the ability to adapt to a strange kind of war, one little understood in the modern world but based on principles twenty-five centuries old.

Whatever the form of combat, the genius of the Marine as a fighter has caused his superiors to place a great deal of confidence in him. They are convinced of his ability, to the point where they will offer unhesitatingly his commitment in an hour of crisis. More important, the American people will accept the offer with the confidence, born of long experience, that when a Marine is called upon, he will be ready and, when committed to a fight, that he may be depended on to win.

CHAPTER 12

A New Kind of War

When Daniel Ellsberg was on trial for stealing the Pentagon Papers, his defense lawyers, to confuse the issue, introduced the claim that U.S. participation in the Vietnam conflict was premeditated, that the Tonkin Gulf incident was a contrived excuse for our intervention. I was one of the witnesses for the federal government. On cross-examination, Ellsberg's attorney, Leonard Weinglass, wanted me to admit that well before we went to Vietnam the Marines were preparing for combat there. I surprised him by confessing. Yes, I said, we were indeed preparing for the eventuality of having to fight in Vietnam. Even more important, I told him, we were preparing to fight in a lot of other places, too.[1]

Unwittingly, Mr. Weinglass had underscored one of the characteristics that has distinguished the Corps—a standing determination to be ready for combat wherever and however it may arise. Total readiness is, nevertheless, more an objective than a reality, because of the enemy—his strengths, his aims, and his resolve. We have learned, to our regret, that while you are certainly the better for preparing, the war you prepare for is rarely the war you get.

Thus, we come to an unusual, and generally unheralded, aspect of the Marines' quality as fighters. Adaptability, initiative, and improvisation are the true fabric of obedience, the ultimate in soldierly conduct, going further than sheer heroism to make the Marines what they are. "The battle is what it's all about," Marines say. "Try as hard as you can to be ready for it but be willing to adapt and improvise when it turns out to be a different battle than the one you expected, because adaptability is where victory will be found." This virtue of adaptability has found expression many times in the Marines' combat history, especially since the beginning of the twentieth century.

In 1916, for example, Marines went to Santo Domingo on short notice with the simple mission of protecting the American Legation in Santo Domingo City. They were still there eight years later, involved in the far broader tasks of both pacifying and governing the country, to which they had adapted readily. In 1950, they went to Korea intending to make a decisive amphibious assault at Inchon to sever the North Korean supply line. Ten weeks later they were still in Korea, fighting quite a different kind of war—a protracted land campaign in the subzero ice and snow of the Chosin Reservoir. And four years later they were still there, fighting an attritional war of position. They stood up to these varied combat challenges because of an instinctive determination to adapt.

The sternest fighting test of all, where the need for adaptability was greatest, came in Vietnam. The onset of that conflict found the Corps in an advanced state of training oriented primarily toward its traditional amphibious mission but with some attention given to counterinsurgency situations. Since 1962, when President Kennedy required all of the services to emphasize counterinsurgency training, the Marines had been preparing to operate in a counterinsurgency environment, not just in Southeast Asia but anywhere in the world.

Serving in the Joint Staff as the focal point in counterinsurgency operations and training, I went to Vietnam eight times between 1962 and 1964. In those early years, I learned something of the complex nature of the conflict there. The problem of seeking out and destroying guerrillas was easy enough to comprehend, but winning the loyalty of the people, why it was so important and how to do it, took longer to understand. Several meetings with Sir Robert Thompson, who contributed so much to the British victory over the guerrillas in Malaya, established a set of basic counterinsurgency principles in my mind. Thompson said, "The peoples' trust is primary. It will come hard because they are fearful and suspicious. Protection is the most important thing you can bring them. After that comes health. And, after that, many things—land, prosperity, education, and privacy to name a few."[2] The more I saw of the situation facing the Vietnamese government and the Vietnamese Army, the more convinced I became—along with many other Americans—that our success in the counterinsurgency conflict would depend on a complete and intimate understanding by all ranks from top to bottom of the principles Thompson had articulated.

In 1964, I assumed command of Fleet Marine Force, Pacific, embracing all the Marines in the Pacific Ocean area. Following the experience of Thompson and based on what I had learned in the preceding two years, we set about orienting our training toward combat in a counterinsurgency environment. The training culminated in early 1965 in a major series of exercises called Silver Lance, patterned as closely as possible upon the emerging situation in Vietnam. All counterinsurgency issues were explored: fighting both large units and small bands of guerrillas; handling situations involving the local civilian population; supporting training and cooperating with the indigenous military; dealing with our own diplomatic representatives; and meeting the challenge of a privileged sanctuary, where a bordering, ostensibly neutral country is used as a base and a route of approach by the enemy. We added realism to the exercise by having Marines, carefully rehearsed for their roles, take the parts of friendly and hostile native forces as well as of our own political and diplomatic personnel.[3] Everyone, from the high command to the individual Marine, was tested, and we all learned from the experience.[4]

The exercise could not have been more timely. About a third of the Silver Lance forces—the air/ground 1st Marine Brigade—were at sea off the California coast when the decision was made to land at Danang. The brigade was turned westward immediately and directed to sail toward the anticipated battle. It was actually disembarked in Okinawa, but it ultimately ended up in Vietnam, as did all the other participants in the exercise. And the 3d Battalion 9th Marines from Okinawa, the first unit to be committed, actually war-gamed a landing at Danang only two weeks before the landing took place.

So the Marines, from colonels to privates, were mentally prepared and reasonably ready for a counterinsurgency conflict. However, it turned out that the mission of the initial force to land at Danang was greatly different from what they had been practicing. The unit was restricted to protecting the Danang air base from enemy incursion, nothing more. It was not permitted to "engage in day-to-day actions against the Vietcong," nor were the Marines allowed to leave the air base or to be involved directly with the local population—which is what counterinsurgency is all about. Soon the force was enlarged to include the whole of the 9th Marine Expeditionary Brigade of five thousand men, but it remained confined to the air base area, tied to what the senior U.S. command, "COMUSMACV,"* termed "protection of the Danang air base from enemy attack."

This was never going to work. We were not going to win any counterinsurgency battles sitting in foxholes around a runway, separated from the very people we wanted to protect. Furthermore, the air base was overlooked by hills to the west and northwest, giving the enemy a clear view of the field. On two sides, the airfield complex was cheek-by-jowl with the city of Danang, only a wire fence separating the base from two hundred thousand people—most of them suspicious of us, some of them hostile. Despite all this, General Nguyen Chan Thi, the Vietnamese commander of the area, termed the I Corps Tactical Zone, agreed with General Westmoreland. He did not want the Marines moving outside the airfield area either. Thi, an intense, mercurial personality, had had no experience with Americans. He

---

* "Commander, U.S. Military Advisory Command, Vietnam," commanded, since 1962, by General William C. Westmoreland, U.S. Army.

had, however, been involved with the French—not altogether favorably—and was determined, at the outset, not to allow the Americans to infringe his authority. Ultimately, Thi became totally confident in the Marines, willing to do just about anything they asked.

As Commanding General, Fleet Marine Force, Pacific, I was responsible for the training of all the Marines in the Pacific, for their equipment, their supply of Marine Corps items, and their readiness, but I had no authority whatever over their operational employment in Vietnam. That was General Westmoreland's business, and he answered to the commander of the Pacific Theater, Admiral U. S. Grant Sharp.

Nevertheless, I felt strongly that American lives, as well as many valuable aircraft, were going to be hazarded if we could not patrol the hills around the Danang field. Furthermore, I believed that we could do little to help the people if we were obliged to shun them. I went, with Brigadier General Frederick Karch, the Marine brigade commander, to remonstrate with Thi. Thi listened. After we were finished, he just said, patiently, "You are not ready." We repeatedly pleaded with him, and he relented slightly. By 20 April, 1965, the Marines were patrolling the hills about two miles west of the airfield and the countryside about four miles north of the field. I suspect, in both cases, that General Thi felt safe—there were few Vietcong in those areas but, as we were to learn, there were many not far distant.

These tiny moves into the hinterland turned out to be the first steps in a massive expansion responding to the siren calls of seeking more favorable terrain and engaging the enemy. The eight-square-mile enclave around the Danang airfield grew, in six months, to more than eight hundred square miles. Another enclave of some one hundred square miles was created fifty miles to the south at Chu Lai to accommodate construction of a second airstrip. A third enclave of some sixty square miles was established at Phu Bai, fifty miles north of Danang, at the direction of General Westmoreland, to protect a communications unit there. The creation and growth of the three enclaves brought a great opportunity to work among the native population, to seek out the Vietcong guerrillas in each area, and to bring a little stability to rich and populous areas, some of which had been under enemy control for a decade.

By mid-1965 the five thousand man force had grown to over eighteen thousand, and there was still a crying hunger for more Marines. This was so because the Marines' concept, from the start, involved fighting the Vietnam battle as a multipronged effort. They aimed to bring peace and security to the people in the highly populated coastal regions by conducting aggressive operations against the guerrillas and expanding the pacified areas as rapidly as they were totally secured. At the same time, they planned to train the local militia and to support the Vietnamese Armed Forces in their fight against the Vietcong. Finally, the Marines were determined to go after the larger organized units whenever they could be definitely located and fixed. They set about this balanced strategy with a will, showing persistence and no small degree of innovative genius.

The Marines' first experience of protecting the people began in May 1965. It was a challenging test of the lessons practiced earlier in the year in exercise Silver Lance. To secure the Danang air base from guerrilla attack from the northwest, it was necessary to cover the broad valley of the Cue De River. They learned quickly that Lc My, a village of about seven hundred people, comprising eight hamlets,* only six miles from the main airstrip, was truly enemy country. Two guerrilla platoons—about forty men—lived in the village, where they had constructed an extensive cave and tunnel system. They moved in and out at will, extorting the people's rice and money, coercing their youth to join the insurgency, and threatening the village officials. Because of the Vietcong oppression, Le My was sick unto death. There was little government, little agriculture, little commerce, no security, no public services, and no schools. The Vietnamese Army and regional troops had made a few feeble passes at chasing the Vietcong away, but the enemy retained control of the area, its resources, and its people. Further complicating the situation was the fact that some of the

---

* The Vietnamese hamlet is the equivalent of our small village. Their village equates to our township, their district to our county, and their province to our state.

active guerrillas had relatives in the village, from whom they received food, sanctuary, and information. Nevertheless, the people at large were despondent and terrified. Even the village chief spent many of his nights in Danang because of his fear of assassination or capture.

In early May, after every patrol in the area reported receiving sniper fire, the Marines decided to clean the guerrillas out of Le My. They launched a two-company operation and found they had undertaken a time-consuming and enervating job. The Vietcong reacted to the American threat strongly—by fire, ambush, and booby trap, giving the Marines a foretaste of the bitter antiguerrilla war that was to absorb them for the next six years.

Eventually, however, the insurgents were rooted out of their caves and tunnels, and killed, captured, or driven away. The people's confidence was slowly restored by the security provided by the Marine units as well as by local militia, which resurfaced as the Marine influence grew. By ministering to the villagers' health, by supporting them in construction projects, and by helping them to dig wells and reestablish schools and markets, the Marines brought the villagers a level of stability unseen in a decade. Concurrently, the Marines encouraged and assisted the local militia, training them, repairing their weapons, and helping them construct strong defensive positions around the village.*

The Marines tried to put into effect in the village of Le My exactly what they had practiced before coming to Vietnam. Although lacking in the polish that comes with experience, the effort turned out to be classic—actually a good pattern for their subsequent actions, in scores of other villages, to deliver the people from terror. Among other things, it illustrated that the pacification process demanded the combined efforts of both Americans and Vietnamese. To this end, Lieutenant General Lewis Walt, the senior Marine

---

* Le My, and its hundreds of successors, was quite different from President Ngo Dinh Diem's Strategic Hamlet program of 1962. In that program, a fortified hamlet was created in a Vietcong-dominated area. People were moved into it without regard for their personal wishes and were required to stay there except for organized and protected trips to and from the fields. They did not like it and it failed.

commander, created a "Joint Coordinating Council," which included representatives from all organizations involved with the pacification process.

I learned a lasting lesson at Le My. In late May 1965, I went there with Lieutenant Colonel David A. Clement, whose battalion had done the entire Le My project. We met the district (county) chief and the village chief, who showed us with much pride and gratitude the rejuvenation of the village—the whitewashed dispensary with two shy nurses wearing white; the one-room schoolhouse filled with serious-faced little children; the thriving marketplace; and, more seriously, the newly constructed outposts and security installations around the village perimeter. Neither of the two officials could speak English, but the district chief could speak French, and, amid all the smiles, bows, thanks, and congratulations, he said to me in a very sober way, "One thing. All of this has meaning only if you are going to stay. Are you going to stay?"

It was a hard question, but basic. The villagers could not risk giving us their trust if we were going to go off and leave them unprotected in the vain belief that the Vietcong, once driven off, would not come back. They had already had the experience of being encouraged and then abandoned by the French, and by their own Army, too. So I said, "These same Marines will not stay here, but others will never be far away, and your own militia will be here all the time." He made it clear that this was not exactly what he wanted to hear but it was better than nothing. It turned out to be good enough to encourage one hundred fifty people from two Vietcong-dominated hamlets some ten miles distant to leave their homes and their precious land and move to Le My just to be under the umbrella of American protection.

Le My had its ups and downs in the next five years—minor forays by guerrillas, assassination of one of its mayors—but the Vietcong never took over the area again. Le My was a microcosm of the entire war at this period, reflecting on a small scale the perspective of ten million rural Vietnamese in fourteen thousand hamlets. They always feared, and sometimes hated, the Vietcong for their extortion, taxation, brutality, and designs on the local youth. They wanted and welcomed our protection but were terrified at the prospect of getting it and then losing it. The nearer we were to them and the more thorough our efforts, the better the system worked. This painstaking, exhausting, and sometimes bloody process of bringing peace, prosperity, and health to a gradually expanding area came to be known as the "spreading ink blot" formula. In the effort to free and then protect the people, it should have been at the heart of the battle for freedom in Indochina. Many people applauded the idea, among them Army generals Maxwell Taylor and James Gavin. General Westmoreland told me, however, that while the ink blot idea seemed to be effective, we just didn't have time to do it that way. I suggested to him that we didn't have time to do it any other way; if we left the people to the enemy, glorious victories in the hinterland would be little more than blows in the air—and we would end up losing the war. But Defense Secretary Robert S. McNamara expressed the same view as Westmoreland to me in the winter of 1965—"A good idea," he said about the ink blot formula, "but too slow." I had told him in a letter dated 11 November 1965, "In the highly populous areas the battle ground is in the peoples' minds. We have to separate the enemy from the people, and clean up the area a bit at a time."

With the tiny experience of Le My to encourage them, the Marines moved assertively into more Le Mys, as well as on to other combatant efforts aimed at breaking the guerrillas' hold on the people. One such endeavor was called "County Fair." It began as a simple U.S.–Vietnamese program for rooting out Vietcong military and political cells from the villages. Under cover of darkness a Marine unit would surround a village believed to be infiltrated by Vietcong. Then a Vietnamese Army unit would enter the village, search for tunnels and caves, and flush out any hiding guerrillas. Concurrently, they would screen the residents for identity cards and take into custody any suspicious persons.

The idea was sound in principle and sometimes effective in execution. But often it went aground on either of two circumstances. First, the Vietnamese Army was never enthusiastic about working among the people, and they were not particularly good at it. Second, the Marines were sometimes anxious to do too much for the same people.

Some County Fairs were immensely complicated. While the Vietnamese Army troops were busy digging out guerrillas, there might be a Marine band concert in progress, a soup kitchen, a medical program, a dental program, a population census, some native entertainment, possibly a film, and even some political speeches—all going on at once. I never saw a County Fair where I did not wonder whether the villagers were absolutely sure of what we were doing. And I wondered how long it would take the Vietcong to percolate back after the Marines and Vietnamese Army had packed up and left.

A more effective project was called "Combined Action," a scheme which brought together a squad of Marines and a platoon of the Vietnamese Popular Forces. The Popular Forces were at the very bottom of the pecking order in the Vietnamese military. They were recruited from and served in their own hamlet and, as soldiers, they were pitiable. Poorly equipped, poorly trained, poorly led, and given only half the pay of the Vietnamese Army, they fought indifferently, if at all, and were notorious for their desertion rate. They were literally afraid of the dark; they were quite unwilling to fight at night when the Vietcong were at large. It is not remarkable that they inspired little confidence among the villagers.

My first experience with the Popular Forces was on a trip I made to Vietnam in 1962 with Defense Secretary McNamara. In a hamlet outside the town of Nha Trang, we saw a Popular Force unit of about twenty-five thin, grave-faced little men, drawn up as a sort of ceremonial honor guard. No two in the same uniform, armed with an assortment of battered rifles, carbines, and shotguns, they were monumentally unimpressive to look at. As we walked down the ragged front rank, McNamara pointed to one rifle and asked me, "Do you think those things will shoot?" I took one from a soldier, had trouble getting the bolt open and, when I did, could not see daylight through the gun barrel. The ammunition in the youngster's belt was green with corrosion.

When I told McNamara, he said, "We are going to have to do something about this. These may well be the most important military people in Vietnam. They have something real to fight for—their own hamlet, their own family."

And he was right. Unfortunately, little was done on their behalf between 1962 and 1965, when the Marines hit upon the possibilities inherent in combining the loyalty and local knowledge of the Popular Forces with our own professional skill. It is hard to say just where the idea for Combined Action originated, but Captains Paul R. Ek and John J. Mullen, Jr., and Major Cullen C. Zimmerman are prominently mentioned as the architects and Lieutenant General Lewis Walt, the overall Marine commander, lent his energetic support.

A Marine squad composed of carefully screened volunteers who already had some combat experience was given basic instruction in Vietnamese culture and customs and then combined with a Popular Forces platoon. The Marine squad leader—a sergeant or corporal—commanded the combined force in tactical operations, and the Popular Forces platoon leader was his operational assistant. The remaining Marines were distributed through the unit in subordinate leadership positions.

The initial effort, organized as a "Combined Action Company,"* involved four such units. In the summer of 1965, the 3d Battalion, 4th Marines, launched the program at Phu Bai. The combined platoons lived together in the hamlets. The Vietnamese taught the Marines the language, customs, and habits of the people and the local geography. The Marines conducted training in weapons and tactics. Together, they fought the Vietcong, gradually acquiring the respect and confidence of the villagers. Living conditions were humble—or less. One platoon I visited was living in two squalid native huts—dirt floor, no doors or windows, a blanket of flies. At the moment the Marines and Vietnamese were busy cooking, sharing their food, and chattering in a mixture of English and Vietnamese. With much pride, they were anxious to tell me that only the night before they had conducted a successful ambush outside the village, killing one Vietcong and capturing another—a triumph, considering that only weeks before the Popular Forces troops could

---

* The title, initially the "Joint Action Company," was changed from "Joint" to "Combined" to signify that the forces of more than one nation were involved.

not be induced to go forth at night. Together the two components were effective in often bloody operations against the Vietcong, bringing a measure of peace to localities that had not known it for years.

The Combined Action program spread quickly to all three of the Marine enclaves. By early 1966, there were nineteen Combined Action units; by the end of 1967, there were seventy-nine. All were engaged in offensive operations against the Vietcong to protect their own home village. As they fought their little engagements they were reminding us of the wisdom of the ancient Chinese military scholar Sun Tzu, to which Mao Tze-tung adhered, who declared that in an insurgent war the revolutionaries are the fish and the people are the medium in which they swim. If the medium is hospitable, you are likely to win; if inhospitable you are sure to lose. North Vietnamese General Vo Nguyen Giap had his own way of saying it, "Protracted war requires a whole ideological struggle among the people. Without the people we have no information. . . . They hide us, protect us, feed us and tend our wounded."[5]

The Vietcong had enjoyed a free ride in the Vietnamese hamlets because of the general incompetence of the Popular Forces and the consequent uncertainty of the people. The Combined Action idea was an effective answer to the problem, helping to free the people to act, speak, and live without fear. It was a multiplier, where the final product had combatant value many times the sum of its individual components. There were hundreds of skirmishes and many casualties, but two extraordinary statistics reveal that the unique organizational arrangement paid off: no village protected by a Combined Action unit was ever repossessed by the Vietcong; and 60 percent of the Marines serving the Combined Action units volunteered to stay on with their Marine and Vietnamese companions for an additional six months when they could have returned to the United States.

Senior Marine officers and those who had an interest in Marine Corps history knew that the Combined Action idea had been applied with success before—in Haiti (1915–34), in Nicaragua (1926–33) and, probably most effectively, in Santo Domingo (1916–22). There the Marines organized, trained, and directed a new national police force, the

Guardia National, later to become the Policia National. Formal training schools imbued the Policia rank and file with a sense of discipline. Under Marine leadership, the Policia exercised their new knowledge of weapons and tactics in hundreds of antiguerrilla patrols. But even more important, the Marines got to the heart of security in the Dominican villages by organizing, equipping, and training "Home Guard" units composed of residents who were willing to defend their own homes and families. Led by a Marine officer and including ten to fifteen Dominicans and two or three Marine enlisted men, these mixed groups successfully brought a measure of peace to their small communities. In Vietnam, half a century later, similar combined formations again validated the concept, proving that their effectiveness far exceeded what might have been expected from their small numbers.*

Even guerrillas have to eat, and the Vietcong had no fields of their own. They depended on the farmers for their sustenance, about 1½ pounds of rice per man per day. At harvest time it was their habit to come down to the coastal plain and extort food from the people who had put in six hard months planting, cultivating, harvesting, and collecting the grain. The Vietcong extortion (called rice taxation) not only drove up the price of rice but, for many poor peasants, dangerously narrowed the margin between survival and starvation, a fact that did not seem to dissuade the guerrillas at all.

Beginning with the autumn rice crop of 1965, the Marines in the Danang and Chu Lai areas moved to free the peasants

* Marine Corps experience in stabilizing governments and combatting guerrilla forces was distilled in lecture form at the Marine Corps Schools in Quantico, Virginia, beginning in 1920. Eventually, the lectures were compiled in a book, *Small Wars Manual, 1930,* which after revision, was adopted as an official publication in 1940—a fifteen-chapter compendium of everything the Corps had learned in its Caribbean experience. Although now largely outdated because of advanced technology, *Small Wars Manual,* like similar prospective writings in the amphibious and helicopter fields, shows the Marines' determination always to record what they have learned and, just incidentally, to make it available to all who want to use it.

from the Vietcong rice tax collector. Using intelligence supplied by the villagers themselves, they launched attacks against Vietcong units massing to commence their rice-collecting operations. The Marines also deployed into the fields to protect the harvesters and then helped transport the rice to central storage areas.

The formula, called Golden Fleece, was a success, assembling in the first harvest season some 870,000 pounds of rice for local use that in other years would have been vulnerable to Vietcong seizure. Put in other terms, the Marines' offensive actions disrupted Vietcong units and, in addition, kept sufficient rice out of the enemy's hands to supply an estimated thirty-five hundred guerrillas for an entire growing season. Subsistence, always a serious problem for the Vietcong, became a crisis.

Another step in winning the battle among the people was to prepare the individual Marine for the contacts he would have with the local residents as he moved about in the densely populated areas. We set about it in a methodical manner, developing a *Unit Leader's Personal Response Handbook*. The idea began back in Exercise Silver Lance at Camp Pendleton in early 1965. Its principal architects were three chaplains—John Craven of my staff, Robert Mole, and Richard McGonigle. Craven persuaded me, in preparing for Silver Lance, that we would never be effective in counterinsurgency unless our troops had not only an understanding of but a respect for the local people, their habits, and customs. The idea grew slowly, as both commanders and troops had to be convinced of its importance. The *Handbook* took a practical, case-example approach, explaining to Marines the simple rights and wrongs of dealing with the shy and sensitive Vietnamese people. It became a standard weapon in our arsenal to deal with the complex problem.

The final prong of the Marines' multipronged strategy was to confront enemy units whenever they could be located. The first such large operation, Starlite in late 1965, was marked by two noteworthy characteristics. First, it was based on good intelligence. Intercepted Vietcong communications plus the report of a Vietcong deserter pinpointed an enemy regiment. There was little doubt what the target was or where it was, which was often not the case as the war wore on. Second, Starlite was conducted under conditions of complete secrecy. It was one of the few large operations planned and launched without the knowledge of the Vietnamese Army. Because of these two factors, the enemy force, holed up on the Batangan Peninsula, twelve miles south of the Marine Chu Lai enclave, was taken by surprise.

The Marine approach to the battle—their planning, tactics, and task organization—exhibited the very best of their combatant stock in trade. Once the intelligence was in hand they did not hesitate. Stripping the defenses of the Chu Lai base and securing the permission of commander-in-chief, Pacific, to use a carrier-based Marine battalion from the U.S. 7th Fleet, they planned in two furious days a combined amphibious and helicopter-borne operation. Heavily supported by Marine fighter and attack aircraft from Danang, as well as by naval gunfire from three ships of the 7th Fleet and by Marine heavy artillery at Chu Lai, the Marine force struck the 1st Vietcong Regiment from three sides. In two days of bitter hedgerow and bunker fighting, the Marines killed 614 of the enemy, rendering the 1st VC Regiment ineffective for six months.

The successful operation showed the power and flexibility that fixed wing and helicopter air support gives to well-trained ground forces. Indeed, a major factor in the procession of Marine ground operations which followed against the growing North Vietnamese strength, from Quang Ngai province in Central South Vietnam to the Demilitarized Zone, was the immense power of the Marine aviation component and the extraordinary tactical momentum and flexibility with which it endowed our ground operations. Nobody else in Vietnam had it, and it was the justified envy of others.

The great combatant quality that Marine aviation brought to Vietnam was adaptability. They came—fixed-wing and helicopters—prepared to cope with the demands of the operational environment and thus enjoyed a great advantage over other aviation formations. Apart from the professionalism of pilots and crews, they were truly organized and equipped as expeditionary forces. Their ability to supply and maintain themselves in the field and their expeditionary hardware—bulk fuel systems, mobile arresting gear, air-transportable airfield operations systems, and unique aluminum planking "Short Airfield for Tactical Support" (SATS)—all gave Marine aviation formations an enviable flexibility.

SATS was not taken seriously by anyone but the Marines until it was decided that a second field was needed to supplement the overworked field at Danang. At a meeting in Honolulu in late April 1966, attended by the secretary of state, the secretary of defense, the U.S. ambassador to Vietnam, and the principal military commanders, we discussed how long it would take to build a field at Chu Lai, some fifty-five miles south of Danang. The conservative figure for a reinforced concrete installation was eleven months. I stated that the Marines already had the ability to construct an articulated aluminum runway and taxiway in far less time and that we already had the material available in the Far East.

The secretary of defense, Robert McNamara, had heard of the aluminum field concept but was not acquainted with its characteristics. He asked questions concerning its components and design and then asked how long it would take to build such a field at Chu Lai. In Marine Corps Schools problems in Quantico we had been talking of building a three thousand-foot strip and essential taxiways in five days. In this case we were considering an eight thousand-foot installation, so I said twenty-five days, thinking that would give us an adequate cushion. McNamara said, "Go ahead. Keep me informed of how you are doing." A few minutes later, Admiral Sharp (CINCPAC) said to me, "You know your neck is out a mile." Which turned out to be true.

Problems with tropical summer heat, where tractor operators could work only in thirty-minute shifts; equipment breakdowns caused by the fine sand; and difficulty in stabilizing the sand subgrade ate up the days all too quickly. Even so, on the twenty-fifth day, we had a four thousand-foot strip from which four 1st Marine Aircraft Wing planes were able to fly eight bombing sorties before sundown. I asked Admiral Sharp to send a message to the secretary of defense, "Chu Lai Expeditionary Airfield operational this date." A few days later I received a longhand note from

McNamara, "Brute: I thought you were dreaming. Nice going."

Well and good. The real significance of this small incident, however, is that it illustrates that the air Marine, like his ground counterpart, had been thinking in terms of the realities of combat, even in times of peace.

All together, the first Marines in Vietnam created an innovative strategy that was well attuned to the problems. It recognized that the people themselves were both the battlefield and the objective and that the usual tactical objectives —hills, bridges, rivers—meant little and the usual battlefield statistics—enemy killed and wounded—meant even less.

Between 1962 and 1968, I went to Vietnam fifty-four times for periods of five to twenty days. I saw a lot of the country, from the DMZ in the north to the Ca Mau Peninsula in the south. And I saw a lot of the people, from French-speaking dilettantes in Saigon to Moslems at Phan Rang on the seacoast to Montagnards in the hills near the Laos border. As far back as 1963, I went on operations with the Vietnamese Army and the Vietnamese Marines and saw how easily sizable enemy forces could melt into a countryside willing to support, or at least to tolerate, them. Everything I saw kept bringing me back to the basic proposition that the war could only be won when the people were protected. If the people were for you, you would triumph in the end. If they were against you, the war would bleed you dry and you would be defeated.

Sound and logical as it appeared, the Marines' strategy had two defects: General Westmoreland did not agree with it; and it was unable to address the reality that the enemy enjoyed a privileged sanctuary in the ports of North Vietnam and in Laos, through which a growing cascade of deadly munitions was flowing.

CHAPTER 13

A Conflict of Strategies

In June 1966 the Marines' multiple approach, hardly begun, was altered by a new philosophy announced by General Westmoreland. His strategy was to turn over the liberation and protection of the heavily populated coastal regions to the Vietnamese and to launch American units into the hinterland to seek out and destroy the larger enemy forces. As he described it later, he proposed to "... forget about the enclaves and take the war to the enemy."[1]

General Westmoreland knew that the North Vietnamese regular units were moving southward down the Ho Chi Minh Trail in growing numbers. They were carrying increasingly sophisticated equipment through Laos, a privileged sanctuary, and then into the central provinces of South Vietnam. He had a reasonable apprehension that their purpose was to drive to the seacoast and cut the country in two. His thinking, generally shared in Washington, was that under these circumstances the North Vietnamese regular forces, with their Soviet artillery, rockets, and mortars, were too much for the Vietnamese Army. The correct action, as they saw it, was to send large U.S. units into the backcountry to face the North Vietnamese formations—in other words, to pit our manpower against theirs. Wiping out the guerrillas and giving the people day-to-day protection would be left to the Vietnamese military, who really had little stomach for the task.

This approach worried a lot of people. Marine Commandant General Wallace M. Greene, for example, believed that the concept was defective in its "failure to make the population secure."[2] Much later, an American observer illuminated the weakness of Westmoreland's strategy: "Force without reform, finally fails."[3]

It became plain that the United States faced a problem that had three distinct parts: one part concerned the geography of the country; another the movement of material on the enemy's side; and, the third, the political implications of any move to deal with the first two elements. Geographically, it was significant that 80 percent of the people in South Vietnam lived in 10 percent of the country, within a few miles of the seacoast. These heavily populated areas—as many as one thousand persons per square mile—are where the rice, salt, and fish are. Indeed, fully 70 percent of the people outside the cities were involved in raising rice. Rice culture requires land and whoever could guarantee the peasants their land—the Vietnamese government, the Vietcong, or the North Vietnamese—would have their loyalty. Vietnamese President Ngo Dinh Diem, who had been assassinated in 1963, had recognized this fact and had instituted a policy of modest land redistribution to put more of the countryside in the hands of the peasants. By the early 1960s, however, it was less a matter of ownership than of protection, and the Vietnamese Army was not enthusiastic about providing the protection the people required.

Outside the rich coastal plain, South Vietnam is generally unproductive, especially in the heavily forested, inhospitable western half, where mountains rise to altitudes of seven thousand feet. There the population is only two people per square mile, and the mountain tribesmen want nothing more than to be left alone. They had little loyalty to the Vietnamese government and no loyalty whatever to the Vietcong or North Vietnamese. Any North Vietnamese forces based in these mountains would either have to be provided food from outside South Vietnam or they would have to come down to the coastal lowlands and take their food away from the rice-growing peasants—or require the Vietcong guerrillas to take it for them.

The North Vietnamese units had to bring all combat material with them—weapons, gasoline, ammunition, medical supplies—from North Vietnam, perhaps four hundred miles. But, beyond that, the critical hardware of war—artillery, antiaircraft, mortars, rockets, radios, transport—had to come from sources outside North Vietnam, a little from Red China by rail, but primarily in ships from the Soviet Union and Bloc countries. The North Vietnamese could not produce sophisticated arms themselves.

If these indispensable warlike things could be prevented from entering North Vietnam, then their fighting forces in the south would soon begin to suffer. The only way to stifle the importation of weapons, however, was to bomb and mine the North Vietnamese ports and to destroy their key airfields. Of course, such action was not without risk. It could introduce a political problem—the possible effect on relations with the Soviet Union of overt American military operations against the North Vietnam ports and logistic centers where Soviet ships or aircraft might be found.

Our national policy assumed that all-out American air and sea operations against the North Vietnam ports, airfields, and transportation systems would risk galvanizing the Russians—and perhaps the Chinese, too—into participation in the conflict. The flow of sophisticated material, so the rationale went, must therefore be dealt with primarily in South Vietnam, with a limited and carefully controlled aerial counterpoint against communication routes in North Vietnam. The ports, harbors, and docks would be left untouched. It was also decided that Americans would take the lead in the ground campaign against the large North Vietnamese units, with the South Vietnamese assigned the role of destroying the guerrillas and providing local security.

As a consequence of this fundamental decision, the Marines were urged in 1965–66 to launch out from their enclaves, to seek out and bring to battle the North Vietnamese regular units that were moving into the northern provinces of South Vietnam in growing strength. Implicitly, because of our limited personnel strength, this so-called search and destroy concept would have to take priority over the spreading ink blot of pacification and stabilization.

This represented a divergence in strategic concept, and it was not just between the Marines and General Westmoreland's Military Advisory Command (MACV). Others —General Maxwell Taylor and General James Gavin, for example—had expressed views similar to those held by the Marines. Their idea was to take advantage of a base on the seacoast, exploit our supporting arms, and bring peace and security to an ever-growing number of people—the spreading ink blot. Marine Commandant Greene summarized this philosophy clearly, pointing out that "I Corps is ideally situated geographically to undertake security operations from the sea against key points on the coast."[4]

The Marines' view of how to fight the war, shared by everyone from General Greene on down, could be articulated in three convergent declarations:

(1) Put the primary emphasis on pacifying the highly populated South Vietnamese coastal plain. In conjunction with South Vietnamese forces, protect the people from the guerrillas so that they will not be forced to provide the enemy with rice, intelligence, and sanctuary. Expand the pacified areas as rapidly as possible, but only as fast as they are secure, tranquil, and effectively policed by Vietnamese military and paramilitary forces.

(2) Degrade the North Vietnamese ability to fight by cutting off their military substance before it ever leaves the North Vietnam ports of entry.

(3) In coordination with South Vietnamese forces, move out of our protected and sanitized areas when a clear opportunity exists to engage the VC Main Force or North Vietnamese units on terms favorable to ourselves.

The MACV concept would make the third point the primary undertaking, even while deemphasizing the need for clearly favorable conditions before engaging the enemy. General Westmoreland was determined to pursue the enemy relentlessly, bring him to battle, and destroy him, a unit at a time. He placed constant urging on the Marine commander, Lieutenant General Lewis Walt, to "get out of the enclaves" and go after the enemy in the hinterland. Furthermore, there was little pressure—and I could never understand why—to organize a campaign to stop the flow of supplies through the port of Haiphong.

The Marines saw the MACV idea as flawed. It would leave the population and the wealth of the land largely uncovered, it would engage the enemy in the hinterland where circumstances favored him, and it would generate very large U.S. manpower requirements. And something else—the Americans' conduct of search-and-destroy operations would be hampered by the fact that, more often than not, the enemy would know in advance what we were going to do. This was exhibited to be true time and again. Almost all of the American ground operations were known to the Vietnamese Army, at least in some degree, before being launched. Because North Vietnamese or Vietcong agents had infiltrated the Vietnamese Army, there was always a possibility that the enemy would be forewarned. This was certainly true of Vietnamese Army operations, many of which were obviously compromised.

I saw what was happening as wasteful of American lives, promising a protracted strength-sapping battle with small likelihood of a successful outcome. I made my views known to General Westmoreland, but, for reasons of his own, he did not concur. So I did what I could. I put my convictions on paper in a seventeen-page strategic appraisal of the situation in Vietnam and set about getting it to people who could take some effective action.

The appraisal began by condemning the current strategy, characterizing it as aiming to do no more than "attrit the enemy to a degree which makes him incapable of prosecuting the war, or unwilling to pay the cost of so doing. . . . If this is indeed the basis for our strategy, it has to be regarded as inadequate . . ."[5]

The study continued with an evaluation of the critical importance of loyalty and support of the people, ". . . it is these simple, provincial people who are the battlefield on which the war must be fought. Their provincialism is exploited by the VC at every turn. Not enough is being done to give the people a feel for a strong central government." I wrote, "A key point is this: the conflict between the North Vietnamese/hard core Vietcong, on the one hand, and the

U.S. on the other, could move to another plane to-day and we would not have won the war. On the other hand, if the subversion and guerrilla efforts were to disappear, the war would soon collapse, as the enemy would be denied food, sanctuary and intelligence."

I also included some sobering statistics on attrition. Calculating it at the then-current rate, about 2.5 enemy killed for one American, it would "cost something like 175,000 lives to reduce the enemy manpower pool by a modest 20 percent." An altogether unacceptable prospect, yet it fit North Vietnamese General Vo Nguyen Giap's own prediction, "It will be . . . a protracted war of attrition."[6] And war of attrition it turned out to be. At its end, in 1972, we had managed to reduce the enemy manpower pool by perhaps 25 percent at a cost of over 220,000 U.S. and South Vietnamese dead. Of these, 59,000 were Americans; 59,000 coffins over which American families grieved without knowing exactly how or why it happened.

The study concluded with four recommendations:

- "Shift the thrust of our effort to the task of delivering the people from guerrilla oppression, and to protecting them thereafter; meanwhile seeking out and attacking the main force elements when the odds can be made overwhelmingly in our favor."
- "Address our attritional efforts primarily to the source of North Vietnamese material introduction, fabrication and distribution;—destroy the port areas, mine the ports, destroy the rail lines, destroy power, fuel and heavy industry . . ."
- "Put the full weight of our effort into bringing all applicable resources—U.S. and Vietnamese—into the pacification process. . . . Increase the level of medical assistance. . . . Increase the level of Popular Forces training. . . . Direct the conduct of comprehensive military civic action programs."
- "Press the Vietnamese Government to move immediately into a major land reform program. . . ."

I took the completed appraisal to Admiral Sharp, commander-in-chief, Pacific. He liked it, and I asked his permission to pass it on to Marine Commandant Greene in Washington. General Greene liked it, too, and encouraged me to show it to Defense Secretary McNamara, with whom I had had extensive contact during the 1962–64 period, when I served in the Joint Staff as the focal point for the military counterinsurgency effort.* My relationship with McNamara had been good, and he saw me immediately. I gave him the study and explained its content in detail.

McNamara made only brief comment. He rationalized his own alternative of a slowly intensifying air campaign, "the tightening screw," he called it, designed to persuade the North Vietnamese that they could not win. He suggested, "Why don't you talk to Governor Harriman?" Averill Harriman, then serving as assistant secretary of state for Far Eastern Affairs, agreed to see me. We had lunch at his Georgetown house, just the two of us.

Over the soup, I spoke of the ineffectiveness of the air campaign as it was being waged and of the impressive quantities of artillery, rockets, mortars, and antiaircraft guns pouring down the Ho Chi Minh Trail. Finally I got to the explicit proposal for action—"destroy the port areas, mine the ports, destroy the rail lines, destroy power, fuel and heavy industry." At that point Harriman stopped me. His forehead wrinkled, his heavy eyebrows bristled. Waving his soup spoon in my direction, he demanded, "Do you want a war with the Soviet Union or the Chinese?" I replied that I did not, that I was sure the Russians were not about to start a war with the United States over a fight in Indochina, and that, if put to the test, the North Vietnamese would probably prefer having Americans in their country to Chinese, whom they hate.[7]

Harriman shook his head; he did not agree. Mining the harbor at Haiphong, he said, would probably bring on hostilities with the Soviets. Conversation flagged and the luncheon moved quickly to a cool conclusion. It was plain he had little enthusiasm for attacking the ports and logistic

---

* My title was "special assistant for counterinsurgency and special activities." The "special activities" part meant anything that the JCS chairman, the secretary of defense or, on occasion, the president, wanted me to do.

bases in North Vietnam, and I winced when I thought about the kind of advice he was giving President Johnson and Secretary of State Rusk.

I have not recited this incident of the strategic estimate to illuminate any prescience on my own part or even on the part of Commandant Greene, General Walt, or the many other Marines who believed as I did. Rather, my purpose is to bring to the surface two qualities that the Marines have always possessed in abundance, two indispensable qualities that our government failed to exhibit in the Vietnam crisis: courage and flexibility. As Governor Harriman made clear —and as our subsequent national conduct verified—we did not have the Washington-level courage to take the war directly to the North Vietnamese ports where every weapon, every bullet, truck, and gallon of fuel that was prevented from entering the country would ultimately contribute to the success of our arms and the preservation of our lives in South Vietnam. I believed then, and still do, that mining Haiphong harbor would have generated Soviet protests but that they would have done nothing more—and the indispensable pipeline to North Vietnam would have been interrupted.

For the next five years nothing happened to alter this appraisal. Until that moment in 1970 when President Nixon ordered the mining of Haiphong harbor and intensified attacks on logistic installations—by which time it was far too late—we were fighting the war the wrong way. A sort of one-sided Marquis of Queensberry situation prevailed, where we voluntarily focused our operations on the geography called South Vietnam while the enemy was free to use neutral Laos, the 17th Parallel Demilitarized Zone, and the material support of their Soviet and Chinese allies. Despite our aerial interdiction of communication routes, four thousand artillery pieces, twenty-five thousand heavy rockets, eight thousand antiaircraft guns, six thousand trucks, a hundred tanks—these and the other sinews of modern war were able to find their way into North Vietnam and into battle in South Vietnam, and their effect was decisive.

The Marines never gave up on their multipronged concept for victory. To the very end, and within the limits of the forces available, they strove to protect and emancipate the people. They never ceased pleading for decisive action against the North Vietnam port and logistic system. And they went into the hinterland after the large enemy units—far more than they really wanted to—but in response to the strong pressures from MACV Headquarters.

This last challenge greatly drained the Marines, as it did the other U.S. and South Vietnamese forces. As Soviet supplies and equipment continued to flow into the ports of Haiphong and Vinh, the North Vietnamese units became more effective and more formidable. More of their operating forces could be supported in the South,* which, in turn, generated a demand for even greater numbers of U.S. troops to pursue General Westmoreland's search-and-destroy strategy. Those battles were fought too often on the enemy's terms, where close-quarters combat in the fog-shrouded hills, forests, and vine-thick jungles, with which he was familiar, stretched our logistic system and diminished the effectiveness of U.S. supporting arms, particularly air. Although we claimed a statistical victory in almost every battle, by our own calculations we were killing only about two and a half North Vietnamese for each U.S. fighting man who lost his life. Under those terms the attritional battle had to be more costly than we could prudently endure. Obviously, we had become involved in a self-punishing, self-defeating cycle brought on by a faulty attritional strategy. Thus, our self-declared victories in the search-and-destroy operations were not relevant to the total outcome of the war. Things were bad and bound to get worse unless our strategy was altered.

On one of my visits to Washington immediately after a Vietnam trip in mid-1966, the commandant arranged for me to see President Johnson. His first question was, "What is it going to take to win?"

I spoke of the need for improvements in the quality of the South Vietnamese government and for acceleration in the training of South Vietnamese forces. But, most of all, I told him we faced a self-defeating attritional cycle involving engagement with large and increasingly sophisticated North

---

* During the first six months of 1966 at least 50,000 additional North Vietnamese were deployed in the South.

Vietnamese units. We had to stop the flow of war materials to those forces. The president asked if I were implying that the air campaign against communication routes in North Vietnam was ineffective, noting that it amounted to as many as four hundred to five hundred sorties a day. That was what I meant, I said, that for the most part we were attacking the wrong targets. I told him that the only real answer was to stop the supplies, not when they were dispersed in the North Vietnam road system or when they got to the Ho Chi Minh Trail in Laos, but before they ever crossed the dock in Haiphong. Then I voiced the critical words, urging that we "mine the ports, destroy the Haiphong dock area."

That was it. As soon as he heard me speak of mining and unrestrained bombing of the ports, Mr. Johnson got to his feet, put his arm around my shoulder, and propelled me firmly toward the door. It was plain to me then that the Washington civilian leadership was taking counsel with its fears. They were willing to spend $30 billion a year on the Vietnam enterprise but they were unwilling to accept the timeless philosophy of John Paul Jones: "It seems to be a truth, inflexible and inexorable, that he who will not risk cannot win."

That was the last time I saw Mr. Johnson. A month or so later I read a speech that he made to the Tennessee legislature. He described our strategy, among other things, as aiming "to limit the flow or substantially increase the cost of infiltrating men and supplies into South Vietnam." Here, I realized, was a losing strategy.

Under the considerable pressure from MACV Headquarters, and at the expense of their efforts among the people, the Marines gave a good account of themselves in bringing to battle the Vietcong Main Force units and the North Vietnamese formations which, by mid-1966, were appearing in regimental and even division size. There was a general sentiment, however, in both Saigon and in Washington, that the Marines were wedded to their enclaves. The common talk was that they were absorbed in caring for the people and in training the native militia, and preferred to leave the unhappy task of going after the large enemy units to others.

Twice during the summer of 1966, by Defense Secretary

McNamara in May and by Navy Secretary Nitze in July, I was questioned directly as to why the Marines were not doing their share in meeting and defeating the major North Vietnamese forces. I responded to them both in writing, in the hope that what the Marines were trying to do would percolate into the Washington sensibility. To McNamara I said,

In the past there seems to have been some question as to the matter of the intensity [of the Marine operations against the large units] although I am hard put to perceive why. Last year they conducted 88 air/ground team operations of battalion and larger size, aggregating 301 battalion days of operation. Every one involved helicopter envelopment and 14 of them involved an amphibious attack too. They were calculated to strike the enemy where the likelihood of doing him substantial hurt was great, not just to trade manpower with him. . . . The Marines are not just addressing one part of the problem, they are covering all the bases. They are not bemused with handing out soap or bushwhacking guerrillas at the expense of attacking the Main Force units. They are treating the whole patient.[8]

To Nitze I said,

The Marines, comprising 21 percent of U.S. and Free World ground forces troops in Vietnam have, since 1 January 1966, participated in 39 percent of all U.S. battalion or larger operations, in 35 percent of all major operations and have been responsible for 28 percent of the total enemy killed in those operations. So, in the precise area where Marines are sometimes alleged not to be carrying their share, they have exceeded the contribution which might have been expected of them.[9]

Although the pursuit of large enemy formations was not the Marines' preferred formula for winning, they continued to seek them out and attack them with skill and aggressiveness throughout the 10,000 square miles of their tactical zone. Their air/ground team performed effectively and certainly visited destruction and confusion on the enemy. But, victories notwithstanding, we were pitting American bodies against North Vietnamese bodies in a backcountry war of attrition, while the enemy was free to make political speeches in the hamlets and villages of the populous coastal littoral.

Some false comfort was taken in the statistics deriving from the air campaign in North Vietnam. Reported destroyed in 1966 were the following: eighty-two hundred buildings; forty-eight hundred motor vehicles; eighteen hundred railroad cars; eighty-nine hundred boats and barges; and twenty-two bridges. The impressive statistics lost their impact when measured against what was actually going on in South Vietnam. There, as everyone had to agree, more and more North Vietnamese units were turning up, equipped with more, bigger, and better weapons.[10]

The truth was that, even at considerable hazard to their lives, our pilots were not allowed to attack the targets that really counted. General William W. Momyer, commander of the 7th Air Force, put it bluntly in 1966: "Our air operations are nowhere near enough. With the current limitations on targets North Vietnamese air defense will become more effective and our losses will grow." And, in January 1967, I told Defense Secretary McNamara that what was needed was "constant bombardment from the sea of every sensitive point on the enemy communications, transportation and air defense system within naval gun range; greatly increased . . . aerial destruction of North Vietnamese transportation, military logistic suport and power resources."[11]

However valiant, however skillful were the Army and Marine operations against the large formations, however impressive were the tonnages of bombs dropped on North Vietnamese communication systems or on the Ho Chi Minh Trail, it was plain that the strategy was futile—analogous to pushing a wet noodle. In the end, in terms of doing what we came to Vietnam to do, the costly, blood-sapping, grinding battles were blows in the air.

The worst of them all was Khe Sanh. There, the Marine air/ground team, with much help from the Air Force and the Navy's 7th Fleet, caused as many as ten thousand enemy casualties* and destroyed large quantities of enemy materiel. But when it was over nothing had changed— nothing.

---

* As estimated in Joint Chiefs of Staff Fact Sheet on Khe Sanh, 26 April 1968.

CHAPTER 14

The Dienbienphu That Wasn't

Khe Sanh is in the far northwestern corner of South Vietnam, four miles from Laos, twelve miles south of the Demilitarized Zone, a way point on Route Coloniale No. 9, the winding road that joins the Vietnam coast with Savannakhet in Laos. I first heard of Khe Sanh when I was in China in 1937. My battalion commander, Major H. N. Stent, went to Indochina to hunt tiger. He returned with stories of his experience hunting in a beautiful valley near a place called Khe Sanh, not far from the city of Hue. He spoke of the plantains, the elephants, the forests full of game, the waterfalls, the gentle people who lived there, and he brought me pictures, which I still have.

My next acquaintance with Khe Sanh was in the autumn of 1964, when General Westmoreland decided to establish a communications station of about thirty Marine specialists at a place called Tiger Tooth Mountain near the point where South Vietnam, North Vietnam, and Laos come together. When I studied the area on the map, it seemed a pretty remote place to hang a few Marine communicators out to dry, so I took the opportunity to inspect it. It turned out to be an impressively wild area, beautiful in its rugged simplicity—and definitely remote. Precipitous, dark green mountains are covered with tangled liana, boulders, bushes, and thorn trees; a little coffee grows in the low ground, as does a lot of four-foot-high elephant grass and bamboo; there are a few small villages. In the middle, rising out of the valley, is the flat Khe Sanh plateau, some three hundred feet above sea level, about a mile in length and a half-mile wide. It was there, in 1949, that the French had established a fifteen hundred-foot dirt airstrip and an outpost which was to be the setting for our own climactic battle nineteen years later.

Khe Sanh is about forty miles from the seacoast. At the time of the American involvement, it was accessible over a bad road that included twelve bridges. It was vulnerable to interdiction at many points. The valley is characterized by some of the most miserable weather in all of Vietnam. Eighty inches of annual rainfall plus fog and low clouds make visibility a major problem for at least six months of the year, affecting tactical observation and limiting both artillery and air operations. By its nature, the Khe Sanh plateau is a hard place to defend. Hills, rising to altitudes of three thousand feet, look down on the airstrip just as the top-row seats in a football stadium look down on the playing field.

Tiger Tooth Mountain, it turned out, was actually Hill 950, one of those peaks overlooking the Khe Sanh plateau from the north and northwest. The area was so wild and isolated that I was reluctant to put the small group of Marine communicators out there without protection. So I reinforced the communications unit with a platoon of Marine infantry from the 3d Marine Division in Okinawa. This was the first organized U.S. infantry unit to be deployed to Vietnam—six months before President Johnson decided to commit our ground forces to the conflict.

In 1964, at about the time I reconnoitered the area, General Westmoreland established an Army Special Forces detachment in the old French redoubt near the Khe Sanh airstrip. Working with the native mountain tribesmen, they kept an alert eye on North Vietnamese infiltration down the Ho Chi Minh Trail from North Vietnam into Laos. In early 1966, Westmoreland urged Lieutenant General Walt, commander of the III Marine Amphibious Force,* to conduct a search-and-destroy operation in the Khe Sanh vicinity based on a report from the Special Forces garrison that North Vietnamese forces were closing in on the area. Accordingly, on 17 April, a reinforced Marine battalion, the 1st Battalion, 1st Marines, was flown into the existing airstrip and spent a week scouring an area some 6 miles in radius. The Marines found nothing. Not a shot was fired. After ten days, instead of flying out, they elected to march all the way back to their base near the coast, some forty miles distant. This they did, without incident, the first major unit to traverse that route on foot since the French withdrawal in 1954.

The first Marine undertaking at Khe Sanh is noted here to show the considerable waste of manpower entailed in searching around in the wilderness for North Vietnamese formations. There were many other less costly ways to gather intelligence on their whereabouts. Electronic, aerial, photographic, seismic, and accoustic surveillance means were available, as well as clandestine operations—eyeball observation—by Vietnamese and hill people who already knew the area.

General Westmoreland felt differently on the matter of information-gathering. On one occasion he said, "I had to have more intelligence on what was going on up north and there was no better way to get it than by sending in reconnaissance elements in force."[1] That is to say, risk exposing large U.S. units to ambush in exchange for information obtainable in less costly ways.

Later that same year, in the autumn of 1966, General Westmoreland again pressured the Marines to establish a presence in the Khe Sanh area, this time a reinforced battalion, for a month. The thought of committing a major force of Marines to the Khe Sanh plateau for a protracted time disturbed me as much as it did the Marine command-

---

* The overall Marine operational command in Vietnam. Initially, it was to be named "III Marine Expeditionary Force" but the expression "Expeditionary Force" was regarded as too reminiscent of the title of the French command in the earlier Indochina war, something generally offensive to the Vietnamese.

ers who were directly involved. While I was not concerned that the enemy would defeat the Marines, I did believe that the undertaking would divert valuable resources from more productive pursuits.

As noted earlier, my responsibilities did not extend to the operational employment of the Marine forces in Vietnam—that was General Westmoreland's business. Even so, I never hesitated to give him my thoughts concerning his tactical use of Marines. He was always kind enough to hear me out. In this case, we met at the Chu Lai airfield and conferred aboard his aircraft. I offered him the view that protracted occupation of the Khe Sanh plateau would be a demanding affair and that one battalion would not be adequate to do the job. The airstrip could not be defended by forces deployed only around the strip itself. Occupation of at least five key hills—located between two and four miles to the north and west—would be necessary. This was the job for at least another battalion. The task of holding the hills, even in the face of limited resistance, would require a major helicopter commitment because the troops could not possibly be supported wholly on foot. I further suggested to Westmoreland that holding Khe Sanh would not deter the North Vietnamese forces from infiltrating southward. They would just continue down the Ho Chi Minh Trail in Laos and enter South Vietnam at other points farther south. They had already proven that they could make their way without roads such as Route 9. Nor would a large presence at Khe Sanh add greatly to our intelligence of enemy movements. There were U.S. Army Special Forces, with several hundred irregular native scouts, doing a competent job in the area; they already knew there was more activity on the Ho Chi Minh Trail than we could handle—some five hundred trucks a day. I reminded General Westmoreland that every Marine tied to the Khe Sanh area would be one less involved in pacification of the critical coastal area where 95 percent of the people lived. Finally, if his purpose was attrition, we already had overwhelming evidence that such a strategy offered little prospect of success.

Westmoreland saw it all quite differently. To him, holding Khe Sanh was critical to monitoring enemy north-south movement, an effective block to enemy use of Route 9, a source of good intelligence, a western anchor to U.S. defense of the Demilitarized Zone, and a strategic jumping-off place should his dream of an expedition into Laos to cut the Ho Chi Minh Trail ever be realized. And he said that he saw Khe Sanh as offering an excellent opportunity to tie down and destroy thousands of enemy soldiers.

Of all these reasons, I was sure that the last was the dominant one in Westmoreland's mind, representing his own conception of how to defeat the large North Vietnamese forces. As he saw it, firepower was the classic answer—locate the enemy formations, fix them, then back off and beat them to death with air and artillery. Ironically, this same attritional strategy impelled General Henri Navarre to establish the French base at Dienbienphu. I am reminded of the Marechal de Saxe who said, "In default of knowing what should be done, they do what they know."[2] Despite our lack of success in the manpower attrition game thus far, it was clear to me that attrition was what he had in mind and further that his decision in this case was firm. Our discussion got nowhere. Although the Marine commanders involved were dead set against it, the Marines went to Khe Sanh.

They went to Khe Sanh over the next year; first one, then two, then three, and, finally, four battalions, reinforced with forty-one light and medium artillery pieces, direct-fire weapons, and six tanks. The force ultimately reached six thousand.

The buildup began with the introduction of the 1st Battalion, 3d Marines, flown in on 29 September 1966. The unit patrolled vigorously to a depth of five or six miles in all directions, finding almost nothing. In response to General Westmoreland's desire, however, the battalion remained at the outpost for three additional months. They continued to patrol and still found only a few enemy.

An interesting sidelight to the unit's four-month deployment to the Khe Sanh area was the troops' almost instinctive response to the opportunity to work with the people. About two miles south of the airstrip, there was a small village peopled by Montagnards—members of the Bru tribe. Gentle, simple little people, they had no understanding of war in general and especially of the war in which they found themselves. To them the conflict was bad because it disturbed their tranquility and their freedom to scratch out a modest food supply. And they were not happy that refugees from the war had swelled the size of their little village.

On a visit I found that the Marines had made friends with the Bru tribesmen and their families, organizing a program of regular medical clinics to care for the usual cases of yaws and ulcerated teeth. They set about building a school, improvised play structures from gasoline drums, ammunition containers, and so forth, and took up a collection to buy equipment for the school. They repaired a church; they adopted an orphanage; and they organized a Combined Action Platoon with the Bru. It was a proud and serious unit, the only one in all the program utilizing mountain tribesmen. The Marines did all these things even while carrying on with their military tasks of patrolling, digging, and, on occasion, fighting.

The battalion was withdrawn in February 1967, leaving behind one company to provide security for a Seabee detachment which was extending the existing fifteen hundred-foot Khe Sanh runway to thirty-nine hundred feet. All the activity of bulldozers and trucks, movement in and out by air, and the many patrols of the countryside had a predictable effect, as Italian correspondent Oriana Fallaci noted, like setting out honey to attract flies.[3] Khe Sanh became a progressively more alluring target to the North Vietnamese. The growing enemy presence around Khe Sanh prompted a prophetic comment by Major General Bruno A. Hochmuth, commanding general of the 3d Marine Division, in whose care responsibility for Khe Sanh rested until his death in a helicopter crash on 14 July. Hochmuth, a quiet matter-of-fact Texan, told me in a letter, "The Khe Sanh business could give us trouble. The place itself doesn't mean anything but if we keep cruising around out there the NVA are going to wait until the weather closes in and jump on us."[4]

That is just about what happened. In April 1967, patrols from the one Marine company remaining in the Khe Sanh area discovered that 861, 881 South, and 881 North, hills dominating the airstrip on the north and west, were occupied by North Vietnamese units holed up in limestone caves, trenches, and bunkers which, local Bru tribesmen said, had been dug into the hills as much as three years earlier. The Marine forces at the outpost could not tolerate enemy observation and weapons looking directly into their airfield positions. The North Vietnamese units had to be thrown out. The result was the bitterest fighting of the entire Khe Sanh battle, perhaps the bitterest fighting of the entire war for the Marines.

The 3d Marine Regiment, with two battalions and a battalion of light artillery, moved into the area in late April 1967. There followed two violent and bloody weeks of fighting in the rain and mud, as the Marines drove the enemy from the key hills. Then, throwing back repeated counterattacks, they made clear that they had no intention of relinquishing their positions. Indeed, had they done so, there would have been no way to continue operations of the base and airstrip. Those hills, it was clear, were the key to Khe Sanh—either to its defense or to its conquest. The North Vietnamese were still not convinced. They continued to hammer at the hills in the hope that the Marines would give way. By late June, they had expended the bulk of two regiments in savage hand-to-hand combat—all to no avail. Ironically, the enemy tactics in the hill fights were similar to Westmoreland's attritional strategy; both sought to entrap enemy units and then decimate them with heavy weapons fire. Americans were seldom able to make the tactic work because of the enemy's excellent intelligence. The North Vietnamese were occasionally more successful, but not this time. In any event, the two months of conflict cost the Marines more than fifty lives. The hills were theirs, but the North Vietnamese would continue to contest them for ten more months.

The price in blood was accompanied by great expenditure of material resources. The forces occupying the hill outposts were sustained almost exclusively by Marine helicopters, upon which the troops depended for their food, ammunition, casualty evacuation, even their water. The steady valor of the helicopter pilots, often operating in full view of the enemy, was an inspiration to the Marines on the hilltops. Although Route 9, from Khe Sanh to the seacoast, was technically open, traffic on it was subject to enemy attack. Transport aircraft, therefore, provided the bulk of the logistic support for the rapidly growing base.

By now there was no doubt in the minds of the Marines—and there should have been no doubt at the Saigon high command either—that the Khe Sanh base, with its miserable weather and unfavorable tactical location, had the makings of a strategic albatross. At about this time (15 May 1967) I told Marine Commandant Greene in a letter that ". . . at great cost to him the enemy is holding our attention and consuming our resources in the area. He may be exploiting the circumstance to move in strength . . . and launch an attack on Quang Tri or Danang," which is exactly what he did a year later.[5]

Although the most intense phase of the hill fights had ended, the North Vietnamese continued to exhibit their interest by occasionally attacking the hill outposts and probing the base's perimeter.

Khe Sanh was not the only trying problem facing the Marines in the summer of 1967. Along the eastern portion of the Demilitarized Zone, twenty-five or thirty miles east of Khe Sanh in the region around Con Thien, Marine units found themselves in heavy combat against North Vietnamese forces that employed the Zone and the area immediately north of it to rest and refurbish their units, as well as to emplace artillery and surface-to-air missiles. At a great cost in blood, they were proving anew—for those who had overlooked it—that a privileged sanctuary confers immense advantages on the adversary possessing it. Nobody involved in those bitter fights along the Demilitarized Zone will forget the unwisdom of accepting battle on such unequal terms.

Khe Sanh was facing problems of a different sort in August 1967. The metal-surfaced airfield was not up to the constant pounding from landings by a procession of sixty-ton transport aircraft. It had to be closed for repairs which would require two months. At almost the same time, the enemy ambushed an artillery column headed for the base and destroyed a key bridge on Route 9, twelve miles east of the airfield. From that moment, the base, now occupied by Colonel David Lownds's 26th Marine Regiment (which had replaced Colonel John P. Lanigan's 3d Marines), was dependent on helicopters and parachute drop by fixed-wing aircraft for resupply. Now, Khe Sanh was truly isolated, and it was about to be besieged.

As autumn came, with its mist and rain, the North Vietnamese stepped up the pressure—more probing activity on the perimeter of the base, more 122-millimeter and 152-millimeter heavy artillery screaming in from Laos and north of the DMZ, more stubborn attacks on the hill outposts, more mortars and rockets pounding the bunkers and supply dumps and making jagged holes in the aluminum airstrip. Pressure on the five critical hill outposts grew until in the early hours of 21 January 1968 there was a powerful attack on one of them, Hill 861, by a North Vietnamese force of about three hundred men. Following a drenching mortar and rocket preparation came five hours of intense fighting, much of it hand-to-hand, where the Marines were supported by the total artillery and mortar resources of the base. The enemy was thrown back, but many a Marine wondered what would have happened had there been three thousand of the enemy instead of three hundred. A few hours later, as the defenders of Hill 861 caught their breath, a cloudburst of artillery, mortar, and rocket fire blanketed the base itself, destroying helicopters and trucks and making a direct hit on the principal munition dump. Some fifteen hundred tons—almost the whole of the Khe Sanh ammunition stock—went up in one immense eruption. Shortly thereafter Khe Sanh village, about two miles south of the combat base, came under attack. A company of provincial militia and a Combined Action Company managed to hold on, with much help from Marine artillery in the combat base. All told, 21 January was a busy day. Over twelve hundred enemy rounds fell and volumes approaching that amount were absorbed on many days to follow. The American high command in Washington began to worry. So far, the numbers of attacking enemy were small, but was a true human wave assault on the base by thousands of North Vietnamese in the offing? If so, when? And would the Marines be able to handle it?

Over the next seventy-seven days and in company with

their helicopters and close support aircraft and with the help of Air Force and Navy aircraft, the Marines gave them their answer. The answer came in a fabric of stubborn resolution, teamwork, and cold heroism that reflected glory and honor on the Marines themselves and on their Corps.

Day after trying day, the weather dominated the battle. It ruled out visual close air support, and it prevented helicopters from supplying the hill outposts or evacuating their casualties. Mortars and rockets churned up the main base and drove everyone underground, while the key hills were under continuing close quarters pressure. It was the hardest kind of fighting, valiantly and efficiently done. But the melancholy truth is when it was over, with all the dirt and blood and fatigue and frustration and heroic sacrifice, it had done little to advance our cause toward victory.

In February 1968, a visit to Khe Sanh gave me a real sense of the pressures involved in being besieged. Jumping from a rolling helicopter and diving into a strip-side bunker while the aircraft got back in the air to avoid the inevitable 120-millimeter mortar reaction was standard procedure. The mist and damp and mud were Khe Sanh's trademarks. The cluttered bunkers were redolent of the smell of dirty bodies. The men's faces were drawn, their eyes deeply shadowed, yet, incredibly enough, their sense of humor was as lively as ever. Beside a muddy foxhole, literally the home of two Marines, I saw a crude hand-drawn sign: "The Rain in Laos Falls Mainly in the House." And by another foxhole, "Home is Where You Dig It." Beside still another: "Want to see a rocket up close? Stand here." And at the end of a mess line, a sign: "No Tipping." It all told an eloquent story of spirit and determination.

Two days later I stopped at Saigon, where a colonel on the MACV staff spoke to me of unfavorable reports they had been receiving on the state of tidiness of the Khe Sanh combat base and the quality of its fortifications. He said he understood that "there is trash everywhere, troops are dirty, ragged and unshaven and their bunkers are disgracefully inadequate." He asked if that was the impression I derived from my visit. I surprised him by agreeing, "It's bad, maybe even worse than you say. A grim sight. What they really need up there is someone with a high sense of order to clean the place up—somebody like you. Why don't you go? Of course, you must remember, every trip you make to one of the trash dumps or to the water point is going to be Russian roulette with a 120-millimeter mortar, and every bag of cement you arrange to fly in will be a gamble that the aircraft will not come home. I suggest you get your butt up there and find out what the word *siege* means." The real problem was that, like the people who were bearing the brunt of it, I hated the bad choice that put them there, and I took it out on an innocent staff officer who had missed a chance to be quiet.

Lost in all the smoke was the question of how the Marines came to be in Khe Sanh in the first place. In its stead, there arose the more dramatic question of whether "the United States had a Dienbienphu on its hands." The media were largely the creators—or at least, willing disseminators—of the Dienbienphu analogy. Americans consistently heard an alarming drumroll in the headlines fashioned by press doomsayers:

- "Reds Gamble for a Knockout" (*U.S. News & World Report*, 5 February 1968)
- "Drawing the Noose; Both Sides Acutely Aware of Similarities Between Khe Sanh and France's Cataclysmic Defeat Fourteen Years Ago" (*Newsweek*, 5 February 1968)
- "Khe Sanh; U.S. Girds for Red Blow. Growing concern that battle could turn into a disaster—an American Dienbienphu" (*U.S. News & World Report*, 26 February 1968)
- "Khe Sanh; Tension, Heavy Casualties, Tightening Ring. Defenders now surrounded by more than 20,000" (*U.S. News & World Report*, 11 March 1968)
- "The Dusty Agony of Khe Sanh" (*Newsweek*, 19 March 1968).

It is little wonder that President Johnson asked General Earl Wheeler, chairman of the Joint Chiefs of Staff, to provide him with the personal assessment of the Khe Sanh situation by every member of the Joint Chiefs. He was worried about the terrifying similarity between the two battles, as portrayed by the press.

In truth, the military differences between the two situations were great. At Dienbienphu, the enemy held all the high ground. At Khe Sanh, by virtue of the bitter hill fights in the spring of 1967 and by the Marines' continuing resolution to hold those hills, our side occupied most of the essential heights. The French Dienbienphu outpost was 175 miles from its supporting base. Khe Sanh was only 40 miles from major support. The Vietminh at Dienbienphu had more artillery than the French. At Khe Sanh, the situation was reversed. The force was supported not only by forty-six tubes of light and medium artillery within the base but by Army heavy artillery only fourteen miles distant. And the contrast between French and American air support was dramatic. No more than two hundred planes of all types were available to sustain the French garrison. The largest of their cargo aircraft could handle only four tons and General Rene Laval, commander of the French air force in Indochina, told General Navarre from the first that he could not support the base. The Americans at Khe Sanh had available over two thousand attack planes, twenty-five hundred helicopters, three hundred cargo aircraft capable of payloads up to twenty tons, and enough of the nation's strategic bombing force to put six B-52s, each with 108 five hundred-pound bombs, over Khe Sanh every three hours. Of even greater importance was the Marines' capability to deliver bombs round-the-clock in any weather, daylight or dark. (See Chapter 7, "The Marines' Push Button.")

These factors made the two situations dissimilar in a military sense. In a political sense, however, the analogy was accurate because Khe Sanh had seized the attention of the American people just as Dienbienphu had captivated the French people in 1954. Khe Sanh troubled our political leadership, to the point where the fortunes of Colonel Lownds and his men were a subject of highest priority in the workday of President Johnson, who insisted that General Westmoreland submit to him a detailed plan for relieving and rescuing the Marine garrison, if necessary. Had we suffered a defeat at Khe Sanh, the tactical and logistical differences between the two battles would have been overshadowed by their political similarity. The effect in Washington of a tragedy on the ground would have been just as disastrous as it had been in Paris in 1954.

The political advantage the North Vietnamese stood to gain only became clear as the struggle approached a climax. But what prompted their initial move into the Khe Sanh hills? What was the true motivation of the North Vietnamese at Khe Sanh? This is one of the great mysteries of the Vietnam conflict. Theories extend all across the spectrum: that General Giap saw Khe Sanh as a perfect replica of Dienbienphu; that he planned it as a diversion for the Tet offensive; or that he would never have come near the place had we not offered him a target that promised him great rewards.

To dispell some of the mystery, it is necessary to understand something of the personality, philosophy, and influence of General Vo Nguyen Giap himself. Giap was much more than the generalissimo in command of the North Vietnamese forces in the Indochina war. A teacher, a philosopher, and as much a political as a military figure, Giap held a position that, in American terms, combined the duties of the secretary of defense with those of the commander of the Pacific theater. He had even served for five months as acting president of the Democratic Republic of Vietnam while Ho Chi Minh was in Geneva negotiating the end of the French war in 1954. He was a broadly experienced Marxist ideologue, hardened by thirty years of fighting dating from World War II. His overall design for victory in the latter phases of the Indochina war reflected this breadth of background. He articulated it often and in many ways. Here is a typical example.

> The people are and always must be our object. If we protect them and earn their trust they will sustain us. We must draw the enemy away from the people and make him scatter his forces where they will be easy prey to our troops.[6]

Anyone who studied Giap's life and aspirations would have to know that his efforts—strategic and tactical—were certain to be focused on the populace of South Vietnam, not on roads or hills or bridges, but on the loyalty and support of those fourteen million people. In that sense, Khe Sanh cannot have meant more to Giap than a convenient mechanism for drawing the Americans away from the populated coastal area. Giap himself provided some contemporary clue of what he had in mind with respect specifically to Khe Sanh: "The primary emphasis [is] to draw American units into remote areas and thereby facilitate control of the population of the lowlands." One of his colleagues, Nguyen Van Mai, expressed the idea in about the same way, "We will entice the Americans close to the border and bleed them without mercy."[7]

My belief at the time—and now—was that the North Vietnamese behavior at Khe Sanh was reactive. First, General Westmoreland dangled the Marine bait at Khe Sanh before them, exactly as the French did at Dienbienphu, aiming to attract large numbers of North Vietnamese soldiers whom we would fix in place and decimate with firepower. As he put it, "We will lure the enemy to their deaths." The North Vietnamese then tested the Khe Sanh situation by attacking the key hill outposts, knowing, if those outposts fell, that the base would be indefensible. They committed a substantial number of their best troops, initially perhaps ten thousand, with the future potential of three times that number. In the process, they drew more and more Americans into the Khe Sanh base to match them. The battle got bigger and bigger and, in consequence, more important to us.

When Giap perceived the immensity of the fire support and logistic resources which General Westmoreland was prepared to invest, I believe that he seized the opportunity to use Khe Sanh to wring us out in a major way. He wanted to drain as much of our substance as he could, to induce us to put our national prestige on the line, to fix our forces in place, and thus to turn them away from their efforts at pacification, which he feared more than bombs. Giap himself stated the case, "I will stretch the Marines as taut as a bow string and draw them away from the populated areas." And French Major Jean Pouget, a Dienbienphu veteran said, "What Giap wants is to control the population of South Vietnam. American attention is concentrated on Khe

Sanh while political commissars are speaking in the public squares of every small village and even in Saigon itself."[8]

Finally, there seemed to have been a third change. Giap, deciding that he had us firmly committed to the Khe Sanh plateau and to expending great resources there daily, felt able to shift at least half and perhaps more of his Khe Sanh forces to the great Tet offensive of February 1968. So the spring saw Giap realizing the better parts of both worlds. He still had us tied down at Khe Sanh, diverted from pacification, expending a thousand tons of bombs plus hundreds of artillery and mortar rounds a day, and delivering two hundred tons of supplies a day by helicopters, fixed-wing aircraft, and air drop. Meanwhile, he was able to free at least three regiments to participate in the Tet attack on Hue.*

This offers support to the conclusion that the North Vietnamese had no intention of undertaking an all-out assault on the base. Their forces were in place around Khe Sanh as the Tet offensive approached—perhaps three divisions of them—and, with all of the other concurrent diversions of American resources, there could not have been a more favorable opportunity for a decisive attack on the base. It did not happen. Although they made many probes of the perimeter, they never tried a one- or two-division human wave run at the defenses of the base itself, as they did at Dienbienphu. Some analysts contend that mass assaults were frustrated by the heavy B-52 attacks. That does not explain, however, why they never chose to interrupt or poison the Marines' water supply, the Rao Quan River, which originated in the area they controlled. Nor does it explain why they did not attempt to tunnel under the defenses, as they did at Dienbienphu. Instead, during the Tet period they elected just to hold at Khe Sanh, keeping pressure on its hill outposts and shelling the base proper, while putting their prime offensive effort on the coastal cities.

There has to be some relationship between the Tet under-

---

* There have probably been a hundred books written on the Indochina war, and of those that I have read analyzing Giap's strategic thoughts, none has said anything that has caused me to change my own view of Giap's purposes as I describe them here.

taking and Khe Sanh. At the least, the conflict for the Khe Sanh outpost served to capture the attention of the Americans and South Vietnamese while the very large deployments of North Vietnamese troops and material into other areas of South Vietnam were taking place. Beyond that, there was the substantial diversion of U.S. resources to Khe Sanh, resources that might better have been addressed to the critical coastal area.

Despite the fact that Tet was a tactical disaster for the enemy, costing them thousands of soldiers and gravely damaging their guerrilla structure in South Vietnam, it provided them the same sort of strategic benefit that they might have realized from a victory at Khe Sanh. It demonstrated to the American people that despite our immense commitment—half a million men, thousands of aircraft, mountains of supplies—the enemy could still go almost anywhere they chose in Vietnam. The sobering knowledge, in Washington, Topeka, and Tallahassee, that the enemy could move heavy howitzers and rockets within range of Hue, Saigon, and a score of district towns represented a strategic victory of Dienbienphu dimensions. And despite the fact that they never gained control of Khe Sanh, they demonstrated to American strategic planners that they were able to make their way to the coastal plain in strength without the use of Route 9. This road, it will be recalled, was frequently described as a necessary element of any North Vietnamese offensive strategy and a key reason for our going to Khe Sanh in the first place.

In the end, Giap, having milked as much out of the Khe Sanh operation as he could, simply caused his forces to melt away. This behavior of the North Vietnamese emphasizes the futility of the American strategy in setting up the Khe Sanh base. They tied us down, they diverted us from the people, they exacted an impressive penalty in men, time, and material while they proceeded with their Tet strategy. Their only investment was blood, to which they assigned a low importance.

It is plain, in retrospect, that a worried U.S. government could have doubled the number of men General Westmoreland had beating the weeds for the large North Vietnamese units. It would have made little difference. So long as the privileged Soviet supply pipeline at Haiphong was allowed to exist, so long as the privileged Laos sanctuary was allowed to exist, and so long as the Vietnamese people were accorded secondary priority, there was no chance of our winning.

The U.S. command was preparing for the promised rescue expedition to relieve the Marines at Khe Sanh. Called Operation Pegasus, it was an unwarranted diversion of resources. A thirty thousand-man effort was built around the 1st Air Cavalry Division. The imposing relief force, however, could not make it to Khe Sanh without a road. Marine engineers from Dongha, along with Army engineers and Seabees, protected by two battalions of Marine infantry, had to improve Route 9 and repair nine bridges so that the airborne unit's land-based tail—jet fuel, tankers, artillery—could follow along. Concurrently, the engineers hacked out a two thousand–foot airstrip, some twelve miles east of Khe Sanh, for the airborne unit.

The engineers' efforts were not needed. By mid-March 1968, it became clear that the enemy strength around Khe Sanh was fading away. Artillery, mortar, and rocket fire dropped off, as did pressure on the hill outposts. It was obvious that the forces and resources being committed to a relief expedition might now better be applied elsewhere. Nevertheless, the project was pursued. General Westmoreland had responded to President Johnson's directive with the great design of Pegasus. It had become a national matter, with a commitment to the commander-in-chief, and it was hard to abandon it, whether it made sense or not.

On the morning of 30 March, I had the satisfaction of observing a company of the 1st Battalion, 26th Marines break out of the perimeter and attack southward toward Khe Sanh town. Their success signaled the fact—already well known—that the siege was ended. Later in the day, I paid a courtesy call on the commanding general of the 1st Air Cavalry Division, whose headquarters was just moving into position near Calu, about twelve miles east of Khe Sanh, in preparation for the long-heralded relief. As we approached, I was sobered by the forest of helicopters, the legions of vehicles, the mass of artillery—all of the sinews of power. But there was little left for them to do at Khe

Sanh. A week later, patrols from the Marines at Khe Sanh and the air cavalrymen had a ceremonial link-up on Route 9 about four miles east of the base. It was all over.

Two months later at Guam, General Westmoreland told the officers of the 3d Air Division (B-52) that Khe Sanh was "a battle won by you and exploited by the 1st Air Cavalry Division of the United States Army and the Marines."[9] While the order in which the general assigned his applause is open to serious question, his opinion in that matter is less significant, in the long run, than the inconsistency of our overall strategy. First, we declared Khe Sanh to be of major importance—worth tying down six thousand elite troops for months and spending mountains of resources—twenty thousand tons delivered by air alone. General Westmoreland declared it to be "a critical blocking position . . . a source of good intelligence . . . crucial anchor of our defense of the Demilitarized Zone . . . strategic jumping off place for an expedition in Laos. . . ." Then, in a reversal that deserves Olympic honors for inconsistency, Khe Sanh was abandoned. General Creighton Abrams, Westmoreland's successor, said that the growth in our troop strength near the DMZ and the increase in our helicopter mobility made it unnecessary for us to keep our forces "tied to specific terrain." In other words, our philosophy that had been initiated in 1966 was suddenly reversed and, by mid-June of 1968, the piece of ground that had been characterized a few months previously as terrain of the utmost importance was abandoned as having no great tactical significance. Unused ammunition, the airfield matting, the supplies were all hauled back to the coast. Things of lesser value were burned, blown up, or buried. Bunkers, fighting holes, and emplacements were bulldozed over. Khe Sanh was abandoned and twelve miles of the road the engineers had prepared at such pains for use by the Army airborne division were destroyed.

I agree with British counterinsurgency specialist Sir Robert Thompson: "The absurdity of Khe Sanh will rate a book by itself"[10] and with General Giap himself: "As long as [the Americans] stayed in Khe Sanh to defend their prestige, they said Khe Sanh was important; when they abandoned it they said Khe Sanh was not important."[11]

There is just one final thing left to say. The Marines who went to Khe Sanh had no idea that they were—or were not—repeating history. Nor did they care. They were warriors, doing nothing more and nothing less than carrying out their orders. They were expected to defend the position and that is what they did. They accepted the mud, the short rations, and the limited water supply. They endured the cascade of mortars and Katyusha rockets raining down on them from positions in the nearby hills and they tolerated the 152-millimeter artillery that came screaming in at them through the Laotian mists. When North Vietnamese assault forces made a run at one or another of their positions, they fought back savagely until the enemy was dead or ran away. When it was all over, the grim-faced Marines in the stinking foxholes ascribed their triumph to the support of the intrepid Marine helicopter crews, or perhaps to the incomparable close air support, or even to the ground-shaking thunder of the B-52s. But as to their own performance, they would characterize it as nothing more than should be expected.

And that is the mark of the true fighting man.

Conclusion

For the Marine Corps there is no Peace.

Sergeant USMC
(later Secretary of the Navy)
Edwin N. Denby

Voltaire, in a disclaimer of atheism, declared, "If there were not a God it would be necessary to invent one." Similarly, some modern-day military philosopher might be inspired to say that if the United States did not have a Marine Corps it would be necessary, in our national interest, to create one. But just to need a Marine Corps and command it to exist would never be enough. To try to duplicate today's Marine Corps would be as hopeless as commanding a sculptor to create another David. The initial vital spark would be missing, as would the character that an object—or an institution—acquires only over time.

As I have tried to show in this book, the U.S. Marine Corps has evolved its mystical appeal slowly, through an unusual combination of circumstance, good fortune, and, most of all, conviction in the hearts of resolute men. It is a combination that has both strengthened and brought glory to the United States.

Although the Corps contains its share of visible heroes, its triumphs, in an aberration of history, are triumphs of the institution itself and not the attainments of individual Marines. We remember that Marlborough defeated the French, that Togo defeated the Russians, that Scipio defeated Carthage. But we know only that it was the Marines who won at Belleau Wood, the Marines who won at Guadalcanal, the Marines who led the way at Inchon. And that is exactly the way the Corp's heroes—big and small—would have it, for the Corps is less of the flesh than of the spirit.

Today, three powerful external factors cloud the Marines' horizon. The first of these is the oppressive influence of threat. Threat, in one way or another, has been a major influence on the growth of the Corps from the start. Rooted in the attitudes or aspirations of the Army, the Navy, or various chief executives, its nature has varied—threat to the Corps's repute, to its right to fight, to its very survival. At present, the threat from these quarters has diminished in intensity. To be sure, there can always be another Theodore Roosevelt or Harry Truman, with an ingrained antipathy to the Corps. And there will always be competition with the other services for dollars in peace and missions in war.

Today, however, the Corps faces a more immediate threat to its ability to perform, created by the times themselves. There is, across the land, an erosion of the work and service ethics, a general failure to provide incentives for excellence, a dimmed sense of industry and frugality, and, most seriously, a degraded sense of national commitment—a reluctance to fight, no matter what the occasion or circumstance. It is from such a society that the young men and women comprising a citizens' Marine Corps must be drawn. It is a dilute reservoir. For the Corps to maintain its standards of dedication, professionalism, and patriotic commitment under the weight of this impediment is a sobering task.

The Marines' second challenge is found in a recurrent military affliction called austerity. Coming in the wake of every war, when eternal peace is prophesied and dollars are appropriated for military purposes only with niggardly reluctance, the consequent enforced austerity wrenches the soul of every fighting man, who sees his ability to perform endangered. Such severe times are not made for the weak, the inflexible, or the faint of heart. Some, whose habits have been molded in free-wheeling periods of war or high military threat, when money is easy to come by, find the world of austerity intolerable. At best, they take their frustrations into the civilian world, where they can do no harm. At worst, they linger in active service and are a hazard to all around them.

The third factor complicating the Marines' quest for excellence is the dead hand of bureaucracy that lies over the entire military establishment. Today, initiative and resourcefulness are immured behind the oppressive gray walls of bureaucratic standardization. The present multilayered defense organization would never have permitted the Corps, on its very own, to give the military world its unique unified air/ground combat organization, the amphibian tractor, the assault helicopter, a working technique of day-and-night close air support, or an entirely new concept of landing operations employing vertical envelopment. Yet the Corps's healthy and useful survival is dependent, as it was yesterday and will be tomorrow, on its being unfettered intellectually and professionally. The Corps must remain on the cutting edge of the technology that will keep its specialty effective.

This condition, in turn, is dependent on there being a niche in the modern U.S. military system that allows an original, independent, and fiercely proud Corps to test new worlds on its own, in the nation's interest.

The Corps is capable of meeting and overcoming the first problem—the quality of the recruit drawn from today's society. Because of the sheer strength of its traditions and the reputation of its standards, the Corps will continue to attract those who want to be the best. The Corps must always be mindful of what it stands for and realize that its willingness to meet any challenge and accept any hardship underlies both its attraction to the best of young recruits and its value to the country. Unpopular and difficult issues will continue to present themselves, but they must be met head-on and without compromise. This is what the Corps did in its unrelenting campaign against drugs. In that matter, the Marines proved once again that they are justified in holding themselves as something more than just a cross-section of society. This same dynamic attitude must prevail wherever societal conditions threaten the standards of the Corps.

Likewise, the challenge of austerity is no stranger to the Marines. It was in the spirit of frugality that Commandant Burrows undertook to build the Washington Marine Barracks with Marine Corps labor and at a total cost of $20,000. It was an instinct of austerity that inspired Commandant Lejeune, after World War I, to establish a policy of returning, each year, to the Treasury, a part of the Marine Corps appropriation. And it was with austere pride that Commandant Vandegrift told the Senate Naval Affairs Committee in 1946 that "in the days of peace preceding the recent war the United States possessed the world's top-ranking Marine Corps at a cost to the nation of $1,500 per Marine, while it had the eighteenth-place Army, at a cost of $2,000 per soldier."

The Marines, by virtue of tradition and habit, will survive the cutbacks and economies that accompany a dramatically changed strategic environment in which the Soviet Union is a less forbidding threat. Their instinct to be always ready to fight, with whatever resources are vouchsafed them, has sustained them in times of peace before, and will again.

The third problem—that of an all-encompassing military bureaucracy—represents a more formidable battlefield than many the Corps has known. The fatty folds of the Defense Department establishment grow ever more ponderous, enveloping and suffocating under their great weight the ability of our armed forces to perform the warlike work for which they were created. The Defense Department substructure, peopled by a combination of appointive birds of passage and career civil servants, is so engrossed in administrative quill-driving and dollar-shuffling that the fundamental issues of combat and combat preparation have trouble getting a hearing.

All of the armed services—not just the Marines—are absorbed in responding to make-work initiatives, sometimes to the degree that military officers themselves lose sight of the relative importance of the things they do, endowing briefcase-carrying in Washington with a patina it does not deserve. In short, the Pentagon is an inflated bureaucratic pyramid, perched precariously on its point, and the first wind of real war is likely to blow it over.

While the larger services may be able to handle the pressures of bureaucracy, the Marine Corps has neither the instinct nor the time for it. The Marines are an assemblage of warriors, nothing more. Paper-messaging and computer competitions do not kill the enemy, which is what Marines are supposed to do. In the past, this unique dedication to combat has been recognized by the nation at large. H. L. Mencken said it well: "An unwarlike Marine is quite as unthinkable as an honest burglar." As representative of the people, Congress has shown the same strong confidence in the Corps's reliability, protecting and nourishing the services's integrity and initiative. This precious confidence can be maintained only by a religious dedication to one thing that impresses congressional members of all dispositions, that one thing being performance.

Performance, in its turn, is geared to readiness—not just readiness to go, but readiness to go and win—and then come home alive. Congress exhibited its belief that the Marines could be trusted to do just that almost four decades ago when it required by law that, in addition to its primary statutory amphibious mission, the Corps be prepared to carry out "such other duties as the President may direct." Not idle words, they charge the Marines with a unique responsibility not specifically borne by any other military service—to fight Boxers in China, to guard the U.S. mails, to fight in the snows of the Chosin Reservoir, or to go on short notice to Korea or Vietnam on missions where politics severely circumscribe the ability to win.

Only through painstaking and realistic preparation can total readiness to do these things be achieved. A forward-looking Corps must envision the full spectrum of possible employment and devise innovative, realistic, challenging, sometimes even hazardous, training. Marines understand, as Revolutionary War General James Wolfe said, that "war is an option of difficulties." They must see no mission as too dangerous, no notice too short, no task too humble.

And now a brief genuflection to a final and unchanging element in the Marines' future. Our globe is three-fourths water, and there is still no way for significant numbers of American ground forces to come to grips with a powerful enemy on a hostile shore other than through the use of the sea. The air alone is not a suitable medium through which to initiate and sustain major assault operations. For this reason assault landing operations in the classic image have an impressive future. Advances in technology, such as helicopters, very high speed landing ships and craft, powerful air and surface fire support weapons, and sophisticated electronics, serve only to make amphibious assaults more formidable to the enemy.

There is little that will sober a defender more surely than the knowledge that somewhere, just over the horizon, lies a force of well-trained, well-equipped Marines in competently manned ships capable of delivering a stunning amphibious blow at a point and time of their own choosing. For the Marines, the maritime nature of the globe creates at once a grave responsibility and an elegant opportunity. It makes a powerful statement of a truth that the Corps must never, never forget—that their future, as has their past, lies with the Navy.

In a more profound sense, I suppose, the future of the Corps lies within itself, because, however large or small its problems are, nobody else is going to find solutions to them. It has been that way for over 200 years and it is that way today. It is a challenge that will demand the very best of a Corps that has been sharpened on challenge for all of its colorful life.

Semper Fidelis

NOTES

Introduction

1. Charles R. Smith, *Marines in the Revolution* (Washington: History and Museums Division, Headquarters, U.S. Marine Corps, 1975), pp. 7–12.

2. Ibid., pp. 90–91; Allan R. Millett, *Semper Fidelis: the History of the United States Marine Corps* (New York: Macmillan, 1980), pp. 13–14.

3. Captain Thomas Truxtun, letter to Marine Commandant W. W. Burrows, 2 April 1901.

4. Millett, *Semper Fidelis,* p. 140.

5. General Gerald C. Thomas, USMC, letter to the author, 20 October 1982.

Part I

1. General Holland M. Smith and Percy Finch, *Coral and Brass* (New York: Charles Scribner's Sons, 1949); James Forrestal, *Forrestal Diaries* (New York: Viking Press, 1951).

2. Author's diary.

Chapter 1

1. General M. B. Twining, letter to the author, 2 February 1982.

2. House Select Committee on Postwar Military Policy, *Hearings on Proposal to Establish a Single Department of Armed Forces,* 78th Cong., 2d sess., 1944, 42.

3. Ibid., 222.

4. General A. A. Vandegrift and Robert Asprey, *Once a Marine* (New York: W. W. Norton, 1964), p. 257.

5. House Select Committee on Postwar Military Policy, 78th Cong., 2d sess., 1944, H. Rept. 1645.

6. Explained in the report by JCS Special Committee for the Reorganization of National Defense, 11 April 1945.

7. Ibid.

8. Senate Committee on Naval Affairs, *Unification of the Armed Forces,* Hearings, S. 2044, 1946.

9. Vandegrift and Asprey, *Once a Marine.*

10. President Harry S. Truman, *Memoirs,* vol.2 (Garden City, N.Y.: Doubleday, 1958).

11. JCS 1478/10, *Mission of the Land, Sea and Air Forces,* 15 March 1946, paragraph 8, p. 53.

12. JCS 1478/11, Ibid., 16 March 1946, paragraph 5, p. 59.

13. JCS 1478/12, Ibid., 30 March 1946, encl. A, pp. 67–70.

14. JCS 1478/16, Ibid., 18 April 1946, paragraph Sh, p. 26.

15. Senate Committee on Naval Affairs, *Unification of the Armed Forces,* Hearings on S.2044, statement of General A. A. Vandegrift, 79th Cong., 2d sess., 10 May 1946.

16. Ibid.

Chapter 2

1. Demetrios Caraley, *The Politics of Military Unification* (New York: Columbia University Press, 1966), p. 140.

2. House Committee on Expenditures in the Executive Departments, *Hearings on H.R. 2319: National Security Act of 1947,* 80th Cong., 1st sess., 1947.

3. Lt. Col. James D. Hittle, "The Unification Controversy" (unpublished essay, 15 May 1948), in the possession of the Marine Corps Historical Center, Washington, D.C.

4. Senate Committee on Armed Services, *National Defense Establishment (Unification of the Armed Services),* Hearings, 80th Cong., 1st sess., 1947, 97.

5. Ibid., 374.

6. Author's diary.

7. In *Once a Marine,* General Vandegrift describes his meeting with the president as cordial and the president's reaction following a reading of the revised (and, as it turned out, greatly watered down) speech, as favorable.

8. Senate Committee on Armed Services, Hearings, 80th Cong., 1st sess., 1947, 758.

9. Ibid., 600.

10. Veterans of Foreign Wars Press Conference, Washington, D.C., 27 March 1947.

11. Gordon W. Keiser, "The U.S. Marine Corps and Unification" (M.A. Thesis, Tufts University, 1971), p. 127; also published as *U.S. Marine Corps and Defense Unification* (Washington: National Defense University Press, 1982), p. 97.

12. House Committee on Expenditures in the Executive Departments, Hearings, 80th Cong., 1st sess., 1947, 264.

13. Ibid., 310.

14. Ibid.

15. Keiser, "U.S. Marine Corps and Unification," p. 162.

16. House Committee on Expenditures in the Executive Departments, Hearings, 80th Cong., 1st sess., 1947, 455.

17. Ibid., 482.

18. Vandegrift and Asprey, *Once a Marine,* p. 324.

Chapter 3

1. Gen. Clifton B. Cates, "Complete Texts of Statements in Defense Dispute," *U.S. News & World Report* (28 October 1949):54.

2. U.S. Department of Defense, *First Report of the Secretary of Defense* (Washington: Government Printing Office, 1948), pp. 3–8.

3. Public Papers of President Harry S. Truman, 1949, National Archives, Washington, D.C., 162–66.

4. Cates, "Complete Text," 54.

5. House Committee on Armed Services, *The National Defense Program—Unification and Strategy,* Hearings, 81st Cong., 2d sess., October 1949.

6. *Congressional Record,* 81st Cong., 2d sess., Appendix, A5942–A5943.

7. Representative Gordon S. McDonough, letter to President

Truman, 21 August 1950, McDonough Papers, University of Southern California.

8. President Harry S. Truman, letter to Congressman Gordon S. McDonough, 29 August 1950, Truman Papers.

9. *Congressional Record,* 81st Cong., 2d sess., 1950, 14165–14166.

10. Adm. Robert L. Dennison, USN (Ret.), *Memoirs.* Adm. Dennison was serving at the time as an aide to President Truman.

11. Adm. Robert L. Dennison, USN (Ret.), Oral History, Truman Library, 131.

12. Ibid., confirmed in discussion between the author and Adm. Dennison, 3 May 1971.

13. Senate Committee on Armed Services, *Marine Corps Strength and Joint Chiefs Representation, Hearings on . . . S.677,* 82d Cong., 1st sess., April 1951.

14. Ibid., 72, 91.

15. Quoted in Franklin D. Mitchell, "An Act of Presidential Indiscretion," *Presidential Studies Quarterly* 2, no. 4 (1981): 565–75.

16. Gen. L. C. Shepherd, Jr., letter to the author, 18 October 1981.

17. Ibid.

18. Secretary of Defense Robert A. Lovett, letter to President Harry S. Truman, 18 November 1956.

19. Report of the Committee on Organization of the Department of the Navy, 16 April 1954.

20. House Committee on Armed Services, *Reorganization of the Department of Defense. Hearings . . . pursuant to H.R. 11001 . . . H.R. 12541* (and others), 85th Cong., 2d sess., 1958, 5974–5977.

21. Ibid., 6754.

22. House Committee on Armed Services, *Department of Defense Reorganization Act of 1958, to Accompany H.R. 12541,* 85th Cong., 2d sess., May 1958, H.R. 1765, 7–11.

23. Ibid., 12–14.

24. Public Law 85-599 (72 Stat. 514) Sec. 202(j).

Chapter 4

1. Gen. Dwight D. Eisenhower, "Harmony in the Armed Services; an Interview," *U.S. News & World Report* (3 February 1950).

2. Testimony before House Armed Services Committee, 17 Octo-

ber 1949. The Navy and Marines never permitted Bradley to forget his indiscretion.

3. John A. Lejeune, "The United States Marine Corps," *U.S. Naval Institute Proceedings* (October 1925): 1858–70.

4. Eli K. Cole, "Joint Overseas Operations," *U.S. Naval Institute Proceedings* (November 1929). Cole himself was one of the truly prospective thinkers in the amphibious arena.

5. Major J. H. Russell, "The Preparation of War Plans for the Establishment and Defense of a Naval Advance Base" (Lecture given at the U.S. Naval War College, 1910), Naval War College Archives, Newport, R.I.

6. The study was approved by Commandant Lejeune as Operation Plan 712 on 25 June 1921.

7. Colonel Dion Williams, "The Winter Maneuvers of 1924," *Marine Corps Gazette* 9 (March 1924): 1–25.

8. CINCLANTFLEET letter to Chief of Naval Operations, A16-3/FLANEX7 of 15 March 1941.

9. Commanding General Atlantic Amphibious Force letter to Commander-in-Chief, U.S. Atlantic Fleet, Serial 02/120, 9 September 1941.

10. J. F. C. Fuller, *The Second World War* (New York: Duell, Sloan, and Pierce, 1949), p. 207.

Chapter 5

1. Reminiscences of Maj. Gen. John T. Selden, USMC (Ret.), author's diary.

2. Smith and Finch, *Coral and Brass*, p. 72.

3. Andrew J. Higgins, letter to the author, 23 February 1942.

4. Quoted in Smith and Finch, *Coral and Brass*, p. 96.

Chapter 6

1. Commandant of the Marine Corps, letter to the Senior Member of the Navy Department Continuing Board for Development of Landing Craft, 18 May 1939.

2. Author's diary.

3. Lieutenant General Julian C. Smith, USMC, Interview, Headquarters, U.S. Marine Corps, 15 October 1962.

4. V Amphibious Corps Action Report, Galvanic Operation.

5. Jeter A. Isely and Philip A. Crowl, *The U.S. Marines and Amphibious War* (Princeton: Princeton University Press, 1951); and

comments of Lt. Gen. Louis Metzger, USMC, to the author, April 1983.

Chapter 7

1. First Lieutenant James H. Alexander, USMC, Oral History Collection, No. 2621, History and Museums Division, Headquarters, U.S. Marine Corps, Washington, D.C.

2. Bernard C. Nalty, *Air Power and the Fight for Khe Sanh* (Washington: Office of Air Force History, U.S. Air Force, 1973).

Chapter 8

1. Michael Langley, *Inchon Landing, MacArthur's Last Triumph* (New York: Times Books, 1979), p. 54.

2. Robert D. Heinl, *Soldiers of the Sea* (Annapolis: U.S. Naval Institute, 1962), p. 527, quoting James D. Stahlman, who was present at the New York event.

3. Author's diary.

4. Ibid.

5. Lt. Gen. A. L. Bowser, USMC, letter to the author, 14 March 1982.

6. Maj. Gen. O. P. Smith, "Korean War Diary," History and Museums Division, Headquarters, U.S. Marine Corps, Washington, D.C.

7. Lt. Gen. L. C. Shepherd, Jr., "Korean War Diary," part 4, p. 3.

8. Ibid., p. 5.

9. Ibid., p. 11.

10. Author's diary.

11. Maj. Gen. O. P. Smith, "Korean War Diary," p. 75.

12. Maj. Gen. R. L. Murray, letter to the author, 28 April 1982.

13. Maj. Gen. O. P. Smith, "Korean War Diary," p. 79.

14. Maj. Gen. R. L. Murray, letter to the author, 28 April 1982.

15. Lt. Gen. A. L. Bowser, letter to the author, 13 May 1982.

16. Lt. Gen. L. C. Shepherd, Jr., "Korean War Diary," part 5, p. 6.

17. Author's diary.

Chapter 11

1. Endorsement to the secretary of the navy on record of proceedings of Court of Inquiry convened at Marine Corps Recruit Depot, Parris Island, 9 April 1956.

2. Richard H. Kohn, "The Social History of the American Soldier: A Review and Prospectus for Research," *American Historical Review* (June 1981):553–67.

3. E. H. McClellan, "A History of the Marine Corps," 2 vols., typescript (Washington, D.C.:1925–33).

4. Maj. Reginald Hargreaves, "Vital Spark," *Military Review* (October 1953):18–22.

5. Gen. Walter Greatsinger Farrell, interview with author, 16 February 1982.

6. General Gerald C. Thomas, interview with author, 11 March 1982.

7. Millett, *Semper Fidelis,* p. 298.

8. Endorsement to the secretary of the navy on record of proceedings of Court of Inquiry, Parris Island, 9 April 1956.

9. The quotes are from the court-martial proceedings as recounted in Colonel W. B. McKean, *Ribbon Creek* (New York: Dial Press, 1958.)

10. Dr. Eugene B. Sledge, "Peleliu, Neglected Battle," *Marine Corps Gazette* (January 1980). Dr. Sledge is now a professor of biology at the University of Montevallo, Montevallo, Alabama.

11. General R. H. Barrow, letter to the author, 31 July 1981.

Chapter 12

1. Proceedings, U.S. v. Anthony J. Russo, Jr., et al., Case no. 9373-WMB-CD, 9th United States District Court (April 1973).

2. Author's diary, 8 May 1963, 19 August 1963.

3. One Marine Reserve officer who took part was Congressman Paul I. McCloskey, later to be known as a foe of our involvement in Vietnam. He had the role of U.S. ambassador.

4. From C. O. "5th Marines, 1st Marine Division Report on Operation Silver Lance," February 1965.

5. Robert J. O'Neill, *General Giap, Politician and Strategist* (Melbourne: Cassell Australia Ltd., 1969.)

Chapter 13

1. General William C. Westmoreland, *A Soldier Reports* (Garden City, N.Y.: Doubleday, 1976), p. 140.

2. Jack Shulimson, *U.S. Marines in Vietnam: An Expanding War, 1966* (Washington: History and Museums Division, Headquarters, U.S. Marine Corps, 1978), p. 14.

3. John M. Collins, *U.S. Defense Planning* (Boulder, Col.: Westview Press, 1982), p. 179.

4. Shulimson, *U.S. Marines in Vietnam, 1966,* p. 14.

5. Lt. Gen. V. H. Krulak, "A Strategic Appraisal, Vietnam, December, 1965," Marine Corps Historical Center, Washington, D.C.

6. Patrick J. McGarvey, comp., *Visions of Victory* (Stanford, Calif.: Hoover Institution on War, Revolution, and Peace, Stanford University, 1969).

7. Author's diary.

8. Lt. Gen. V. H. Krulak, letter to the Honorable Robert S. McNamara, 9 May 1966.

9. Lt. Gen. V. H. Krulak, letter to the Honorable Paul Nitze, 17 July 1966.

10. Shulimson, *U.S. Marines in Vietnam,* 1966.

11. Lt. Gen. V. H. Krulak, letter to the Honorable Robert S. McNamara, 4 January 1967.

Chapter 14

1. Robert E. Shaplen, *The Road from War, Vietnam, 1965–1970* (New York: Harper and Row, 1970).

2. Saxe M. de, *Memoires de l'Art de la Guerre, 1757* (Westport, Conn.: Greenwood Press, 1971).

3. Oriana Fallaci, *Nothing and So Be It* (New York: Doubleday, 1972), p. 226.

4. Maj. Gen. Bruno A. Hochmuth, letter to the author, 21 January 1967. When Hochmuth died in a helicopter crash he was replaced by Maj. Gen. Rathvon M. Tompkins, who, despite his reservations about the Khe Sanh enterprise, spent much of his time at the base and with the gallant men on its hill outposts.

5. Commanding General Fleet Marine Force Pacific Trip Summary, 30 April–4 May 1967. Archives, Headquarters U.S. Marine Corps.

6. Vo Nguyen Giap, *Peoples' War, Peoples' Army* (Hanoi: Foreign Language Publishing House, 1961).

7. Fleet Marine Force Pacific, "Marine Operations in Vietnam, 1967."

8. Robert Pisor, *The End of the Line; the Siege of Khe Sanh* (New York: W. W. Norton, 1982), p. 265.

9. General William Westmoreland, Address, 3d Air Division Guam, from the Unit History, 3d Air Division, January–June 1968.

10. Sir Robert Thompson, *No Exit from Vietnam* (New York: D. McKay Co., 1969), p. 182.

11. An interview with Oriana Fallaci, quoted in *Nothing and So Be It.*

BIBLIOGRAPHIC ESSAY

Introduction

A variety of material contributed to this section. In addition to Marine Corps personnel records the following also influenced the text: Jeter A. Isely and Philip A. Crowl, *U.S. Marines and Amphibious War* (Princeton: Princeton University Press, 1951); Allan Millett, *Semper Fidelis* (New York: Macmillan, 1980); Charles R. Smith, *Marines in the Revolution* (Washington: History and Museums Division, Headquarters, U.S. Marine Corps, 1975); Colonel Robert D. Heinl, *Soldiers of the Sea* (Annapolis: U.S. Naval Institute, 1962); Charles O Paullin, *The Navy of the American Revolution* (Chicago: The Burrows Brothers Co., 1906); M. Almy Aldrich, *History of the U.S. Marine Corps* (Boston: Henry L. Shepard Co., 1875); and Colonel Clyde Metcalf, *History of the Marine Corps* (New York: G.P. Putnam's Sons, 1939). Articles include Dennis Showalter, "Evolution of the U.S. Marine Corps as a Military Elite," *Marine Corps Gazette* (November 1979); and Major Edwin McClellan, "Marine Officers of the Revolution," *Daughters of the American Revolution* (July 1923).

I occasionally relied on my own diary, which will pass from my possession to the Marine Corps Historical Center, Washington,

D.C., when I die. The structure and content of much of the Introduction were influenced by discussions with Brigadier General S. B. Griffith, USMC, retired.

The chronicle of the Marines' trials in self-defense over two centuries began with the early days of our nation. Available to me, as pertinent background reading, were both early and recent histories, such as Gardner W. Allen, *A Naval History of the American Revolution* (Boston and New York: Houghton Mifflin Co., 1913); Charles O. Paullin, *The Navy of the American Revolution* (Chicago: The Burrows Brothers Co., 1906); William Clark, *Ben Franklin's Privateers* (New York: Greenwood Press, 1956, 1969); James F. Cooper, *History of the Navy of the United States* (Philadelphia: Lea and Blanchard, 1839); Robert Neeser, *Statistical and Chronological History of the United States Navy*, 2 vols. (New York: Macmillan, 1980); Alfred Thayer Mahan, *The Influence of Sea Power on History*, 2 vols. (New York: The Macmillan Co., 1909); Allan Millett, *Semper Fidelis* (New York: Macmillan, 1980); and, of course, Colonel Robert D. Heinl, *Soldiers of the Sea* (Annapolis: U.S. Naval Institute, 1962).

The more history I studied, the more I came to understand that, at the beginning, the Marines, while not much less competent than the Continental Army, amounted to little and were fortunate to survive the retrenchment that followed the Revolution. This view is reinforced as one reads from the rich reservoir of official documents affecting the Corps that is available in the Library of Congress and the National Archives—the George Washington Papers, the John Paul Jones Papers, the Naval Records Collection, and the official Records of the U.S. Marine Corps.

The Navy-Marine Corps crises of the early and mid-nineteenth century are richly and fully reflected in the commandants' correspondence, found in the records of Headquarters, U.S. Marine Corps, with secretaries of the navy, members of Congress, commanding officers of Navy ships, and his own officers.

Among the other writings that made clear to me the nature and depth of the Navy-Marine Corps jurisdictional controversy of the period were: Edwin N. McClellan, "History of the U.S. Marine Corps," 1st ed., 2 vols. in forty-five chs. (Washington, D.C.: 1925–33. Typescript); Cadmus Wilcox, *History of the Mexican War* (Washington, Church News Publishing Co., 1982); Harold and Margaret Sprout, *The Rise of American Naval Power* (Princeton, N.J.: Princeton University Press, 1946); William F. Fullam, "The

System of Naval Training and Discipline Required to Promote Efficiency and Attract Americans," *U.S. Naval Institute Proceedings* 4 (1890); Fullam, "The Organization, Training, and Discipline of the Navy Personnel as Viewed from the Ship," *Proceedings* (1896); and Fullam, "Discussion," *Proceedings* 3 (1902).

Chapter 1

Reports of hearings before the House and Senate Military and Naval Affairs Committees show clearly the Marines' unpreparedness during the first phase of the postwar unification struggle as well as the aspirations of the other services where the Marines were concerned. They are invaluable in reconstructing the fast-moving events.

Likewise, a full perception of the problems facing the Marine Corps in the tempestuous 1945–46 period can only be achieved through a complete familiarity with the series of Joint Chiefs of Staff documents designated "JCS 1478-8" through "JCS 1478-16." Originally of high (too high) classification, they are now declassified and are available either in the Library of Congress or the files of the Joint Chiefs of Staff. They document the ignominious fate planned for the Corps by its post–World War II enemies, leaving no doubt that the Corps's apprehensions at the time were justified.

I found items of interest in Demetrios Caraley, *The Politics of Military Unification* (New York: Columbia University Press, 1966); in Samuel P. Huntington, *The Soldier and the State* (Cambridge: Belknap Press of Harvard University Press, 1957); and particularly in Gordon W. Keiser, "The U.S. Marine Corps and Unification," M.A. thesis, Tufts University, 1971 (also published as *U.S. Marine Corps and Defense Unification, 1944–1947* [Washington: National Defense University Press, 1982]). But most useful of all were my own experiences in the middle of the battle, experiences that were made vastly more meaningful by my daily association with General M. B. Twining, whose sensitive understanding of what was going on and of what ought to be done about it were at the heart of the Marine Corps's strategy.

Chapter 2

The bulk of this chapter reflects my direct participation in the events described, underscored and documented by material in the archives of the Marine Corps Historical Center and in the hearings of the House and Senate Armed Services Committees as well as in the reports of the House Committee on Expenditures in the Executive Department, where, it turned out, the climactic hearings on unification were held. Pertinent also were written and oral reflections of others who were involved directly—Generals Thomas and Twining, Brigadier General S. R. Shaw, Brigadier Generals J. D. Hittle and E. H. Hurst, and Colonel Lyford Hutchins.

Chapter 3

This chapter also reflects much personal observation and participation. Reports of congressional committee hearings were valuable. Two books were helpful: Paul R. Schratz, ed., *Evolution of the American Military Establishment* (Lexington, Va.: George C. Marshall Research Foundation Publication, 1978); and Admiral U. S. G. Sharp, *Strategic Direction of the Armed Forces* (Newport, R.I.: Naval War College, 1977). So, too, were discussions, as reflected in my diary, with participants in the key events: General Shepherd, General Cates, General Twining, Admiral Forrest Sherman, Admiral R. L. Dennison, Vice Admiral R. E. Libby, Navy Secretary Robert V. Anderson, Senator Paul Douglas, and Congressmen Carl Vinson, Mike Mansfield, Gordon McDonough, Bob Wilson, and Paul Hoffman.

Chapter 4

The historical writings that influenced this chapter are the following: Jeter A. Isely and Philip A. Crowl, *U.S. Marines and Amphibious War* (Princeton: Princeton University Press, 1951); Sir Charles Callwell, *The Dardanelles* (Boston and New York: Houghton Mifflin, 1919); Colonel R. H. Dunlap, "Lessons for Marines from the Gallipoli Campaign," *Marine Corps Gazette* (September 1921); Antoine H. Jomini, *Précis de l'Art de la Guerre* (Bruxelles: Meline, Cans et Compagnie, 1838); Allan Millett, *Semper Fidelis* (New York, Macmillan, 1980); Clyde H. Metcalf, *A History of the United States Marine Corps* (New York: G.P. Putnam's Sons, 1939); and H. M. Smith and Percy Finch, *Coral and Brass* (New York: Charles Scribner's Sons, 1949). I also found helpful the Naval War College lectures of John A. Lejeune and John H. Russell; the official records of Fleet Landing Exercises 3 through 7; Earl H. Ellis, "Naval Bases, their Locations, Resources and Security" and his "Advanced Base Operations in Micronesia"; Commandant of the Marine Corps,

Annual Reports, 1922, 1928, 1931, and 1932 (Washington: Government Printing Office, 1922–1932); Major General Donald M. Weller's unedited tapes on the development of Naval gunfire support; and Colonel Robert D. Heinl, "Naval Gunfire Training in the Pacific," *Marine Corps Gazette* (June 1948).

Chapter 5

In addition to the general source material just described for chapter 4, I relied here on Kenneth J. Clifford's "Progress and Purpose: A Developmental History of the U.S. Marine Corps," on my own 1937 report from China on Japanese landing craft in the Sino-Japanese War, on my own and General Smith's correspondence with Andrew J. Higgins, and on the records of the Oral History Program of the History and Museums Division, Headquarters, U.S. Marine Corps.

Chapter 6

The sources employed were official Marine Corps records; Frank O. Hough, V. E. Ludwig, and H. I. Shaw, *Pearl Harbor to Guadalcanal* (Washington, D.C.: Historical Branch, G-3 Division, Headquarters, U.S. Marine Corps, 1958); General H. M. Smith and Percy Finch, *Coral and Brass* (New York: Charles Scribner's Sons, 1949); Marine Corps Oral History records, including the interview with Lieutenant Colonel E. E. Linsert, USMC, and discussions with Brigadier General W. W. Davies and Lieutenant General Louis Metzger; and my own diary.

Chapter 7

Little has been written concerning this quantum step in the delivery of close and accurate air support in the dark and in bad weather. Although the U.S. Air Force had made excellent strides in the late 1940s in developing a practical capability for high-level bombing in all weather, nobody had ever solved the problem of achieving a bombing accuracy that would surely and safely place bombs within 100 yards of a frontline soldier in pitch darkness.

The story of how a few unusual Marines did it is based on the papers and reminiscences of Colonel M. C. Dalby, USMC (retired), and on the reminiscences of Brigadier General H. G. Hutchinson, USMC (retired), and Captain Grayson Merrill, USN (retired). Facts concerning identification of personnel are from official Marine Corps records. An excellent reflection of Air Force opinion concerning the quality of the Marine development is found in Bernard C. Nalty, *Air Power and the Fight for Khe Sanh* (Washington, D.C.: Office of Air Force History, USAF, 1973); and the impact of the Marine system on an actual operation is found in Captain Moyers S. Shore, *The Battle for Khe Sanh* (Washington: Historical Branch, G-3 Division, Headquarters, U.S. Marine Corps, 1969).

Chapter 8

Few battles have been more fully chronicled than Inchon. Robert D. Heinl, *Victory at High Tide* (Philadelphia: Lippincott, 1968) is a brilliant portrait. Adding greatly to the general story are Michael Langley, *Inchon Landing* (New York: Times Books, 1979); Lynn Montross et al., *U.S. Marine Corps Operations in Korea, 1950–1953*, 5 vols. (Washington, D.C.: Historical Branch, G-3 Division, Headquarters, U.S. Marine Corps, 1954–1972); Malcolm W. Cagle and F. A. Manson, *The Sea War in Korea* (Annapolis: U.S. Naval Institute, 1957); David Rees, *Korea: The Limited War* (New York: St. Martin's Press, 1964); and Edgar O'Ballance, *Korea: 1950–1953* (Hamden, Ct.: Archon Books, 1969). Hearings before the Senate Committee on Armed Services, 82d Congress; William R. Manchester, *American Caesar* (Boston/Toronto: Little Brown, 1978); and Trumbull Higgins, *Korea and the Fall of MacArthur* (New York: Oxford University Press, 1960) were of general usefulness. But the entire reservoir of good writing and careful research still does not catch the spirit of Marine and Navy improvisation that proved to be the golden thread that held the entire Inchon idea together. For this I turned to the official after-action reports and to the words of the actual participants—diaries and memoranda by Generals Shepherd and O.P. Smith, discussions with others who were there, particularly Generals R. L. Murray and A. L. Bowser, who bore heavy responsibilities in the operation, my own diary for discussions with Admiral J. H. Doyle, Generals Field Harris, E. K. Wright, and E. A. Almond, and my own observations at and before Inchon as recorded in my diary.

Chapters 9 and 10

Conversations with veterans of the Old Corps—Generals Thomas, Shepherd, Noble, Hogaboom, Farrell, Craig, and Curtis, to name a few—provide some of the legend that animates these two chapters. Color is added, in the case of General Hill, by talks with his widow. The stories of Sergeants Holzworth and Walkovitz come from my own diary and recollections. The other stories are purely apocryphal. One may be sure that there are as many stories about Marines's corner-cutting and penny-pinching as there are Marines —and that is a lot of stories.

Chapter 11

Woven through all of the writings about the Marines from Continental days to the present is the thread of brotherhood. Fashioned and strengthened by their small numbers and by their unusual relationship with the Navy, this fierce internal loyalty is reflected in histories going back beyond 1850. Fraternity was indeed the Marines' earliest characteristic.

Certainly the most eloquent portrait of this quality is General Lejeune's 1921 *Marine Corps Manual* essay, "Relations between Officers and Men" (changed in 1948 to "Relations between Officers and Enlisted Marines" and reprinted in the *Marine Corps Manual).* Unaltered, except for the title, the essay stands out as a bright island of enduring reality in a sea of cold administrative and bureaucratic language that characterizes today's *Marine Corps Manual.* Lejeune, not content just to adjure his officers, took pains to ensure that each of the six paragraphs contained clear and mandatory instructions that would result in round-the-clock guidance and care of the enlisted Marine. His essay is a basic document for understanding the sensitive, interpersonal relationships that characterize the Marine Corps.

During the writing of this chapter, I was privileged to have access to the records, files, and publications at the Marine Corps Recruit Depot, San Diego. Additionally, I had access to the views and recollections of Marines of the present and earlier days, some of whom could contribute firsthand accounts of their recruit training in World War I. General G. C. Thomas and Brigadier General Walter G. Farrell both were privates at Parris Island at the war's beginning in 1917. Their oral and written comments to me were most valuable, and are now in the hands of the Marine Corps Historical Center, Washington, D.C., under *Krulak Papers.*

Further insight came from a study of the proceedings of the Court of Inquiry convened on 9 April 1956 to investigate the Ribbon

Creek tragedy at the Marine Corps Recruit Depot, Parris Island, as well as from the eloquent endorsements on the record by the commandant of the Marine Corps and the secretary of the navy. (General Twining wrote both.)

Finally, I leaned on my own experience of more than two years as commanding general of a recruit depot (San Diego), where my diary entries chronicled my reactions to the mystique of the incredible thing called Boot Camp.

Part VI

There is so much historical evidence of the Marines' combatant quality that it was difficult to decide which of the many great stories to recount as representative of the Marine fighter. I could have chosen battles planned and executed on a shoestring—in the Philippines, Nicaragua, or at Guadalcanal—where determination was the coin; bloody detonations like Belleau Wood, Tarawa, and Peleliu; grinding tests of will, endurance, and spirit like the Meuse-Argonne, Saipan, Okinawa, and, particularly, the Chosin Reservoir.

But then there was Vietnam. Vietnam, where a whole procession of circumstances stood stubbornly in the way of victory. There were weighty political restraints, problems with our ally, grave, almost decisive, problems with the privileged sanctuary, and broad internal disagreements at home as to strategy and in the field as to tactics. All of these things challenged not just the ability to win but even the will to win that has so characterized the Marines over the years. It slowly became plain to me that when Vietnam was over something from the best of everything that had ever been said about Marines as fighters found its validation there—innovativeness, resolution, obedience, patience, endurance, and the ultimate in raw courage. Vietnam had to be the real exemplification of "The Fighters," and I enjoyed writing about it.

My principal foundation were the many primary sources available—in my own possession, at the Marine Corps Historical Center, and at the National Archives. At the center and Archives, I looked at unit action reports, Fleet Marine Force Pacific reports of III Marine Amphibious Force Operations for the years 1965–68, the Fleet Marine Force Pacific publication "Marine Forces in Vietnam 1965–1967," U.S. Military Assistance Command, Vietnam Command Histories, command chronologies from the 1st Marine Aircraft Wing and the 3d Marine Division, exercise reports from the Fleet Marine Force, Pacific; my own 1964 to 1968 West Pac trip summaries, and interviews from the Marine Corps Oral History Collection. I drew also from a multitude of personal discussions with participants in the events and, of course, from my diary. In addition, I found much of value in Jack Shulimson and Major Charles M. Johnson, *U.S. Marines in Vietnam, . . . 1965* (Washington, D.C.: History and Museums Division, Headquarters, U.S. Marine Corps, 1978); and in Jack Shulimson, *U.S. Marines in Vietnam, . . . 1966* (Washington, D.C.: History and Museums Division, Headquarters, U.S. Marine Corps, 1982).

Chapter 12

This chapter embodies much of my own opinion, formed, in large measure, during my two years (1962–64) in the Pentagon as special assistant to the Joint Chiefs of Staff and the secretary of defense for counterinsurgency. I had abundant opportunity on the ground in Vietnam to observe our involvement, to perceive the disabilities under which the South Vietnamese operated, to understand the great impact of the privileged sanctuary, and to learn firsthand what Mao Tze-tung meant when he said that the people are the sea and the revolutionaries are the fish within it.

My knowledge was broadened by visits with leaders of the Vietnamese military, with General Paul Harkins and others in the U.S. Military Advisory system, with Dr. P. J. Honey, an expert on Asian Communism, and with Sir Robert Thompson, whose Malayan experience had much similarity with Vietnam.

Helpful reading during the early period came largely from the French experience—Bernard Fall, *Vietnam Dernières Réflexions sur une Guerre* (Paris: R. Laffon, 1968); Philippe Devillers, *Histoire du Vietnam, 1940 d' 1952* (Paris: Editions du Seuil, 1952); General Henri Navarre, *Agonie d l'Indochine, 1953–1954* (Paris: Plon, 1956); and from General Vo Nguyen Giap, *Peoples' War, Peoples' Army* (Hanoi: Foreign Language Publishing House, 1961).

Later there occurred a deluge of writing, some valuable, some questionable, but all educational—*The Pentagon Papers* (New York: Quadrangle Books, 1971), and as published by *The New York Times;* Douglas Pike, *War and Peace and the Vietcong* (Cambridge: MIT Press, 1969); the incomparable Richard Tregaskis, *Vietnam Diary* (New York: Holt, Rinehart and Winston, 1963); Hilaire du Berrier, *Background to Betrayal* (Boston: Western Islands, 1965);

Samuel B. Griffith, *Mao Tze-tung on Guerrilla Warfare* (Garden City, N.Y.: Anchor Press/Doubleday, 1978); Dr. P.J. Honey, *Communism in North Vietnam* (Cambridge: MIT Press, 1963); Robert J. O'Neill, *General Giap, Politician and Strategist* (Melbourne: Cassell Australia, Ltd., 1969); *Case Studies on Insurgency and Revolutionary Warfare* (Washington, D.C.: American University, Special Operations Research Office, 1963–1964); Franklin M. Osanka, *Modern Guerrilla Warfare* (New York: Free Press of Glencoe, 1962); U.S. Naval Institute, *Studies in Guerrilla Warfare* (Annapolis: The Naval Institute, 1963); and the sensitive and accurate portrait in Marguerite Higgins, *Our Vietnam Nightmare* (New York: Harper & Row, 1965).

Additionally, I utilized Fleet Marine Force Pacific and III Marine Amphibious Force Operations summaries, my own Fleet Marine Force Pacific Trip Reports, and my personal diary.

My comments concerning civic action in the Dominican Republic are drawn from Edward A. Fellowes, "Training Native Troops in Santo Domingo," *Marine Corps Gazette* (December 1923); Robert C. Kilmartin, "Indoctrination in Santo Domingo," *Marine Corps Gazette* (December 1922); and Edward McClellan, "Down in the Dominican Republic," *Marine Corps Gazette* (May 1932).

Chapter 13

The sources for Chapter 12 apply also in this chapter. In addition, I derived my understanding of General Westmoreland's strategic views from his postwar reminiscences, *A Soldier Reports* (Garden City, N.Y.: Doubleday, 1976) and from frequent discussions with him and his staff as the events themselves unfolded. The representation of my strategic ideas is based mainly on two documents I prepared at the time: "A Strategic Concept for the Republic of Vietnam, June 1965" and "A Strategic Appraisal, Vietnam, December, 1965," both on file in the archives of the Marine Corps Historical Center, *Krulak Papers*. Those strategic ideas are further protrayed in my diary and in my correspondence with the secretary of defense and the secretary of the navy, which is located in the archives, Marine Corps Historical Center.

Chapter 14

In writing about Khe Sanh I sought to do two things—to exhibit the wide variation in strategic approach between the Marines and the

U.S. Military Advisory Command, and to portray the steadfast, stubborn obedience of the Marines of all ranks in doing a fighting job for which they had no stomach.

The battle for Khe Sanh has been generously reported, so much that no single scholar could study it all. To accomplish my narrow purposes I relied mainly on official records: Fleet Marine Force Pacific "Operations in Vietnam 1965–1968," Fleet Marine Force Pacific, "U.S. Marine Corps Forces in Vietnam March 1965 to April 1965," my own official trip reports for the period, Marine unit command chronologies, Marine unit after action reports. Also consulted were the following: U.S. Pacific Command, *Report on the War in Vietnam, as of 30 June, 1968* (Washington, D.C.: Government Printing Office, 1969); Bernard C. Nalty, *Air Power and the Fight for Khe Sanh* (Washington, D.C.: Office of Air Force History, USAF, 1973); and Captain Moyers S. Shore, *The Battle for Khe Sanh* (Washington: Historical Branch, G-3 Division, Headquarters, U.S. Marine Corps, 1969). Particularly helpful as general background were Robert Pisor, *The End of the Line: the Siege of Khe Sanh* (New York: W. W. Norton, 1982), an excellent history; Francois d'Orcival and Jacques Francois Chaunac, *Les Marines à Khe Sanh* (Paris: Presses de la cité, 1979), which may just be the best layman's portrayal of the battle. My perceptions of Nguyen Giap derive from many sources, among them Robert J. O'Neill, *General Giap, Politician and Strategist* (Melbourne: Cassell Australia, Ltd., 1969); Oriana Fallaci, *Nothing and So Be It* (New York: Doubleday & Co., 1972); Vo Nguyen Giap, *Peoples' War, Peoples' Army* (Hanoi: Foreign Language Publishing House, 1961); Philippe Devillers, *La Fin d'une Guerre: Indochine 1954* (Paris: Editions du Seuil, 1960); Bernard Fall, "Power and Pressure Groups in North Vietnam," *China Quarterly* (January-March, 1962); and the impressive Jules Roy, *The Battle of Dien Bien Phu* (New York: Harper and Row, 1965).

I must add, however, that the conclusions as to the North Vietnamese aims at Khe Sanh and the relationship of Khe Sanh with the Tet offensive are mine alone, deriving from my own observations and my own deductions at the time.

INDEX

ABOUT THE AUTHOR

LIEUTENANT GENERAL VICTOR H. KRULAK served in the U.S. Marine Corps from 1934 to 1968, distinguishing himself in a career that spanned three wars and involved command of Marine Combat Organization from the platoon to a fleet marine force.

During World War II he commanded a parachute battalion in the Pacific, earning the Navy Cross and the Purple Heart. He later served as operations officer of the Sixth Marine Division in the 82-day Okinawa campaign, and took part in arranging the surrender of Japanese forces in northern China. When the Korean conflict began, he was assistant chief of staff of the Fleet Marine Force Pacific, later moving to Korea as chief of staff of the First Marine Division. In 1964 General Krulak assumed command of the Fleet Marine Force Pacific, with responsibility for all Marines in the Pacific Ocean area, including Vietnam. After four years of command he earned the Distinguished Service Medal for exceptionally meritorious service of great responsibility. He then retired from active duty.

General Krulak is a graduate of the U.S. Naval Academy and received a Ph.D. from the University of San Diego in 1970.

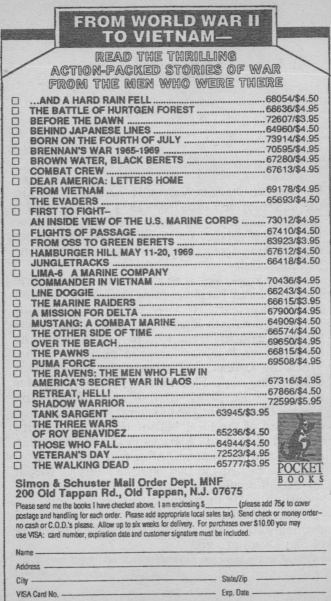